Shaw, G. B.

Androcles and the Lion

DATE DUE			

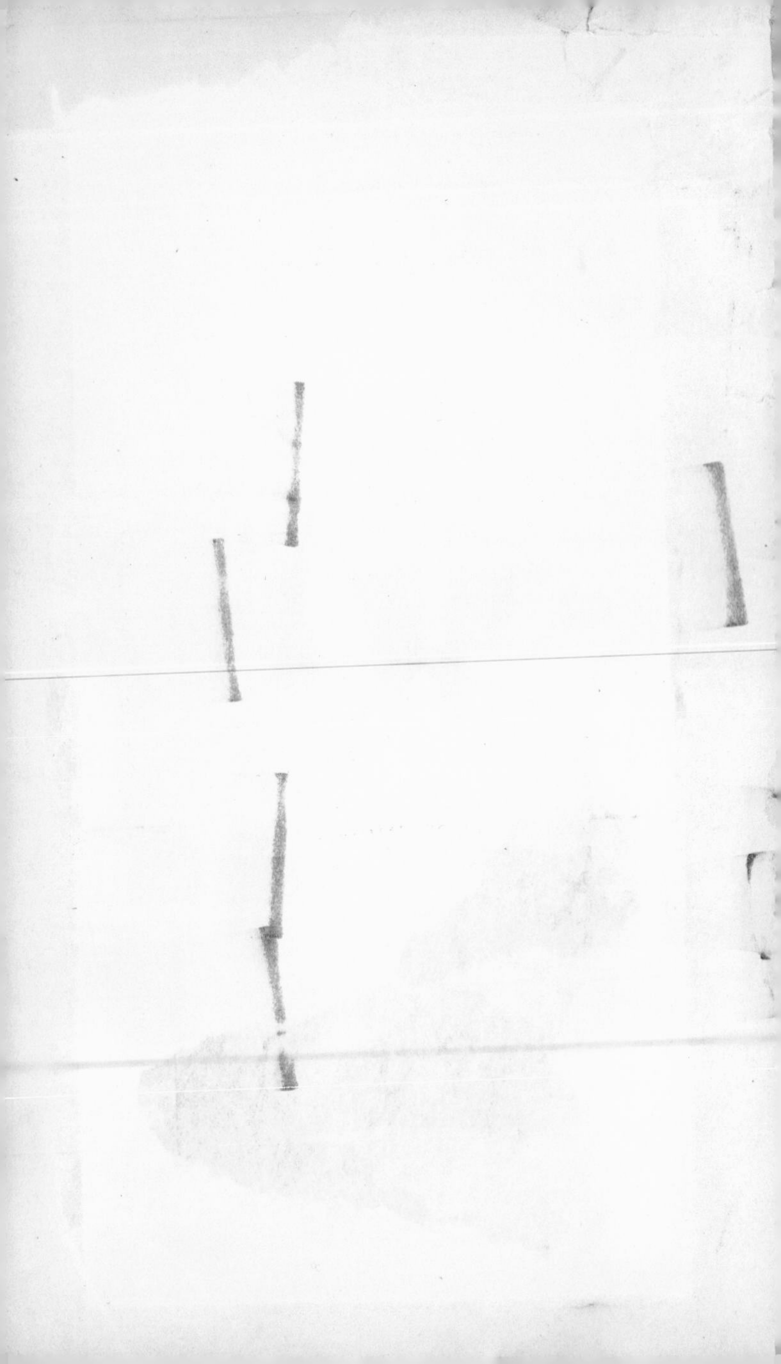

ANDROCLES AND THE LION

BERNARD SHAW

—

The Shaw Alphabet Edition

Q 29

This presentation copy of

ANDROCLES AND THE LION

is furnished to you, free of charge, under Shaw's Will by the Public Trustee, London.

If copies of the corresponding Penguin edition are required, please apply *not* to the Public Trustee, but to Penguin Books Ltd., Harmondsworth, Middlesex, England, making it clear that it is the Shaw's Alphabet edition which is required.

ANDROCLES AND THE LION

AN OLD FABLE RENOVATED

BY

BERNARD SHAW

—

WITH A PARALLEL TEXT IN

SHAW'S ALPHABET

TO BE READ IN CONJUNCTION
SHOWING ITS ECONOMIES
IN WRITING AND
READING

PENGUIN BOOKS

Penguin Books Ltd, Harmondsworth, Middlesex
U.S.A.: Penguin Books Inc., 3300 Clipper Mill Road, Baltimore 11, Md
AUSTRALIA: Penguin Books Pty Ltd, 762 Whitehorse Road, Mitcham, Victoria

—

Androcles and the Lion first performed in London 1913
First published 1913
Published in Penguin Books 1946
This Shaw Alphabet Edition
first published 1962

—

Made and printed in Great Britain
by Stephen Austin and Sons, Ltd, Hertford

—

Cover design by Germano Facetti

THIS BOOK IS DEDICATED TO

SIR JAMES PITMAN

K.B.E. M.P.

in grateful acknowledgement of his unstinted co-operation and continuous support over a period of nine years in carrying out Bernard Shaw's wishes

C.R.S.

PUBLIC TRUSTEE

—

1962

CONTENTS

Foreword
by C. R. Sopwith, Public Trustee 9

Introduction to Shaw's Alphabet
by Sir James Pitman, K.B.E., M.P. 12

Detachable Key Card
for Writers and Readers *facing* 16

Typography and Reading Key 17

Androcles and the Lion
in parallel texts 20

Notes on the Spelling
by Peter MacCarthy 143

Suggestions for Writing
by Kingsley Read 147

The Shaw Alphabet for Writers 150

The Shaw Alphabet Reading Key 151

FOREWORD
BY THE PUBLIC TRUSTEE

BERNARD SHAW died on 2 November 1950 and his Will, by which he appointed the Public Trustee to be executor and trustee, contained provisions for a new 'Proposed British Alphabet', a subject in which he always had a great interest.

Shaw imposed on his trustee the duty of seeking and publishing a more efficient alphabet of at least forty letters than the existing one of twenty-six letters to enable 'the said language to be written without indicating single sounds by groups of letters or by diacritical marks'. The Public Trustee was also directed to

> employ a phonetic expert to transliterate my play entitled *Androcles and the Lion* into the proposed British Alphabet assuming the pronunciation to resemble that recorded of His Majesty our late King George V and sometimes described as Northern English; to employ an artist calligrapher to copy the transliteration for reproduction by lithography, photography or any other method that may serve in the absence of printers' types; to advertise and publish the transliteration with the original Doctor Johnson's lettering opposite the transliteration page by page and a glossary of the two alphabets at the end and to present copies to public libraries in the British Isles, the British Commonwealth, the American States North and South and to national libraries everywhere in that order.

Shaw directed his trustee

> to bear in mind that the proposed British Alphabet does not pretend to be exhaustive as it contains only sixteen vowels whereas by infinitesimal movements of the tongue countless different vowels can be produced all of them in use among speakers of English who utter the same vowels no oftener than they make the same fingerprints.

Shaw's residuary estate was directed to be held for a period on certain trusts for these purposes, but such purposes were declared by a Judge of the Chancery Division of the High Court of Justice in England to be invalid in law. The Public Trustee appealed from this decision, and by way of compromise the British Museum, the Royal Academy of Dramatic Art, and the National Gallery of Ireland (who in default of the alphabet provisions in the Will were entitled to the residuary estate) agreed to pay a certain sum to the Public Trustee to be applied in furtherance of the Alphabet trusts.

At the end of 1957 the Public Trustee let it be known that he would award a prize of £500 for the design of a new alphabet complying most nearly with the provisions of Shaw's Will.

In the course of 1958 about 450 designs were submitted from all parts of the world.

On New Year's Eve 1959 the Public Trustee announced that there did not appear to be one outstanding design which might with confidence be said to be as satisfactory as what might be achieved by further effort and that he was not prepared at that time to single out one as the new Alphabet to be adopted for the purposes of the Will. There were, however, four designers who were judged to be of such outstanding merit that the prize money of £500 was divided equally between them, thus closing the competition. Those four designers were Mrs Pauline M. Barrett (of Canada), Mr J. F. Magrath, Dr S. L. Pugmire, and Mr Kingsley Read.

The Public Trustee then asked an expert in this field to collaborate with one or all of the four designers mentioned above to produce the best possible alphabet as is envisaged by Shaw's Will. The result is the design which appears in the Key on page 151 and on the detachable bookmark between pages 16 and 17 and which has been applied in this publication.

In authorizing the publication of this book the Public Trustee gratefully acknowledges the encouragement he has received from a large number of correspondents throughout the world but must single out for special mention the technical advice given by Mr Alan T. Dodson formerly of H.M. Stationery Office, and by Mr Peter MacCarthy of the Department of Phonetics at Leeds University, and to the latter he is also indebted for the transliteration now published. He also thanks all the very many designers, particularly Mrs Barrett, Mr Magrath, and Dr Pugmire, whose own designs and observations contributed so much to helping the Public Trustee to make a final choice. He is especially grateful, however, to Mr Kingsley Read, whose design has been adopted and to whose typographic artistry the transliteration in this book is its own tribute.

C. R. SOPWITH
Public Trustee

Kingsway
London WC 2
1962

INTRODUCTION TO SHAW'S ALPHABET

HERE is Shaw's alphabet. It has been proved that those who wish to read it can do so after only a few hours of concentrated deciphering.

Why should anyone wish to use it? And why should there be any departure from the familiar forms of the Roman alphabet in which English is printed and written?

You will notice from the comparisons that Shaw's alphabet is both more legible and one-third more economical in space than traditional printing, and this should lead to a great increase in reading speed. The characters themselves are very distinct. To prove them more legible, open the book and hold it upside down in front of a mirror. Both mirrored pages will thus become equally unfamiliar. Keep the back of the book pressed against your lips, and advance towards the mirror until you are able to see individual characters clearly enough to be able to copy them. Note that the Shaw characters are clearly seen at a greater distance.

The economy in space and greater simplicity of characters ought also to increase the speed and ease of *writing* – even more than it does the ease of reading. Many of the characters easily join into pairs and trios to form syllables which recur frequently in English words; the sounds of the language are completely characterized, thus permitting abbreviation with great reliability. Shaw found traditional script too laborious, and Pitman's shorthand too economical. Though at this time we can only guess, it is probable that an abbreviated handwriting speed of 60–100 words a minute, with complete reliability of reading, will be possible for those who attain 'automatic' facility with Shaw's alphabet. In other words, reading may be 50–75 per cent, and writing 80–100 per cent faster, and even 200–300 per cent, by using simple abbreviations.

Shaw insisted that, unless his alphabet were to offer the substantial advantages he himself desired, there would be no reason for adding to the existing media of communication, which include: typewriting, shorthand, morse, semaphore, and braille, in addition to the Roman alphabet which is itself represented by three quite different sets of signs (as in 'ALPHABET', 'alphabet', and '*alphabet*').

The Key on page 151 (duplicated on the bookmark) will enable you to achieve the beginnings of skill and the satisfaction of success within three or four hours. Although this means starting from scratch, remember that Isaac Pitman, whose shorthand Shaw used for all his writings, also did so with a system offering the same advantages as Shaw's alphabet: that is, the saving of time, effort, and money.

Shaw did not want you and me to *abandon* the Roman alphabet. The long-established Roman figures (I,II,III, IV,V,VI,VII,VIII,IX) remain even after the Arabic figures (the newer and handier 0,1,2,3,4,5,6,7,8,9) have found favour. We now use both, with greater convenience. The new figures were not imposed, nor the old supplanted. Similarly, Shaw believed, uses would be found for a new and handier alphabet *without* abandoning the old one.

If those who tried it found it advantageous, they would use it, and by their example it would gain what following it deserved. If its benefits were substantial enough, it would spread and establish itself through merit – as

Arabic numerals did despite the then complete satisfaction with Roman numerals.

Utilitarian advantage is thus the principle governing the new alphabet. Shaw was unique in pointing out that substantial economy could be attained only (*a*) if the designer were to *depart* from a system evolved by the Romans 2,000 years ago for carving their public notices in stone; (*b*) if a single set of alphabetical characters were used – abolishing the different look of words in capitals, small letters, and linked handwritten letters; and (*c*) if each distinct sound of the language were spelt with its own unvarying character.

These three factors in designing, taken together, made a non-Roman alphabet essential. Of course, there is nothing revolutionary in that. There are hundreds of non-Roman alphabets – and there are several variations within the Roman alphabet, e.g.

Roman variations	HERE IS A SENTENCE here is a sentence *here is a sentence*
Greek	ἡρ ις α σεντενς
Russian	ир ис а сентенс

Thus these four *English* words may already be represented in a number of existing alphabets.

Those who know Greek and English, Russian and English, etc., will have no difficulty in reading that sentence immediately in as many alphabets as they know – and it is considered at school that once a child has learned his A, B, C, D he is well placed to learn also his a, b, c, d, his *a, b, c, d,* his α, β, γ, δ (Greek), and his а, б, в, г (Russian).

Only a few hours will be needed to persuade you that the new alphabet has the potential advantages Shaw intended for it. At first you will read and write it in a plodding childlike way, as you once did Roman. Much more rapidly than a child's, your familiarity and ease will grow, until the use of Shaw's alphabet becomes as natural and automatic as your use of Roman – but faster.

In personal and intimate writing the forty-eight (40 + 8) characters of the Shaw alphabet may faithfully portray the pronunciation of the individual; but, as Shaw pointed out, too eccentric a dialect may hamper, and even destroy, effective communication. He considered that, though there was no need to standardize writing if not intended for publication, there was every need for conformity in print; standard spellings being particularly desirable when that print is intended for circulation throughout the English-speaking world.

In his Will, Shaw specified just such a standardization for this play. He laid down for it a 'pronunciation to resemble that recorded of His Majesty our late King George V and sometimes described as Northern English'. He was an expert in stage direction and, so it may be supposed, considered this pronunciation to be the best basis for comprehension with acceptability in reading as he had found it to be in speech from the stage.

But by all means *write* as you think fit, and leave experts to standardize printers' spelling.

This book costs very little. Get your friends to buy one and to learn the alphabet so that you can write to one another – or, if you become so skilled that you no longer need to 'keep your eye in', give it away.

JAMES PITMAN

House of Commons
London
1962

NOTE: I have offered, if there is the demand, to organize what were known as 'ever-circulators' in the early days of my grandfather. Send me a letter in Shaw's alphabet, mentioning your particular interests or circumstances. Give me your name and address in ordinary writing on an enclosed envelope. I will then try to arrange 'circles' of five or six who, drawn together in a friendship by Shaw's alphabet, will all circulate their own letters to which each in turn will add.

I have also offered, if there is a demand, to get further material published in the Shaw alphabet. When you have learnt to read and write fluently, and want more than your ever-circulator correspondence to read, please write to me, Sir James Pitman, K.B.E., M.P., at the House of Commons, London, S.W. 1, England, saying which of Shaw's works or other literature you would like to read in a printed transcription. I can make no promises – other than to consider your suggestions most sympathetically. Meanwhile, if anyone wishes to get printed their own material in Shaw's alphabet, they are permitted to do so, since the copyright for the alphabet and for the type-faces is public property. Messrs Stephen Austin & Sons, Ltd, of Caxton Hill, Ware Road, Hertford, England, hold a supply of the types and are willing to undertake the work. For the moment, type available is confined to 12-point size in the three founts exemplified in this book.

TYPOGRAPHY AND READING KEY

THE orthodox version of the play appears on right-hand pages. On the left is a line-for-line equivalent in the Shaw Alphabet, which occupies one-third less space, though both versions are set in type of the same size.

Three styles of type are used – to distinguish between the dialogue words spoken ('Normal' style), the names of speakers ('Bold'), and the scattered stage directions ('Sloping').

As readers should first become accustomed to Normal type, this style is used for lengthy stage directions introducing the Prologue and each Act. The 'Shavian' text's stage directions are all placed within brackets [] irrespective of what is done with them in the orthodox text.

To help unpractised readers, many apostrophes omitted in the orthodox version are restored in this Shavian text; but any negative verb (dont, wouldnt etc) is transcribed without an apostrophe.

Emphasis is indicated by the use of bold type.

To convert letters into sounds, look for any Tall letter in the Reading Key's first line, for any Deep letter in the second line, for any Short letter in the lower lines. Only the last letter of all is a Tall-and-Short compound.

The reader will find the Key's top edge a handy guide from the line he is deciphering to its 'crib-line' opposite.

Notes on the spelling are given on page 143.

ANDROCLES AND THE LION

·𐑨𐑯𐑛𐑮𐑩𐑒𐑤𐑰𐑟 𐑯 𐑞 𐑤𐑲𐑩𐑯

𐑐𐑮𐑴𐑤𐑪𐑜

[𐑴𐑝𐑼𐑗𐑫𐑼: 𐑓𐑪𐑮𐑦𐑕𐑑 𐑕𐑬𐑯𐑛𐑟, 𐑮𐑹𐑦𐑙 𐑝 𐑤𐑲𐑩𐑯𐑟, 𐑒𐑮𐑦𐑕𐑑𐑘𐑩𐑯 𐑣𐑦𐑥 𐑓𐑱𐑯𐑑𐑤𐑦.

𐑩 𐑡𐑳𐑙𐑜𐑩𐑤 𐑐𐑭𐑔. 𐑩 𐑤𐑲𐑩𐑯𐑟 𐑮𐑹, 𐑩 𐑥𐑧𐑤𐑩𐑙𐑒𐑩𐑤𐑦 𐑕𐑳𐑓𐑼𐑦𐑙 𐑮𐑹, 𐑒𐑳𐑥𐑟 𐑓𐑮𐑪𐑥 𐑞 𐑡𐑳𐑙𐑜𐑩𐑤. 𐑦𐑑 𐑦𐑟 𐑮𐑦𐑐𐑰𐑑𐑩𐑛 𐑯𐑽𐑼. 𐑞 𐑤𐑲𐑩𐑯 𐑤𐑦𐑥𐑐𐑕 𐑓𐑮𐑪𐑥 𐑞 𐑡𐑳𐑙𐑜𐑩𐑤 𐑪𐑯 𐑔𐑮𐑰 𐑤𐑧𐑜𐑟, 𐑣𐑴𐑤𐑛𐑦𐑙 𐑳𐑐 𐑣𐑦𐑟 𐑮𐑲𐑑 𐑓𐑹𐑐𐑷, 𐑦𐑯 𐑢𐑦𐑗 𐑩 𐑣𐑿𐑡 𐑔𐑹𐑯 𐑕𐑑𐑦𐑒𐑕. 𐑣𐑰 𐑕𐑦𐑑𐑕 𐑛𐑬𐑯 𐑯 𐑒𐑪𐑯𐑑𐑧𐑥𐑐𐑤𐑱𐑑𐑕 𐑦𐑑. 𐑣𐑰 𐑤𐑦𐑒𐑕 𐑦𐑑. 𐑣𐑰 𐑖𐑱𐑒𐑕 𐑦𐑑. 𐑣𐑰 𐑑𐑮𐑲𐑟 𐑑 𐑦𐑒𐑕𐑑𐑮𐑨𐑒𐑑 𐑦𐑑 𐑚𐑲 𐑕𐑒𐑮𐑱𐑐𐑦𐑙 𐑦𐑑 𐑩𐑤𐑪𐑙 𐑞 𐑜𐑮𐑬𐑯𐑛, 𐑯 𐑣𐑻𐑑𐑕 𐑣𐑦𐑥𐑕𐑧𐑤𐑓 𐑢𐑻𐑕. 𐑣𐑰 𐑮𐑹𐑟 𐑐𐑦𐑑𐑦𐑩𐑕𐑤𐑦. 𐑣𐑰 𐑤𐑦𐑒𐑕 𐑦𐑑 𐑩𐑜𐑱𐑯. 𐑑𐑽𐑟 𐑛𐑮𐑪𐑐 𐑓𐑮𐑪𐑥 𐑣𐑦𐑟 𐑲𐑟. 𐑣𐑰 𐑤𐑦𐑥𐑐𐑕 𐑐𐑱𐑯𐑓𐑩𐑤𐑦 𐑪𐑓 𐑞 𐑐𐑭𐑔 𐑯 𐑤𐑲𐑟 𐑛𐑬𐑯 𐑳𐑯𐑛𐑼 𐑞 𐑑𐑮𐑰𐑟, 𐑦𐑜𐑟𐑷𐑕𐑑𐑦𐑛 𐑢𐑦𐑞 𐑐𐑱𐑯. 𐑣𐑰𐑝𐑦𐑙 𐑩 𐑤𐑪𐑙 𐑕𐑲, 𐑤𐑲𐑒 𐑢𐑦𐑯𐑛 𐑦𐑯 𐑩 𐑑𐑮𐑪𐑥𐑚𐑴𐑯, 𐑣𐑰 𐑜𐑴𐑟 𐑑 𐑕𐑤𐑰𐑐.

·𐑨𐑯𐑛𐑮𐑩𐑒𐑤𐑰𐑟 𐑯 𐑣𐑦𐑟 𐑢𐑲𐑓 ·𐑥𐑩𐑡𐑽𐑩 𐑒𐑳𐑥 𐑩𐑤𐑪𐑙 𐑞 𐑐𐑭𐑔. 𐑣𐑰 𐑦𐑟 𐑩 𐑕𐑥𐑷𐑤, 𐑔𐑦𐑯, 𐑮𐑦𐑛𐑦𐑒𐑿𐑤𐑩𐑕 𐑤𐑦𐑑𐑩𐑤 𐑥𐑨𐑯 𐑣𐑵 𐑥𐑲𐑑 𐑚𐑰 𐑧𐑯𐑦 𐑱𐑡 𐑓𐑮𐑪𐑥 𐑔𐑻𐑑𐑦 𐑑 𐑓𐑦𐑓𐑑𐑦-𐑓𐑲𐑝. 𐑣𐑰 𐑣𐑨𐑟 𐑕𐑨𐑯𐑛𐑦 𐑣𐑺, 𐑢𐑷𐑑𐑼𐑦 𐑒𐑩𐑥𐑐𐑨𐑖𐑩𐑯𐑩𐑑 𐑚𐑤𐑵 𐑲𐑟, 𐑕𐑧𐑯𐑕𐑦𐑑𐑦𐑝 𐑯𐑪𐑕𐑑𐑮𐑦𐑤𐑟, 𐑯 𐑩 𐑝𐑧𐑮𐑦 𐑐𐑮𐑦𐑟𐑧𐑯𐑑𐑩𐑚𐑩𐑤 𐑓𐑪𐑮𐑦𐑛; 𐑚𐑳𐑑 𐑣𐑦𐑟 𐑜𐑫𐑛 𐑐𐑶𐑯𐑑𐑕 𐑜𐑴 𐑯𐑴 𐑓𐑻𐑞𐑼: 𐑣𐑦𐑟 𐑸𐑥𐑟 𐑯 𐑤𐑧𐑜𐑟 𐑯 𐑚𐑨𐑒, 𐑞𐑴 𐑢𐑲𐑼𐑦 𐑝 𐑞𐑺 𐑒𐑲𐑯𐑛, 𐑤𐑫𐑒 𐑖𐑮𐑦𐑝𐑩𐑤𐑛 𐑯 𐑕𐑑𐑸𐑝𐑛. 𐑣𐑰 𐑒𐑨𐑮𐑦𐑟 𐑩 𐑚𐑦𐑜 𐑚𐑳𐑯𐑛𐑩𐑤, 𐑦𐑟 𐑝𐑧𐑮𐑦 𐑐𐑫𐑼𐑤𐑦 𐑒𐑤𐑨𐑛, 𐑯 𐑕𐑰𐑥𐑟 𐑑𐑲𐑼𐑛 𐑯 𐑣𐑳𐑙𐑜𐑮𐑦.

𐑣𐑦𐑟 𐑢𐑲𐑓 𐑦𐑟 𐑩 𐑮𐑭𐑞𐑼 𐑣𐑨𐑯𐑕𐑩𐑥 𐑐𐑨𐑥𐑐𐑼𐑛 𐑕𐑤𐑨𐑑𐑼𐑯, 𐑢𐑧𐑤 𐑓𐑧𐑛 𐑯 𐑦𐑯 𐑞 𐑐𐑮𐑲𐑥 𐑝 𐑤𐑲𐑓. 𐑖𐑰 𐑣𐑨𐑟 𐑯𐑳𐑔𐑦𐑙 𐑑 𐑒𐑨𐑮𐑦, 𐑯 𐑣𐑨𐑟 𐑩 𐑕𐑑𐑬𐑑 𐑕𐑑𐑦𐑒 𐑑 𐑣𐑧𐑤𐑐 𐑣𐑻 𐑩𐑤𐑪𐑙].

ANDROCLES AND THE LION

PROLOGUE

Overture: forest sounds, roaring of lions, Christian hymn faintly.

A jungle path. A lion's roar, a melancholy suffering roar, comes from the jungle. It is repeated nearer. The lion limps from the jungle on three legs, holding up his right forepaw, in which a huge thorn sticks. He sits down and contemplates it. He licks it. He shakes it. He tries to extract it by scraping it along the ground, and hurts himself worse. He roars piteously. He licks it again. Tears drop from his eyes. He limps painfully off the path and lies down under the trees, exhausted with pain. Heaving a long sigh, like wind in a trombone, he goes to sleep.

Androcles and his wife Megaera come along the path. He is a small, thin, ridiculous little man who might be any age from thirty to fifty-five. He has sandy hair, watery compassionate blue eyes, sensitive nostrils, and a very presentable forehead; but his good points go no further: his arms and legs and back, though wiry of their kind, look shrivelled and starved. He carries a big bundle, is very poorly clad, and seems tired and hungry.

His wife is a rather handsome pampered slattern, well fed and in the prime of life. She has nothing to carry, and has a stout stick to help her along.

𐑨𐑯𐑛𐑮𐑩𐑒𐑤𐑰𐑟 𐑯 𐑞 𐑤𐑲𐑩𐑯

𐑥𐑩𐑡𐑽𐑮𐑩 [𐑕𐑳𐑛𐑩𐑯𐑤𐑦 𐑔𐑮𐑴𐑦𐑙 𐑛𐑬𐑯 𐑣𐑻 𐑚𐑳𐑯𐑛𐑩𐑤] 𐑲 𐑢𐑴𐑯𐑑 𐑜𐑴 𐑩𐑯𐑳𐑞𐑼 𐑕𐑑𐑧𐑐.

𐑨𐑯𐑛𐑮𐑩𐑒𐑤𐑰𐑟 [𐑐𐑤𐑰𐑛𐑦𐑙 𐑢𐑽𐑮𐑦𐑤𐑦] 𐑴, 𐑯𐑪𐑑 𐑩𐑜𐑱𐑯, 𐑛𐑽. 𐑢𐑪𐑑𐑕 𐑞 𐑜𐑫𐑛 𐑝 𐑕𐑑𐑪𐑐𐑦𐑙 𐑧𐑝𐑮𐑦 𐑑𐑵 𐑥𐑲𐑤𐑟 𐑯 𐑕𐑱𐑦𐑙 𐑿 𐑢𐑴𐑯𐑑 𐑜𐑴 𐑩𐑯𐑳𐑞𐑼 𐑕𐑑𐑧𐑐? 𐑢𐑰 𐑥𐑳𐑕𐑑 𐑜𐑧𐑑 𐑪𐑯 𐑑 𐑞 𐑯𐑧𐑒𐑕𐑑 𐑝𐑦𐑤𐑦𐑡 𐑚𐑦𐑓𐑹 𐑯𐑲𐑑. 𐑞𐑺 𐑸 𐑢𐑲𐑤𐑛 𐑚𐑰𐑕𐑑𐑕 𐑦𐑯 𐑞𐑦𐑕 𐑢𐑫𐑛: 𐑤𐑲𐑩𐑯𐑟, 𐑞𐑱 𐑕𐑱.

𐑥𐑩𐑡𐑽𐑮𐑩. 𐑲 𐑛𐑴𐑯𐑑 𐑚𐑦𐑤𐑰𐑝 𐑩 𐑢𐑻𐑛 𐑝 𐑦𐑑. 𐑿 𐑸 𐑷𐑤𐑢𐑱𐑟 𐑔𐑮𐑧𐑑𐑩𐑯𐑦𐑙 𐑥𐑰 𐑢𐑦𐑞 𐑢𐑲𐑤𐑛 𐑚𐑰𐑕𐑑𐑕 𐑑 𐑥𐑱𐑒 𐑥𐑰 𐑢𐑷𐑒 𐑞 𐑝𐑧𐑮𐑦 𐑕𐑴𐑤 𐑬𐑑 𐑝 𐑥𐑲 𐑚𐑪𐑛𐑦 𐑢𐑧𐑯 𐑲 𐑒𐑨𐑯 𐑣𐑸𐑛𐑤𐑦 𐑛𐑮𐑨𐑜 𐑢𐑳𐑯 𐑓𐑫𐑑 𐑚𐑦𐑓𐑹 𐑩𐑯𐑳𐑞𐑼. 𐑢𐑰 𐑣𐑨𐑝𐑩𐑯𐑑 𐑕𐑰𐑯 𐑩 𐑕𐑦𐑙𐑜𐑩𐑤 𐑤𐑲𐑩𐑯 𐑘𐑧𐑑.

𐑨𐑯𐑛𐑮𐑩𐑒𐑤𐑰𐑟. 𐑢𐑧𐑤, 𐑛𐑽, 𐑛𐑵 𐑿 𐑢𐑪𐑯𐑑 𐑑 𐑕𐑰 𐑢𐑳𐑯?

𐑥𐑩𐑡𐑽𐑮𐑩 [𐑑𐑺𐑦𐑙 𐑞 𐑚𐑨𐑜 𐑓𐑮𐑪𐑥 𐑣𐑦𐑟 𐑚𐑨𐑒] 𐑿 𐑒𐑮𐑵𐑩𐑤 𐑚𐑮𐑵𐑑, 𐑿 𐑛𐑴𐑯𐑑 𐑒𐑺 𐑣𐑬 𐑑𐑲𐑼𐑛 𐑲 𐑨𐑥, 𐑹 𐑢𐑪𐑑 𐑚𐑦𐑒𐑳𐑥𐑟 𐑝 𐑥𐑰 [𐑖𐑰 𐑔𐑮𐑴𐑟 𐑞 𐑚𐑨𐑜 𐑪𐑯 𐑞 𐑜𐑮𐑬𐑯𐑛]: 𐑷𐑤𐑢𐑱𐑟 𐑔𐑦𐑙𐑒𐑦𐑙 𐑝 𐑿𐑼𐑕𐑧𐑤𐑓. 𐑕𐑧𐑤𐑓! 𐑕𐑧𐑤𐑓! 𐑕𐑧𐑤𐑓! 𐑷𐑤𐑢𐑱𐑟 𐑿𐑼𐑕𐑧𐑤𐑓! [𐑖𐑰 𐑕𐑦𐑑𐑕 𐑛𐑬𐑯 𐑪𐑯 𐑞 𐑚𐑨𐑜].

𐑨𐑯𐑛𐑮𐑩𐑒𐑤𐑰𐑟 [𐑕𐑦𐑑𐑦𐑙 𐑛𐑬𐑯 𐑕𐑨𐑛𐑤𐑦 𐑪𐑯 𐑞 𐑜𐑮𐑬𐑯𐑛 𐑢𐑦𐑞 𐑣𐑦𐑟 𐑧𐑤𐑚𐑴𐑟 𐑪𐑯 𐑣𐑦𐑟 𐑯𐑰𐑟 𐑯 𐑣𐑦𐑟 𐑣𐑧𐑛 𐑦𐑯 𐑣𐑦𐑟 𐑣𐑨𐑯𐑛𐑟] 𐑢𐑰 𐑷𐑤 𐑣𐑨𐑝 𐑑 𐑔𐑦𐑙𐑒 𐑝 𐑬𐑼𐑕𐑧𐑤𐑝𐑟 𐑩𐑒𐑱𐑠𐑩𐑯𐑩𐑤𐑦, 𐑛𐑽.

𐑥𐑩𐑡𐑽𐑮𐑩. 𐑩 𐑥𐑨𐑯 𐑷𐑑 𐑑 𐑔𐑦𐑙𐑒 𐑝 𐑣𐑦𐑟 𐑢𐑲𐑓 𐑕𐑳𐑥𐑑𐑲𐑥𐑟.

𐑨𐑯𐑛𐑮𐑩𐑒𐑤𐑰𐑟. 𐑣𐑰 𐑒𐑭𐑯𐑑 𐑷𐑤𐑢𐑱𐑟 𐑣𐑧𐑤𐑐 𐑦𐑑, 𐑛𐑽. 𐑿 𐑥𐑱𐑒 𐑥𐑰 𐑔𐑦𐑙𐑒 𐑝 𐑿 𐑩 𐑜𐑫𐑛 𐑛𐑰𐑤. 𐑯𐑪𐑑 𐑞𐑨𐑑 𐑲 𐑚𐑤𐑱𐑥 𐑿.

𐑥𐑩𐑡𐑽𐑮𐑩. 𐑚𐑤𐑱𐑥 𐑥𐑰! 𐑲 𐑖𐑫𐑛 𐑔𐑦𐑙𐑒 𐑯𐑪𐑑 𐑦𐑯𐑛𐑰𐑛. 𐑦𐑟 𐑦𐑑 𐑥𐑲 𐑓𐑷𐑤𐑑 𐑞𐑨𐑑 𐑲'𐑥 𐑥𐑨𐑮𐑦𐑛 𐑑 𐑿?

𐑨𐑯𐑛𐑮𐑩𐑒𐑤𐑰𐑟. 𐑯𐑴, 𐑛𐑽: 𐑞𐑨𐑑 𐑦𐑟 𐑥𐑲 𐑓𐑷𐑤𐑑.

MEGAERA [*suddenly throwing down her stick*] I wont go another step.

ANDROCLES [*pleading wearily*] Oh, not again, dear. Whats the good of stopping every two miles and saying you wont go another step? We must get on to the next village before night. There are wild beasts in this wood: lions, they say.

MEGAERA. I dont believe a word of it. You are always threatening me with wild beasts to make me walk the very soul out of my body when I can hardly drag one foot before another. We havnt seen a single lion yet.

ANDROCLES. Well, dear, do you want to see one?

MEGAERA [*tearing the bundle from his back*] You cruel brute, you dont care how tired I am, or what becomes of me [*she throws the bundle on the ground*]: always thinking of yourself. Self! self! self! always yourself! [*She sits down on the bundle*].

ANDROCLES [*sitting down sadly on the ground with his elbows on his knees and his head in his hands*] We all have to think of ourselves occasionally, dear.

MEGAERA. A man ought to think of his wife sometimes.

ANDROCLES. He cant always help it, dear. You make me think of you a good deal. Not that I blame you.

MEGAERA. Blame me! I should think not indeed. Is it my fault that I'm married to you?

ANDROCLES. No, dear: that is my fault.

𐑥𐑩𐑡𐑽𐑩. 𐑞𐑨𐑑'𐑕 𐑩 𐑯𐑲𐑕 𐑔𐑦𐑙 𐑑 𐑕𐑱 𐑑 𐑥𐑰. 𐑸𐑯𐑑 𐑿 𐑣𐑨𐑐𐑦 𐑢𐑦𐑞 𐑥𐑰?

𐑨𐑯𐑛𐑮𐑩𐑒𐑤𐑰𐑟. 𐑲 𐑛𐑴𐑯𐑑 𐑒𐑩𐑥𐑐𐑤𐑱𐑯, 𐑥𐑲 𐑤𐑳𐑝.

𐑥𐑩𐑡𐑽𐑩. 𐑿 𐑷𐑑 𐑑 𐑚𐑰 𐑩𐑖𐑱𐑥𐑛 𐑝 𐑿𐑼𐑕𐑧𐑤𐑓.

𐑨𐑯𐑛𐑮𐑩𐑒𐑤𐑰𐑟. 𐑲 𐑨𐑥, 𐑥𐑲 𐑛𐑽.

𐑥𐑩𐑡𐑽𐑩. 𐑿'𐑼 𐑯𐑪𐑑: 𐑿 𐑜𐑤𐑹𐑦 𐑦𐑯 𐑦𐑑.

𐑨𐑯𐑛𐑮𐑩𐑒𐑤𐑰𐑟. 𐑦𐑯 𐑢𐑪𐑑, 𐑛𐑸𐑤𐑦𐑙?

𐑥𐑩𐑡𐑽𐑩. 𐑦𐑯 𐑧𐑝𐑮𐑦𐑔𐑦𐑙. 𐑦𐑯 𐑥𐑱𐑒𐑦𐑙 𐑥𐑰 𐑩 𐑕𐑤𐑱𐑝, 𐑯 𐑥𐑱𐑒𐑦𐑙 𐑿𐑼𐑕𐑧𐑤𐑓 𐑩 𐑤𐑭𐑓𐑦𐑙-𐑕𐑑𐑪𐑒. 𐑦𐑑'𐑕 𐑯𐑪𐑑 𐑓𐑺. 𐑿 𐑜𐑧𐑑 𐑥𐑰 𐑞 𐑯𐑱𐑥 𐑝 𐑚𐑰𐑦𐑙 𐑩 𐑖𐑮𐑵 𐑢𐑦𐑞 𐑿𐑼 𐑥𐑰𐑒 𐑢𐑱𐑟, 𐑷𐑤𐑢𐑱𐑟 𐑑𐑷𐑒𐑦𐑙 𐑨𐑟 𐑦𐑓 𐑚𐑳𐑑𐑼 𐑢𐑫𐑛𐑩𐑯𐑑 𐑥𐑧𐑤𐑑 𐑦𐑯 𐑿𐑼 𐑥𐑬𐑔. 𐑯 𐑡𐑳𐑕𐑑 𐑚𐑦𐑒𐑪𐑟 𐑲 𐑤𐑫𐑒 𐑩 𐑚𐑦𐑜 𐑕𐑑𐑮𐑪𐑙 𐑢𐑫𐑥𐑩𐑯, 𐑯 𐑚𐑦𐑒𐑪𐑟 𐑲'𐑥 𐑜𐑫𐑛𐑣𐑸𐑑𐑩𐑛 𐑯 𐑩 𐑚𐑦𐑑 𐑣𐑱𐑕𐑑𐑦, 𐑯 𐑚𐑦𐑒𐑪𐑟 𐑿'𐑼 𐑷𐑤𐑢𐑱𐑟 𐑛𐑮𐑲𐑝𐑦𐑙 𐑥𐑰 𐑑 𐑛𐑵 𐑔𐑦𐑙𐑟 𐑲'𐑥 𐑕𐑪𐑮𐑦 𐑓𐑹 𐑭𐑓𐑑𐑼𐑢𐑼𐑛𐑟, 𐑐𐑰𐑐𐑩𐑤 𐑕𐑱 '𐑐𐑫𐑼 𐑥𐑨𐑯: 𐑢𐑪𐑑 𐑩 𐑤𐑲𐑓 𐑣𐑦𐑟 𐑢𐑲𐑓 𐑤𐑰𐑛𐑟 𐑣𐑦𐑥!' 𐑴, 𐑦𐑓 𐑞𐑱 𐑴𐑯𐑤𐑦 𐑯𐑿! 𐑯 𐑿 𐑔𐑦𐑙𐑒 𐑲 𐑛𐑴𐑯𐑑 𐑯𐑴. 𐑚𐑳𐑑 𐑲 𐑛𐑵, 𐑲 𐑛𐑵, [𐑕𐑒𐑮𐑰𐑥𐑦𐑙] 𐑲 𐑛𐑵.

𐑨𐑯𐑛𐑮𐑩𐑒𐑤𐑰𐑟. 𐑘𐑧𐑕, 𐑥𐑲 𐑛𐑽: 𐑲 𐑯𐑴 𐑿 𐑛𐑵.

𐑥𐑩𐑡𐑽𐑩. 𐑞𐑧𐑯 𐑢𐑲 𐑛𐑴𐑯𐑑 𐑿 𐑑𐑮𐑰𐑑 𐑥𐑰 𐑐𐑮𐑪𐑐𐑼𐑤𐑦 𐑯 𐑚𐑰 𐑩 𐑜𐑫𐑛 𐑣𐑳𐑟𐑚𐑩𐑯𐑛 𐑑 𐑥𐑰?

𐑨𐑯𐑛𐑮𐑩𐑒𐑤𐑰𐑟. 𐑢𐑪𐑑 𐑒𐑨𐑯 𐑲 𐑛𐑵, 𐑥𐑲 𐑛𐑽?

𐑥𐑩𐑡𐑽𐑩. 𐑢𐑪𐑑 𐑒𐑨𐑯 𐑿 𐑛𐑵! 𐑿 𐑒𐑨𐑯 𐑮𐑦𐑑𐑻𐑯 𐑑 𐑿𐑼 𐑛𐑿𐑑𐑦, 𐑯 𐑒𐑳𐑥 𐑚𐑨𐑒 𐑑 𐑿𐑼 𐑣𐑴𐑥 𐑯 𐑿𐑼 𐑓𐑮𐑧𐑯𐑛𐑟, 𐑯 𐑕𐑨𐑒𐑮𐑦𐑓𐑲𐑕 𐑑 𐑞 𐑜𐑪𐑛𐑟 𐑨𐑟 𐑷𐑤 𐑮𐑦𐑕𐑐𐑧𐑒𐑑𐑩𐑚𐑩𐑤 𐑐𐑰𐑐𐑩𐑤 𐑛𐑵, 𐑦𐑯𐑕𐑑𐑧𐑛 𐑝 𐑣𐑨𐑝𐑦𐑙 𐑳𐑕 𐑣𐑳𐑯𐑑𐑩𐑛 𐑬𐑑 𐑝 𐑣𐑬𐑕 𐑯 𐑣𐑴𐑥 𐑓𐑹 𐑚𐑰𐑦𐑙 𐑛𐑻𐑑𐑦 𐑛𐑦𐑕𐑮𐑧𐑐𐑿𐑑𐑩𐑚𐑩𐑤 𐑚𐑤𐑨𐑕𐑓𐑰𐑥𐑦𐑙 𐑱𐑔𐑰𐑦𐑕𐑑𐑕.

𐑨𐑯𐑛𐑮𐑩𐑒𐑤𐑰𐑟. 𐑲'𐑥 𐑯𐑪𐑑 𐑩𐑯 𐑱𐑔𐑰𐑦𐑕𐑑, 𐑛𐑽: 𐑲 𐑨𐑥 𐑩 𐑒𐑮𐑦𐑕𐑗𐑩𐑯.

𐑥𐑩𐑡𐑽𐑩. 𐑢𐑧𐑤, 𐑦𐑟𐑯𐑑 𐑞𐑨𐑑 𐑞 𐑕𐑱𐑥 𐑔𐑦𐑙, 𐑴𐑯𐑤𐑦 𐑑𐑧𐑯

MEGAERA. Thats a nice thing to say to me. Arnt you happy with me?

ANDROCLES. I dont complain, my love.

MEGAERA. You ought to be ashamed of yourself.

ANDROCLES. I am, my dear.

MEGAERA. Youre not: you glory in it.

ANDROCLES. In what, darling?

MEGAERA. In everything. In making me a slave, and making yourself a laughing-stock. It's not fair. You get me the name of being a shrew with your meek ways, always talking as if butter wouldnt melt in your mouth. And just because I look a big strong woman, and because I'm goodhearted and a bit hasty, and because youre always driving me to do things I'm sorry for afterwards, people say 'Poor man: what a life his wife leads him!' Oh, if they only knew! And you think I dont know. But I do, I do, [*screaming*] I do.

ANDROCLES. Yes, my dear: I know you do.

MEGAERA. Then why dont you treat me properly and be a good husband to me?

ANDROCLES. What can I do, my dear?

MEGAERA. What can you do! You can return to your duty, and come back to your home and your friends, and sacrifice to the gods as all respectable people do, instead of having us hunted out of house and home for being dirty disreputable blaspheming atheists.

ANDROCLES. I'm not an atheist, dear: I am a Christian.

MEGAERA. Well, isnt that the same thing, only ten

𐑑𐑲𐑥𐑟 𐑢𐑻𐑕? 𐑧𐑝𐑮𐑦𐑚𐑪𐑛𐑦 𐑯𐑴𐑟 𐑞𐑨𐑑 𐑞 𐑒𐑮𐑦𐑕𐑗𐑩𐑯𐑟 𐑸 𐑞 𐑝𐑧𐑮𐑦 𐑤𐑴𐑩𐑕𐑑 𐑝 𐑞 𐑤𐑴.

𐑨𐑯𐑛𐑮𐑩𐑒𐑤𐑰𐑟. 𐑡𐑳𐑕𐑑 𐑤𐑲𐑒 𐑳𐑕, 𐑛𐑽.

𐑥𐑩𐑜𐑽𐑩. 𐑕𐑐𐑰𐑒 𐑓𐑹 𐑿𐑹𐑕𐑧𐑤𐑓. 𐑛𐑴𐑯𐑑 𐑿 𐑛𐑺 𐑑 𐑒𐑩𐑥𐑐𐑺 𐑥𐑰 𐑑 𐑒𐑪𐑥𐑩𐑯 𐑐𐑰𐑐𐑩𐑤. 𐑥𐑲 𐑓𐑭𐑞𐑼 𐑴𐑯𐑛 𐑣𐑦𐑟 𐑴𐑯 𐑐𐑳𐑚𐑤𐑦𐑒-𐑣𐑬𐑕; 𐑯 𐑕𐑪𐑮𐑴𐑓𐑩𐑤 𐑢𐑪𐑟 𐑞 𐑛𐑱 𐑓𐑹 𐑥𐑰 𐑢𐑧𐑯 𐑿 𐑓𐑻𐑕𐑑 𐑒𐑱𐑥 𐑛𐑮𐑦𐑙𐑒𐑦𐑙 𐑦𐑯 𐑬𐑼 𐑚𐑸.

𐑨𐑯𐑛𐑮𐑩𐑒𐑤𐑰𐑟. 𐑲 𐑒𐑩𐑯𐑓𐑧𐑕 𐑲 𐑢𐑪𐑟 𐑩𐑛𐑦𐑒𐑑𐑦𐑛 𐑑 𐑦𐑑, 𐑛𐑽. 𐑚𐑳𐑑 𐑲 𐑜𐑱𐑝 𐑦𐑑 𐑳𐑐 𐑢𐑧𐑯 𐑲 𐑚𐑦𐑒𐑱𐑥 𐑩 𐑒𐑮𐑦𐑕𐑗𐑩𐑯.

𐑥𐑩𐑜𐑽𐑩. 𐑿'𐑛 𐑥𐑳𐑗 𐑚𐑧𐑑𐑼 𐑣𐑨𐑝 𐑮𐑦𐑥𐑱𐑯𐑛 𐑩 𐑛𐑮𐑳𐑙𐑒𐑼𐑛. 𐑲 𐑒𐑨𐑯 𐑓𐑹𐑜𐑦𐑝 𐑩 𐑥𐑨𐑯 𐑚𐑰𐑦𐑙 𐑩𐑛𐑦𐑒𐑑𐑦𐑛 𐑑 𐑛𐑮𐑦𐑙𐑒: 𐑦𐑑'𐑕 𐑴𐑯𐑤𐑦 𐑯𐑨𐑗𐑼𐑩𐑤; 𐑯 𐑲 𐑛𐑴𐑯𐑑 𐑛𐑦𐑯𐑲 𐑲 𐑤𐑲𐑒 𐑩 𐑛𐑮𐑪𐑐 𐑥𐑲𐑕𐑧𐑤𐑓 𐑕𐑳𐑥𐑑𐑲𐑥𐑟. 𐑢𐑪𐑑 𐑲 𐑒𐑭𐑯𐑑 𐑕𐑑𐑨𐑯𐑛 𐑦𐑟 𐑿𐑼 𐑚𐑰𐑦𐑙 𐑩𐑛𐑦𐑒𐑑𐑦𐑛 𐑑 𐑒𐑮𐑦𐑕𐑑𐑦𐑨𐑯𐑦𐑑𐑦. 𐑯 𐑢𐑪𐑑'𐑕 𐑢𐑻𐑕 𐑩𐑜𐑱𐑯, 𐑿𐑼 𐑚𐑰𐑦𐑙 𐑩𐑛𐑦𐑒𐑑𐑦𐑛 𐑑 𐑨𐑯𐑦𐑥𐑩𐑤𐑟. 𐑣𐑬 𐑦𐑟 𐑧𐑯𐑦 𐑢𐑫𐑥𐑩𐑯 𐑑 𐑒𐑰𐑐 𐑣𐑻 𐑣𐑬𐑕 𐑒𐑤𐑰𐑯 𐑢𐑧𐑯 𐑿 𐑚𐑮𐑦𐑙 𐑦𐑯 𐑧𐑝𐑮𐑦 𐑕𐑑𐑮𐑱 𐑒𐑨𐑑 𐑯 𐑤𐑪𐑕𐑑 𐑒𐑻 𐑯 𐑤𐑱𐑥 𐑛𐑳𐑒 𐑦𐑯 𐑞 𐑣𐑴𐑤 𐑒𐑳𐑯𐑑𐑮𐑦𐑕𐑲𐑛? 𐑿 𐑑𐑫𐑒 𐑞 𐑚𐑮𐑧𐑛 𐑬𐑑 𐑝 𐑥𐑲 𐑥𐑬𐑔 𐑑 𐑓𐑰𐑛 𐑞𐑧𐑥: 𐑿 𐑯𐑴 𐑿 𐑛𐑦𐑛: 𐑛𐑴𐑯𐑑 𐑩𐑑𐑧𐑥𐑐𐑑 𐑑 𐑛𐑦𐑯𐑲 𐑦𐑑.

𐑨𐑯𐑛𐑮𐑩𐑒𐑤𐑰𐑟. 𐑴𐑯𐑤𐑦 𐑢𐑧𐑯 𐑞𐑱 𐑢𐑻 𐑣𐑳𐑙𐑜𐑮𐑦 𐑯 𐑿 𐑢𐑻 𐑜𐑧𐑑𐑦𐑙 𐑑𐑵 𐑕𐑑𐑬𐑑, 𐑛𐑽𐑦.

𐑥𐑩𐑜𐑽𐑩. 𐑘𐑧𐑕: 𐑦𐑯𐑕𐑳𐑤𐑑 𐑥𐑰, 𐑛𐑵. [𐑮𐑲𐑟𐑦𐑙] 𐑴! 𐑲 𐑢𐑴𐑯𐑑 𐑚𐑺 𐑦𐑑 𐑩𐑯𐑳𐑞𐑼 𐑥𐑴𐑥𐑩𐑯𐑑. 𐑿 𐑿𐑕𐑑 𐑑 𐑕𐑦𐑑 𐑯 𐑑𐑷𐑒 𐑑 𐑞𐑴𐑟 𐑛𐑳𐑥 𐑚𐑮𐑵𐑑𐑕 𐑓𐑹 𐑬𐑼𐑟, 𐑢𐑧𐑯 𐑿 𐑣𐑨𐑛𐑯𐑑 𐑩 𐑢𐑻𐑛 𐑓𐑹 𐑥𐑰.

𐑨𐑯𐑛𐑮𐑩𐑒𐑤𐑰𐑟. 𐑞𐑱 𐑯𐑧𐑝𐑼 𐑨𐑯𐑕𐑼𐑛 𐑚𐑨𐑒, 𐑛𐑸𐑤𐑦𐑙. [𐑣𐑰 𐑮𐑲𐑟𐑩𐑟 𐑯 𐑩𐑜𐑱𐑯 𐑖𐑴𐑤𐑛𐑼𐑟 𐑞 𐑚𐑳𐑯𐑛𐑩𐑤].

𐑥𐑩𐑜𐑽𐑩. 𐑢𐑧𐑤, 𐑦𐑓 𐑿'𐑼 𐑓𐑪𐑯𐑛𐑼 𐑝 𐑨𐑯𐑦𐑥𐑩𐑤𐑟 𐑞𐑨𐑯 𐑝 𐑿𐑼 𐑴𐑯 𐑢𐑲𐑓, 𐑿 𐑒𐑨𐑯 𐑤𐑦𐑝 𐑢𐑦𐑞 𐑞𐑧𐑥 𐑣𐑽 𐑦𐑯 𐑞

times worse? Everybody knows that the Christians are the very lowest of the low.

ANDROCLES. Just like us, dear.

MEGAERA. Speak for yourself. Dont you dare to compare me to common people. My father owned his own public-house; and sorrowful was the day for me when you first came drinking in our bar.

ANDROCLES. I confess I was addicted to it, dear. But I gave it up when I became a Christian.

MEGAERA. Youd much better have remained a drunkard. I can forgive a man being addicted to drink: it's only natural; and I dont deny I like a drop myself sometimes. What I cant stand is your being addicted to Christianity. And whats worse again, your being addicted to animals. How is any woman to keep her house clean when you bring in every stray cat and lost cur and lame duck in the whole countryside? You took the bread out of my mouth to feed them: you know you did: dont attempt to deny it.

ANDROCLES. Only when they were hungry and you were getting too stout, dearie.

MEGAERA. Yes: insult me, do. [*Rising*] Oh! I wont bear it another moment. You used to sit and talk to those dumb brute beasts for hours, when you hadnt a word for me.

ANDROCLES. They never answered back, darling. [*He rises and again shoulders the bundle*].

MEGAERA. Well, if youre fonder of animals than of your own wife, you can live with them here in the

𐑡𐑳𐑙𐑜𐑩𐑤. 𐑲'𐑝 𐑣𐑨𐑛 𐑦𐑯𐑳𐑓 𐑝 𐑞𐑧𐑥 𐑯 𐑦𐑯𐑳𐑓 𐑝 𐑿. 𐑲'𐑥 𐑜𐑴𐑦𐑙 𐑚𐑨𐑒. 𐑲'𐑥 𐑜𐑴𐑦𐑙 𐑣𐑴𐑥.

𐑨𐑯𐑛𐑮𐑩𐑒𐑤𐑰𐑟 [𐑚𐑸𐑦𐑙 𐑞 𐑢𐑱 𐑚𐑨𐑒] 𐑯𐑴, 𐑛𐑽𐑦: 𐑛𐑴𐑯𐑑 𐑑𐑱𐑒 𐑪𐑯 𐑤𐑲𐑒 𐑞𐑨𐑑. 𐑢𐑰 𐑒𐑭𐑯𐑑 𐑜𐑴 𐑚𐑨𐑒. 𐑢𐑰'𐑝 𐑕𐑴𐑤𐑛 𐑧𐑝𐑮𐑦𐑔𐑦𐑙: 𐑢𐑰 𐑖𐑫𐑛 𐑕𐑑𐑸𐑝; 𐑯 𐑲 𐑖𐑫𐑛 𐑚𐑰 𐑕𐑧𐑯𐑑 𐑑 ·𐑮𐑴𐑥 𐑯 𐑔𐑮𐑴𐑯 𐑑 𐑞 𐑤𐑲𐑩𐑯𐑟 –

𐑥𐑩𐑜𐑽𐑩. 𐑕𐑻𐑝 𐑿 𐑮𐑲𐑑! 𐑲 𐑢𐑦𐑖 𐑞 𐑤𐑲𐑩𐑯𐑟 𐑡𐑶 𐑝 𐑿. [𐑕𐑒𐑮𐑰𐑥𐑦𐑙] 𐑸 𐑿 𐑜𐑴𐑦𐑙 𐑑 𐑜𐑧𐑑 𐑬𐑑 𐑝 𐑥𐑲 𐑢𐑱 𐑯 𐑤𐑧𐑑 𐑥𐑰 𐑜𐑴 𐑣𐑴𐑥?

𐑨𐑯𐑛𐑮𐑩𐑒𐑤𐑰𐑟. 𐑯𐑴, 𐑛𐑽 –

𐑥𐑩𐑜𐑽𐑩. 𐑞𐑧𐑯 𐑲'𐑤 𐑥𐑱𐑒 𐑥𐑲 𐑢𐑱 𐑔𐑮𐑵 𐑞 𐑓𐑪𐑮𐑦𐑕𐑑; 𐑯 𐑢𐑧𐑯 𐑲'𐑥 𐑰𐑑𐑩𐑯 𐑚𐑲 𐑞 𐑢𐑲𐑤𐑛 𐑚𐑰𐑕𐑑𐑕 𐑿'𐑤 𐑯𐑴 𐑢𐑪𐑑 𐑩 𐑢𐑲𐑓 𐑿'𐑝 𐑤𐑪𐑕𐑑. [𐑖𐑰 𐑛𐑨𐑖𐑩𐑟 𐑦𐑯𐑑𐑵 𐑞 𐑡𐑳𐑙𐑜𐑩𐑤 𐑯 𐑯𐑽𐑤𐑦 𐑓𐑷𐑤𐑟 𐑴𐑝𐑼 𐑞 𐑕𐑤𐑰𐑐𐑦𐑙 𐑤𐑲𐑩𐑯]. 𐑴! 𐑴! ·𐑨𐑯𐑛𐑦! ·𐑨𐑯𐑛𐑦! [𐑖𐑰 𐑑𐑪𐑑𐑼𐑟 𐑚𐑨𐑒 𐑯 𐑒𐑩𐑤𐑨𐑐𐑕𐑩𐑟 𐑦𐑯𐑑𐑵 𐑞 𐑸𐑥𐑟 𐑝 ·𐑨𐑯𐑛𐑮𐑩𐑒𐑤𐑰𐑟, 𐑣𐑵, 𐑒𐑮𐑳𐑖𐑑 𐑚𐑲 𐑣𐑻 𐑢𐑱𐑑, 𐑓𐑷𐑤𐑟 𐑪𐑯 𐑣𐑦𐑟 𐑚𐑳𐑯𐑛𐑩𐑤].

𐑨𐑯𐑛𐑮𐑩𐑒𐑤𐑰𐑟 [𐑦𐑒𐑕𐑑𐑮𐑨𐑒𐑑𐑦𐑙 𐑣𐑦𐑥𐑕𐑧𐑤𐑓 𐑓𐑮𐑪𐑥 𐑚𐑦𐑯𐑰𐑔 𐑣𐑻, 𐑕𐑤𐑨𐑐𐑦𐑙 𐑣𐑻 𐑣𐑨𐑯𐑛𐑟 𐑦𐑯 𐑜𐑮𐑱𐑑 𐑨𐑙𐑟𐑲𐑩𐑑𐑦] 𐑢𐑪𐑑 𐑦𐑟 𐑦𐑑, 𐑥𐑲 𐑐𐑮𐑧𐑖𐑩𐑕, 𐑥𐑲 𐑐𐑧𐑑? 𐑢𐑪𐑑𐑕 𐑞 𐑥𐑨𐑑𐑼? [𐑣𐑰 𐑮𐑱𐑟𐑩𐑟 𐑣𐑻 𐑣𐑧𐑛. 𐑕𐑐𐑰𐑗𐑤𐑩𐑕 𐑢𐑦𐑞 𐑑𐑧𐑮𐑼, 𐑖𐑰 𐑐𐑶𐑯𐑑𐑕 𐑦𐑯 𐑞 𐑛𐑦𐑮𐑧𐑒𐑖𐑩𐑯 𐑝 𐑞 𐑕𐑤𐑰𐑐𐑦𐑙 𐑤𐑲𐑩𐑯. 𐑣𐑰 𐑕𐑑𐑰𐑤𐑟 𐑒𐑷𐑖𐑩𐑕𐑤𐑦 𐑑𐑫𐑢𐑹𐑛𐑟 𐑞 𐑕𐑐𐑪𐑑 𐑦𐑯𐑛𐑦𐑒𐑱𐑑𐑩𐑛 𐑚𐑲 ·𐑥𐑩𐑜𐑽𐑩. 𐑖𐑰 𐑮𐑲𐑟𐑩𐑟 𐑢𐑦𐑞 𐑩𐑯 𐑧𐑓𐑼𐑑 𐑯 𐑑𐑪𐑑𐑼𐑟 𐑭𐑓𐑑𐑼 𐑣𐑦𐑥].

𐑥𐑩𐑜𐑽𐑩. 𐑯𐑴, ·𐑨𐑯𐑛𐑦: 𐑿'𐑤 𐑚𐑰 𐑒𐑦𐑤𐑛. 𐑒𐑳𐑥 𐑚𐑨𐑒.

[𐑞 𐑤𐑲𐑩𐑯 𐑳𐑑𐑼𐑟 𐑩 𐑤𐑪𐑙 𐑕𐑯𐑹𐑦𐑙 𐑕𐑲. ·𐑨𐑯𐑛𐑮𐑩𐑒𐑤𐑰𐑟 𐑕𐑰𐑟 𐑞 𐑤𐑲𐑩𐑯, 𐑯 𐑮𐑦𐑒𐑶𐑤𐑟 𐑓𐑱𐑯𐑑𐑦𐑙 𐑦𐑯𐑑𐑵 𐑞 𐑸𐑥𐑟 𐑝 ·𐑥𐑩𐑜𐑽𐑩, 𐑣𐑵 𐑓𐑷𐑤𐑟 𐑚𐑨𐑒 𐑪𐑯 𐑞 𐑚𐑳𐑯𐑛𐑩𐑤. 𐑞𐑱 𐑮𐑴𐑤 𐑩𐑐𐑸𐑑 𐑯 𐑤𐑲 𐑕𐑑𐑺𐑦𐑙 𐑦𐑯 𐑑𐑧𐑮𐑼 𐑨𐑑 𐑢𐑳𐑯 𐑩𐑯𐑳𐑞𐑼. 𐑞 𐑤𐑲𐑩𐑯 𐑦𐑟 𐑣𐑻𐑛 𐑜𐑮𐑴𐑯𐑦𐑙 𐑣𐑧𐑝𐑦𐑤𐑦 𐑦𐑯 𐑞 𐑡𐑳𐑙𐑜𐑩𐑤].

jungle. Ive had enough of them and enough of you. I'm going back. I'm going home.

ANDROCLES [*barring the way back*] No, dearie: dont take on like that. We cant go back. Weve sold everything: we should starve; and I should be sent to Rome and thrown to the lions –

MEGAERA. Serve you right! I wish the lions joy of you. [*Screaming*] Are you going to get out of my way and let me go home?

ANDROCLES. No, dear –

MEGAERA. Then I'll make my way through the forest; and when I'm eaten by the wild beasts youll know what a wife youve lost. [*She dashes into the jungle and nearly falls over the sleeping lion*]. Oh! Oh! Andy! Andy! [*She totters back and collapses into the arms of Androcles, who, crushed by her weight, falls on his bundle*].

ANDROCLES [*extracting himself from beneath her and slapping her hands in great anxiety*] What is it, my precious, my pet? Whats the matter? [*He raises her head. Speechless with terror, she points in the direction of the sleeping lion. He steals cautiously towards the spot indicated by Megaera. She rises with an effort and totters after him*].

MEGAERA. No, Andy: youll be killed. Come back.

The lion utters a long snoring sigh. Androcles sees the lion, and recoils fainting into the arms of Megaera, who falls back on the bundle. They roll apart and lie staring in terror at one another. The lion is heard groaning heavily in the jungle.

𐑨𐑯𐑛𐑮𐑩𐑒𐑤𐑰𐑟 𐑯 𐑞 𐑤𐑲𐑩𐑯

𐑨𐑯𐑛𐑮𐑩𐑒𐑤𐑰𐑟 [𐑢𐑦𐑕𐑐𐑼𐑦𐑙] 𐑛𐑦𐑛 𐑿 𐑕𐑰? 𐑩 𐑤𐑲𐑩𐑯.

𐑥𐑧𐑜𐑽𐑩 [𐑛𐑦𐑕𐑐𐑺𐑦𐑙] 𐑞 𐑜𐑷𐑛𐑟 𐑣𐑨𐑝 𐑕𐑧𐑯𐑑 𐑣𐑦𐑥 𐑑 𐑐𐑳𐑯𐑦𐑖 𐑳𐑕 𐑚𐑦𐑒𐑪𐑟 𐑿'𐑼 𐑩 𐑒𐑮𐑦𐑕𐑗𐑩𐑯. 𐑑𐑱𐑒 𐑥𐑰 𐑩𐑢𐑱, ·𐑨𐑯𐑛𐑦. 𐑕𐑱𐑝 𐑥𐑰.

𐑨𐑯𐑛𐑮𐑩𐑒𐑤𐑰𐑟 [𐑮𐑲𐑟𐑦𐑙] ·𐑥𐑧𐑜𐑦: 𐑞𐑺'𐑟 𐑢𐑳𐑯 𐑗𐑭𐑯𐑕 𐑓𐑹 𐑿. 𐑦𐑑'𐑤 𐑑𐑱𐑒 𐑣𐑦𐑥 𐑐𐑮𐑦𐑑𐑦 𐑯𐑲 𐑑𐑢𐑧𐑯𐑑𐑦 𐑥𐑦𐑯𐑦𐑑𐑕 𐑑 𐑰𐑑 𐑥𐑰 (𐑲'𐑥 𐑮𐑭𐑞𐑼 𐑕𐑑𐑮𐑦𐑙𐑦 𐑯 𐑑𐑳𐑓) 𐑯 𐑿 𐑒𐑨𐑯 𐑦𐑕𐑒𐑱𐑐 𐑦𐑯 𐑤𐑧𐑕 𐑑𐑲𐑥 𐑞𐑨𐑯 𐑞𐑨𐑑.

𐑥𐑧𐑜𐑽𐑩. 𐑴, 𐑛𐑴𐑯𐑑 𐑑𐑷𐑒 𐑩𐑚𐑬𐑑 𐑰𐑑𐑦𐑙. [𐑞 𐑤𐑲𐑩𐑯 𐑮𐑲𐑟𐑩𐑟 𐑢𐑦𐑞 𐑩 𐑜𐑮𐑱𐑑 𐑜𐑮𐑴𐑯 𐑯 𐑤𐑦𐑥𐑐𐑕 𐑑𐑩𐑢𐑹𐑛𐑟 𐑞𐑧𐑥]. 𐑴! [𐑖𐑰 𐑓𐑱𐑯𐑑𐑕].

𐑨𐑯𐑛𐑮𐑩𐑒𐑤𐑰𐑟 [𐑒𐑢𐑱𐑒𐑦𐑙, 𐑚𐑳𐑑 𐑒𐑰𐑐𐑦𐑙 𐑚𐑦𐑑𐑢𐑰𐑯 𐑞 𐑤𐑲𐑩𐑯 𐑯 ·𐑥𐑧𐑜𐑽𐑩] 𐑛𐑴𐑯𐑑 𐑿 𐑒𐑳𐑥 𐑯𐑽 𐑥𐑲 𐑢𐑲𐑓, 𐑛𐑵 𐑿 𐑣𐑽? [𐑞 𐑤𐑲𐑩𐑯 𐑜𐑮𐑴𐑯𐑟. ·𐑨𐑯𐑛𐑮𐑩𐑒𐑤𐑰𐑟 𐑒𐑨𐑯 𐑣𐑸𐑛𐑤𐑦 𐑕𐑑𐑨𐑯𐑛 𐑓𐑹 𐑑𐑮𐑧𐑥𐑚𐑤𐑦𐑙]. ·𐑥𐑧𐑜𐑦: 𐑮𐑳𐑯. 𐑮𐑳𐑯 𐑓𐑹 𐑿𐑼 𐑤𐑲𐑓. 𐑦𐑓 𐑲 𐑑𐑱𐑒 𐑥𐑲 𐑲 𐑪𐑓 𐑣𐑦𐑥, 𐑦𐑑𐑕 𐑷𐑤 𐑳𐑐. [𐑞 𐑤𐑲𐑩𐑯 𐑣𐑴𐑤𐑛𐑟 𐑳𐑐 𐑣𐑦𐑟 𐑢𐑵𐑯𐑛𐑩𐑛 𐑐𐑷 𐑯 𐑓𐑤𐑨𐑐𐑕 𐑦𐑑 𐑐𐑦𐑑𐑦𐑩𐑕𐑤𐑦 𐑚𐑦𐑓𐑹 ·𐑨𐑯𐑛𐑮𐑩𐑒𐑤𐑰𐑟]. 𐑴, 𐑣𐑰'𐑟 𐑤𐑱𐑥, 𐑐𐑫𐑼 𐑴𐑤𐑛 𐑗𐑨𐑐! 𐑣𐑰'𐑟 𐑜𐑪𐑑 𐑩 𐑔𐑹𐑯 𐑦𐑯 𐑣𐑦𐑟 𐑐𐑷. 𐑩 𐑓𐑮𐑲𐑑𐑓𐑫𐑤𐑦 𐑚𐑦𐑜 𐑔𐑹𐑯. [𐑓𐑫𐑤 𐑝 𐑕𐑦𐑥𐑐𐑩𐑔𐑦] 𐑴, 𐑐𐑫𐑼 𐑴𐑤𐑛 𐑥𐑨𐑯! 𐑛𐑦𐑛 𐑳𐑥 𐑜𐑧𐑑 𐑩𐑯 𐑷𐑓𐑫𐑤 𐑔𐑹𐑯 𐑦𐑯𐑑𐑫 𐑳𐑥'𐑟 𐑑𐑫𐑑𐑕𐑳𐑥𐑟 𐑢𐑫𐑑𐑕𐑳𐑥𐑟? 𐑣𐑨𐑟 𐑦𐑑 𐑥𐑱𐑛 𐑳𐑥 𐑑𐑵 𐑕𐑦𐑒 𐑑 𐑰𐑑 𐑩 𐑯𐑲𐑕 𐑤𐑦𐑑𐑩𐑤 𐑒𐑮𐑦𐑕𐑗𐑩𐑯 𐑥𐑨𐑯 𐑓𐑹 𐑳𐑥'𐑟 𐑚𐑮𐑧𐑒𐑓𐑩𐑕𐑑? 𐑴, 𐑩 𐑯𐑲𐑕 𐑤𐑦𐑑𐑩𐑤 𐑒𐑮𐑦𐑕𐑗𐑩𐑯 𐑥𐑨𐑯 𐑢𐑦𐑤 𐑜𐑧𐑑 𐑳𐑥'𐑟 𐑔𐑹𐑯 𐑬𐑑 𐑓𐑹 𐑳𐑥; 𐑯 𐑞𐑧𐑯 𐑳𐑥 𐑖𐑨𐑤 𐑰𐑑 𐑞 𐑯𐑲𐑕 𐑒𐑮𐑦𐑕𐑗𐑩𐑯 𐑥𐑨𐑯 𐑯 𐑞 𐑯𐑲𐑕 𐑒𐑮𐑦𐑕𐑗𐑩𐑯 𐑥𐑨𐑯'𐑟 𐑯𐑲𐑕 𐑚𐑦𐑜 𐑑𐑧𐑯𐑛𐑼 𐑢𐑲𐑓𐑦-𐑐𐑲𐑓𐑦. [𐑞 𐑤𐑲𐑩𐑯 𐑮𐑦𐑕𐑐𐑪𐑯𐑛𐑟 𐑚𐑲 𐑥𐑴𐑯𐑟 𐑝 𐑕𐑧𐑤𐑓-𐑐𐑦𐑑𐑦]. 𐑘𐑧𐑕, 𐑘𐑧𐑕, 𐑘𐑧𐑕, 𐑘𐑧𐑕, 𐑘𐑧𐑕. 𐑯𐑬, 𐑯𐑬 [𐑑𐑱𐑒𐑦𐑙 𐑞 𐑐𐑷 𐑦𐑯 𐑣𐑦𐑟 𐑣𐑨𐑯𐑛], 𐑳𐑥 𐑦𐑟 𐑯𐑪𐑑 𐑑 𐑚𐑲𐑑 𐑯 𐑯𐑪𐑑 𐑑 𐑕𐑒𐑮𐑨𐑗, 𐑯𐑪𐑑 𐑰𐑝𐑩𐑯 𐑦𐑓 𐑦𐑑 𐑣𐑻𐑑𐑕 𐑩 𐑝𐑧𐑮𐑦 𐑝𐑧𐑮𐑦 𐑤𐑦𐑑𐑩𐑤. 𐑯𐑬 𐑥𐑱𐑒 𐑝𐑧𐑤𐑝𐑩𐑑 𐑐𐑷𐑟. 𐑞𐑨𐑑'𐑕 𐑮𐑲𐑑. [𐑣𐑰 𐑐𐑫𐑤𐑟 𐑡𐑦𐑯𐑡𐑼𐑤𐑦 𐑨𐑑 𐑞 𐑔𐑹𐑯. 𐑞

ANDROCLES [*whispering*] Did you see? A lion.

MEGAERA [*despairing*] The gods have sent him to punish us because youre a Christian. Take me away, Andy. Save me.

ANDROCLES [*rising*] Meggy: theres one chance for you. Itll take him pretty nigh twenty minutes to eat me (I'm rather stringy and tough) and you can escape in less time than that.

MEGAERA. Oh, dont talk about eating. [*The lion rises with a great groan and limps towards them*]. Oh! [*She faints*].

ANDROCLES [*quaking, but keeping between the lion and Megaera*] Dont you come near my wife, do you hear? [*The lion groans. Androcles can hardly stand for trembling*]. Meggy: run. Run for your life. If I take my eye off him, it's all up. [*The lion holds up his wounded paw and flaps it piteously before Androcles*]. Oh, he's lame, poor old chap! He's got a thorn in his paw. A frightfully big thorn. [*Full of sympathy*] Oh, poor old man! Did um get an awful thorn into um's tootsums wootsums? Has it made um too sick to eat a nice little Christian man for um's breakfast? Oh, a nice little Christian man will get um's thorn out for um; and then um shall eat the nice Christian man and the nice Christian man's nice big tender wifey pifey. [*The lion responds by moans of self-pity*]. Yes, yes, yes, yes, yes. Now, now [*taking the paw in his hand*], um is not to bite and not to scratch, not even if it hurts a very very little. Now make velvet paws. Thats right. [*He pulls gingerly at the thorn. The*

𐑤𐑲𐑩𐑯, 𐑢𐑦𐑞 𐑩𐑯 𐑨𐑙𐑜𐑮𐑦 𐑘𐑧𐑤 𐑝 𐑐𐑱𐑯, 𐑡𐑻𐑒𐑕 𐑚𐑨𐑒 𐑣𐑦𐑟 𐑐𐑷 𐑕𐑴 𐑩𐑚𐑮𐑳𐑐𐑑𐑤𐑦 𐑞𐑨𐑑 ·𐑨𐑯𐑛𐑮𐑩𐑒𐑤𐑰𐑟 𐑦𐑟 𐑔𐑮𐑴𐑯 𐑪𐑯 𐑣𐑦𐑟 𐑚𐑨𐑒]. 𐑕𐑑𐑧𐑛𐑰𐑰𐑰! 𐑴, 𐑛𐑦𐑛 𐑞 𐑯𐑨𐑕𐑑𐑦 𐑒𐑮𐑵𐑩𐑤 𐑤𐑦𐑑𐑩𐑤 𐑒𐑮𐑦𐑕𐑗𐑩𐑯 𐑥𐑨𐑯 𐑣𐑻𐑑 𐑞 𐑕𐑹 𐑐𐑷? [𐑞 𐑤𐑲𐑩𐑯 𐑥𐑴𐑯𐑟 𐑩𐑕𐑧𐑯𐑑𐑦𐑙𐑤𐑦 𐑚𐑳𐑑 𐑩𐑐𐑪𐑤𐑩𐑡𐑧𐑑𐑦𐑒𐑤𐑦]. 𐑢𐑧𐑤, 𐑢𐑳𐑯 𐑥𐑹 𐑤𐑦𐑑𐑩𐑤 𐑐𐑫𐑤 𐑯 𐑦𐑑 𐑢𐑦𐑤 𐑚𐑰 𐑷𐑤 𐑴𐑝𐑼. 𐑡𐑳𐑕𐑑 𐑢𐑳𐑯 𐑤𐑦𐑑𐑩𐑤, 𐑤𐑦𐑑𐑩𐑤, 𐑤𐑰𐑑𐑩𐑤 𐑐𐑫𐑤; 𐑯 𐑞𐑧𐑯 𐑳𐑥 𐑢𐑦𐑤 𐑤𐑦𐑝 𐑣𐑨𐑐𐑦𐑤𐑦 𐑧𐑝𐑼 𐑭𐑓𐑑𐑼. [𐑣𐑰 𐑜𐑦𐑝𐑟 𐑞 𐑔𐑹𐑯 𐑩𐑯𐑳𐑞𐑼 𐑐𐑫𐑤. 𐑞 𐑤𐑲𐑩𐑯 𐑮𐑹𐑟 𐑯 𐑕𐑯𐑨𐑐𐑕 𐑦𐑑𐑕 𐑡𐑷𐑟 𐑢𐑦𐑞 𐑩 𐑑𐑧𐑮𐑦𐑓𐑲𐑦𐑙 𐑒𐑤𐑨𐑖]. 𐑴, 𐑥𐑳𐑕𐑯𐑑 𐑓𐑮𐑲𐑑𐑩𐑯 𐑳𐑥'𐑟 𐑜𐑫𐑛 𐑒𐑲𐑯𐑛 𐑛𐑪𐑒𐑑𐑼, 𐑳𐑥'𐑟 𐑩𐑓𐑧𐑒𐑖𐑩𐑯𐑩𐑑 𐑯𐑻𐑕𐑦. 𐑞𐑨𐑑 𐑛𐑦𐑛𐑯𐑑 𐑣𐑻𐑑 𐑨𐑑 𐑷𐑤: 𐑯𐑪𐑑 𐑩 𐑚𐑦𐑑. 𐑡𐑳𐑕𐑑 𐑢𐑳𐑯 𐑥𐑹. 𐑡𐑳𐑕𐑑 𐑑 𐑖𐑴 𐑣𐑬 𐑞 𐑚𐑮𐑱𐑝 𐑚𐑦𐑜 𐑤𐑲𐑩𐑯 𐑒𐑨𐑯 𐑚𐑺 𐑐𐑱𐑯, 𐑯𐑪𐑑 𐑤𐑲𐑒 𐑞 𐑤𐑦𐑑𐑩𐑤 𐑒𐑮𐑲𐑚𐑱𐑚𐑦 𐑒𐑮𐑦𐑕𐑗𐑩𐑯 𐑥𐑨𐑯. 𐑵𐑐𐑖! [𐑞 𐑔𐑹𐑯 𐑒𐑳𐑥𐑟 𐑬𐑑. 𐑞 𐑤𐑲𐑩𐑯 𐑘𐑧𐑤𐑟 𐑢𐑦𐑞 𐑐𐑱𐑯, 𐑯 𐑖𐑱𐑒𐑕 𐑣𐑦𐑟 𐑐𐑷 𐑢𐑲𐑤𐑛𐑤𐑦]. 𐑞𐑨𐑑'𐑕 𐑦𐑑! [𐑣𐑴𐑤𐑛𐑦𐑙 𐑳𐑐 𐑞 𐑔𐑹𐑯]. 𐑯𐑬 𐑦𐑑'𐑕 𐑬𐑑. 𐑯𐑬 𐑤𐑦𐑒 𐑳𐑥'𐑟 𐑐𐑷 𐑑 𐑑𐑱𐑒 𐑩𐑢𐑱 𐑞 𐑯𐑨𐑕𐑑𐑦 𐑦𐑯𐑓𐑤𐑩𐑥𐑱𐑖𐑩𐑯. 𐑕𐑰? [𐑣𐑰 𐑤𐑦𐑒𐑕 𐑣𐑦𐑟 𐑴𐑯 𐑣𐑨𐑯𐑛. 𐑞 𐑤𐑲𐑩𐑯 𐑯𐑪𐑛𐑟 𐑦𐑯𐑑𐑧𐑤𐑦𐑡𐑩𐑯𐑑𐑤𐑦 𐑯 𐑤𐑦𐑒𐑕 𐑣𐑦𐑟 𐑐𐑷 𐑦𐑯𐑛𐑳𐑕𐑑𐑮𐑦𐑩𐑕𐑤𐑦]. 𐑒𐑤𐑧𐑝𐑼 𐑤𐑦𐑑𐑩𐑤 𐑤𐑲𐑩𐑯𐑦-𐑐𐑲𐑩𐑯𐑦! 𐑳𐑯𐑛𐑼𐑕𐑑𐑨𐑯𐑛𐑟 𐑳𐑥'𐑟 𐑛𐑽 𐑴𐑤𐑛 𐑓𐑮𐑧𐑯𐑛 ·𐑨𐑯𐑛𐑦 ·𐑢𐑪𐑯𐑛𐑦. [𐑞 𐑤𐑲𐑩𐑯 𐑤𐑦𐑒𐑕 𐑣𐑦𐑟 𐑓𐑱𐑕]. 𐑘𐑧𐑕, 𐑒𐑦𐑕𐑳𐑥𐑟 ·𐑨𐑯𐑛𐑦 ·𐑢𐑪𐑯𐑛𐑦. [𐑞 𐑤𐑲𐑩𐑯, 𐑢𐑨𐑜𐑦𐑙 𐑣𐑦𐑟 𐑑𐑱𐑤 𐑝𐑲𐑩𐑤𐑩𐑯𐑑𐑤𐑦, 𐑮𐑲𐑟𐑩𐑟 𐑪𐑯 𐑣𐑦𐑟 𐑣𐑲𐑯𐑛 𐑤𐑧𐑜𐑟, 𐑯 𐑦𐑥𐑚𐑮𐑱𐑕𐑩𐑟 ·𐑨𐑯𐑛𐑮𐑩𐑒𐑤𐑰𐑟, 𐑣𐑵 𐑥𐑱𐑒𐑕 𐑩 𐑮𐑲 𐑓𐑱𐑕 𐑯 𐑒𐑮𐑲𐑟] 𐑝𐑧𐑤𐑝𐑩𐑑 𐑐𐑷𐑟! 𐑝𐑧𐑤𐑝𐑩𐑑 𐑐𐑷𐑟! [𐑞 𐑤𐑲𐑩𐑯 𐑛𐑮𐑷𐑟 𐑦𐑯 𐑣𐑦𐑟 𐑒𐑤𐑷𐑟]. 𐑞𐑨𐑑'𐑕 𐑮𐑲𐑑. [𐑣𐑰 𐑦𐑥𐑚𐑮𐑱𐑕𐑩𐑟 𐑞 𐑤𐑲𐑩𐑯, 𐑣𐑵 𐑓𐑲𐑯𐑩𐑤𐑦 𐑑𐑱𐑒𐑕 𐑞 𐑧𐑯𐑛 𐑝 𐑣𐑦𐑟 𐑑𐑱𐑤 𐑦𐑯 𐑢𐑳𐑯 𐑐𐑷, 𐑐𐑤𐑱𐑕𐑩𐑟 𐑞𐑨𐑑 𐑑𐑲𐑑 𐑮𐑬𐑯𐑛 ·𐑨𐑯𐑛𐑮𐑩𐑒𐑤𐑰𐑟'𐑩𐑟 𐑢𐑱𐑕𐑑, 𐑮𐑧𐑕𐑑𐑦𐑙 𐑦𐑑 𐑪𐑯 𐑣𐑦𐑟 𐑣𐑦𐑐. ·𐑨𐑯𐑛𐑮𐑩𐑒𐑤𐑰𐑟 𐑑𐑱𐑒𐑕 𐑞 𐑳𐑞𐑼 𐑐𐑷 𐑦𐑯 𐑣𐑦𐑟 𐑣𐑨𐑯𐑛, 𐑕𐑑𐑮𐑧𐑗𐑩𐑟 𐑬𐑑

lion, with an angry yell of pain, jerks back his paw so abruptly that Androcles is thrown on his back]. Steadeee! Oh, did the nasty cruel little Christian man hurt the sore paw? [*The lion moans assentingly but apologetically*]. Well, one more little pull and it will be all over. Just one little, little, leetle pull; and then um will live happily ever after. [*He gives the thorn another pull. The lion roars and snaps his jaws with a terrifying clash*]. Oh, mustnt frighten um's good kind doctor, um's affectionate nursey. That didnt hurt at all: not a bit. Just one more. Just to shew how the brave big lion can bear pain, not like the little crybaby Christian man. Oopsh! [*The thorn comes out. The lion yells with pain, and shakes his paw wildly*]. Thats it! [*Holding up the thorn*]. Now it's out. Now lick um's paw to take away the nasty inflammation. See? [*He licks his own hand. The lion nods intelligently and licks his paw industriously*]. Clever little liony-piony! Understands um's dear old friend Andy Wandy. [*The lion licks his face*]. Yes, kissums Andy Wandy. [*The lion wagging his tail violently, rises on his hind legs, and embraces Androcles, who makes a wry face and cries*] Velvet paws! Velvet paws! [*The lion draws in his claws*]. Thats right. [*He embraces the lion, who finally takes the end of his tail in one paw, places that tight round Androcles' waist, resting it on his hip. Androcles takes the other paw in his hand, stretches out*

𐑣𐑦𐑟 𐑸𐑥, 𐑯 𐑞 𐑑𐑵 𐑢𐑷𐑤𐑕 𐑮𐑨𐑐𐑗𐑼𐑩𐑕𐑤𐑦 𐑮𐑬𐑯𐑛 𐑯 𐑮𐑬𐑯𐑛 𐑯 𐑓𐑲𐑯𐑩𐑤𐑦 𐑩𐑢𐑱 𐑔𐑮𐑵 𐑞 𐑡𐑳𐑙𐑜𐑩𐑤].

𐑥𐑦𐑡𐑽𐑩 [𐑣𐑵 𐑣𐑨𐑟 𐑮𐑦𐑝𐑲𐑝𐑛 𐑛𐑘𐑫𐑼𐑦𐑙 𐑞 𐑢𐑷𐑤𐑕] 𐑴, 𐑿 𐑒𐑬𐑼𐑛, 𐑿 𐑣𐑨𐑝𐑯𐑑 𐑛𐑭𐑯𐑕𐑑 𐑢𐑦𐑞 𐑥𐑰 𐑓𐑹 𐑘𐑦𐑼𐑟; 𐑯 𐑯𐑬 𐑿 𐑜𐑴 𐑪𐑓 𐑛𐑭𐑯𐑕𐑦𐑙 𐑢𐑦𐑞 𐑩 𐑜𐑮𐑱𐑑 𐑚𐑮𐑵𐑑 𐑚𐑰𐑕𐑑 𐑞𐑨𐑑 𐑿 𐑣𐑨𐑝𐑯𐑑 𐑯𐑴𐑯 𐑓𐑹 𐑑𐑧𐑯 𐑥𐑦𐑯𐑦𐑑𐑕 𐑯 𐑞𐑨𐑑 𐑢𐑪𐑯𐑑𐑦𐑛 𐑑 𐑰𐑑 𐑿𐑼 𐑴𐑯 𐑢𐑲𐑓. 𐑒𐑬𐑼𐑛. 𐑒𐑬𐑼𐑛! 𐑒𐑬𐑼𐑛! [𐑖𐑰 𐑮𐑳𐑖𐑩𐑟 𐑪𐑓 𐑭𐑓𐑑𐑼 𐑞𐑧𐑥 𐑦𐑯𐑑𐑵 𐑞 𐑡𐑳𐑙𐑜𐑩𐑤].

his arm, and the two waltz rapturously round and round and finally away through the jungle].

MEGAERA [*who has revived during the waltz*] Oh, you coward, you havnt danced with me for years; and now you go off dancing with a great brute beast that you havnt known for ten minutes and that wants to eat your own wife. Coward. Coward! Coward! [*She rushes off after them into the jungle*].

𐑨𐑒𐑑 I

[𐑰𐑝𐑯𐑦𐑙. 𐑞 𐑧𐑯𐑛 𐑝 𐑔𐑮𐑰 𐑒𐑩𐑯𐑝𐑻𐑡𐑦𐑙 𐑮𐑴𐑛𐑟 𐑑 ·𐑮𐑴𐑥. 𐑔𐑮𐑰 𐑑𐑮𐑲𐑳𐑥𐑓𐑩𐑤 𐑸𐑗𐑩𐑟 𐑕𐑐𐑨𐑯 𐑞𐑧𐑥 𐑢𐑺 𐑞𐑱 𐑛𐑦𐑚𐑬𐑗 𐑪𐑯 𐑩 𐑕𐑒𐑢𐑺 𐑨𐑑 𐑞 𐑜𐑱𐑑 𐑝 𐑞 𐑕𐑦𐑑𐑦. 𐑤𐑫𐑒𐑦𐑙 𐑯𐑹𐑔 𐑔𐑮𐑵 𐑞 𐑸𐑗𐑩𐑟 𐑢𐑳𐑯 𐑒𐑨𐑯 𐑕𐑰 𐑞 𐑒𐑨𐑥𐑐𐑭𐑯𐑘𐑩 𐑔𐑮𐑧𐑛𐑩𐑛 𐑚𐑲 𐑞 𐑔𐑮𐑰 𐑤𐑪𐑙 𐑛𐑳𐑕𐑑𐑦 𐑑𐑮𐑨𐑒𐑕. 𐑪𐑯 𐑞 𐑰𐑕𐑑 𐑯 𐑢𐑧𐑕𐑑 𐑕𐑲𐑛𐑟 𐑝 𐑞 𐑕𐑒𐑢𐑺 𐑸 𐑤𐑪𐑙 𐑕𐑑𐑴𐑯 𐑚𐑧𐑯𐑗𐑩𐑟. 𐑩𐑯 𐑴𐑤𐑛 𐑚𐑧𐑜𐑼 𐑕𐑦𐑑𐑕 𐑪𐑯 𐑞 𐑰𐑕𐑑 𐑕𐑲𐑛, 𐑣𐑦𐑟 𐑚𐑴𐑤 𐑨𐑑 𐑣𐑦𐑟 𐑓𐑰𐑑.

𐑔𐑮𐑵 𐑞 𐑰𐑕𐑑𐑼𐑯 𐑸𐑗 𐑩 𐑕𐑒𐑢𐑪𐑛 𐑝 𐑮𐑴𐑥𐑩𐑯 𐑕𐑴𐑤𐑡𐑼𐑟 𐑑𐑮𐑨𐑥𐑐 𐑩𐑤𐑪𐑙 𐑧𐑕𐑒𐑹𐑑𐑦𐑙 𐑩 𐑚𐑨𐑗 𐑝 𐑒𐑮𐑦𐑕𐑗𐑩𐑯 𐑐𐑮𐑦𐑟𐑩𐑯𐑼𐑟 𐑝 𐑚𐑴𐑔 𐑕𐑧𐑒𐑕𐑩𐑟 𐑯 𐑷𐑤 𐑱𐑡𐑩𐑟, 𐑩𐑥𐑳𐑙 𐑞𐑧𐑥 𐑢𐑳𐑯 ·𐑤𐑩𐑝𐑦𐑯𐑾, 𐑩 ·𐑜𐑫𐑛-𐑤𐑫𐑒𐑦𐑙 𐑮𐑧𐑟𐑩𐑤𐑵𐑑 𐑘𐑳𐑙 𐑢𐑫𐑥𐑩𐑯, 𐑩𐑐𐑸𐑩𐑯𐑑𐑤𐑦 𐑝 𐑣𐑲𐑼 𐑕𐑴𐑖𐑩𐑤 𐑕𐑑𐑨𐑯𐑛𐑦𐑙 𐑞𐑨𐑯 𐑣𐑻 𐑓𐑧𐑤𐑴-𐑐𐑮𐑦𐑟𐑩𐑯𐑼𐑟. 𐑩 ·𐑕𐑧𐑯𐑑𐑘𐑫𐑼𐑾𐑯, 𐑒𐑨𐑮𐑦𐑦𐑙 𐑣𐑦𐑟 𐑝𐑲𐑯𐑢𐑫𐑛 𐑒𐑳𐑡𐑩𐑤, 𐑑𐑮𐑳𐑡𐑩𐑟 𐑩𐑤𐑪𐑙𐑕𐑲𐑛 𐑞 𐑕𐑒𐑢𐑪𐑛, 𐑪𐑯 𐑦𐑑𐑕 𐑮𐑲𐑑, 𐑦𐑯 𐑗𐑸𐑡 𐑝 𐑦𐑑. 𐑷𐑤 𐑸 𐑑𐑲𐑼𐑛 𐑯 𐑛𐑳𐑕𐑑𐑦; 𐑚𐑳𐑑 𐑞 𐑕𐑴𐑤𐑡𐑼𐑟 𐑸 𐑛𐑪𐑜𐑛 𐑯 𐑦𐑯𐑛𐑦𐑓𐑼𐑩𐑯𐑑, 𐑞 𐑒𐑮𐑦𐑕𐑗𐑩𐑯𐑟 𐑤𐑲𐑑𐑣𐑸𐑑𐑦𐑛 𐑯 𐑛𐑦𐑑𐑻𐑥𐑦𐑯𐑛 𐑑 𐑑𐑮𐑰𐑑 𐑞𐑺 𐑣𐑸𐑛𐑖𐑦𐑐𐑕 𐑨𐑟 𐑩 𐑡𐑴𐑒 𐑯 𐑦𐑯𐑒𐑳𐑮𐑦𐑡 𐑢𐑳𐑯 𐑩𐑯𐑳𐑞𐑼.

𐑩 𐑚𐑿𐑜𐑩𐑤 𐑦𐑟 𐑣𐑻𐑛 𐑓𐑸 𐑚𐑦𐑣𐑲𐑯𐑛 𐑦𐑯 𐑞 𐑮𐑽, 𐑢𐑺 𐑞 𐑮𐑧𐑕𐑑 𐑝 𐑞 𐑒𐑪𐑤𐑩𐑥 𐑦𐑟 𐑓𐑪𐑤𐑴𐑦𐑙].

𐑕𐑧𐑯𐑑𐑘𐑫𐑼𐑾𐑯 [*𐑕𐑑𐑪𐑐𐑦𐑙*] 𐑣𐑷𐑤𐑑! 𐑹𐑛𐑼𐑟 𐑓𐑮𐑪𐑥 𐑞 𐑒𐑨𐑐𐑑𐑦𐑯. [*𐑞𐑱 𐑣𐑷𐑤𐑑 𐑯 𐑢𐑱𐑑*]. 𐑯𐑬 𐑞𐑧𐑯, 𐑿 𐑒𐑮𐑦𐑕𐑗𐑩𐑯𐑟, 𐑯𐑳𐑯 𐑝 𐑿𐑼 𐑤𐑸𐑒𐑕. 𐑞 𐑒𐑨𐑐𐑑𐑦𐑯'𐑟 𐑒𐑳𐑥𐑦𐑙. 𐑥𐑲𐑯𐑛 𐑿 𐑚𐑦𐑣𐑱𐑝 𐑿𐑼𐑕𐑧𐑤𐑝𐑟. 𐑯𐑴 𐑕𐑦𐑙𐑦𐑙. 𐑤𐑫𐑒 𐑮𐑦𐑕𐑐𐑧𐑒𐑑𐑓𐑩𐑤. 𐑤𐑫𐑒 𐑕𐑽𐑾𐑕, 𐑦𐑓 𐑿'𐑮 𐑒𐑱𐑐𐑩𐑚𐑩𐑤 𐑝 𐑦𐑑. 𐑕𐑰 𐑞𐑨𐑑 𐑚𐑦𐑜 𐑚𐑦𐑤𐑛𐑦𐑙 𐑴𐑝𐑼 𐑞𐑺! 𐑞𐑨𐑑'𐑕 𐑞 𐑒𐑩𐑤𐑩𐑕𐑰𐑩𐑥. 𐑞𐑨𐑑'𐑕 𐑢𐑺 𐑿'𐑤 𐑚𐑰 𐑔𐑮𐑴𐑯 𐑑 𐑞 𐑤𐑲𐑩𐑯𐑟 𐑹 𐑕𐑧𐑑 𐑑 𐑓𐑲𐑑 𐑞 𐑜𐑤𐑨𐑛𐑦𐑱𐑑𐑼𐑟 𐑐𐑮𐑧𐑟𐑩𐑯𐑑𐑤𐑦. 𐑔𐑦𐑙𐑒 𐑝 𐑞𐑨𐑑; 𐑯 𐑦𐑑'𐑤 𐑣𐑧𐑤𐑐 𐑿 𐑑 𐑚𐑦𐑣𐑱𐑝 𐑐𐑮𐑪𐑐𐑼𐑤𐑦 𐑚𐑦𐑓𐑹

ACT I

Evening. The end of three converging roads to Rome. Three triumphal arches span them where they debouch on a square at the gate of the city. Looking north through the arches one can see the campagna threaded by the three long dusty tracks. On the east and west sides of the square are long stone benches. An old beggar sits on the east side, his bowl at his feet.

Through the eastern arch a squad of Roman soldiers tramps along escorting a batch of Christian prisoners of both sexes and all ages, among them one Lavinia, a good-looking resolute young woman, apparently of higher social standing than her fellow-prisoners. A centurion, carrying his vinewood cudgel, trudges alongside the squad, on its right, in command of it. All are tired and dusty; but the soldiers are dogged and indifferent, the Christians lighthearted and determined to treat their hardships as a joke and encourage one another.

A bugle is heard far behind on the road, where the rest of the cohort is following.

CENTURION [*stopping*] Halt! Orders from the Captain. [*They halt and wait*]. Now then, you Christians, none of your larks. The captain's coming. Mind you behave yourselves. No singing. Look respectful. Look serious, if youre capable of it. See that big building over there! Thats the Coliseum. Thats where youll be thrown to the lions or set to fight the gladiators presently. Think of that; and itll help you to behave properly before

𐑞 𐑒𐑨𐑐𐑑𐑦𐑯. [𐑞 𐑒𐑨𐑐𐑑𐑦𐑯 𐑩𐑮𐑲𐑝𐑟]. 𐑩𐑑𐑧𐑯𐑖𐑩𐑯! 𐑕𐑩𐑤𐑵𐑑! [𐑞 𐑕𐑴𐑤𐑡𐑼𐑟 𐑕𐑩𐑤𐑵𐑑].

𐑩 𐑒𐑮𐑦𐑕𐑗𐑩𐑯 [𐑗𐑽𐑓𐑫𐑤𐑦] ·𐑜𐑪𐑛 𐑚𐑤𐑧𐑕 𐑿, 𐑒𐑨𐑐𐑑𐑦𐑯!

𐑕𐑧𐑯𐑑𐑿𐑼𐑾𐑯 [𐑕𐑒𐑨𐑯𐑛𐑩𐑤𐑲𐑟𐑛] 𐑕𐑲𐑤𐑩𐑯𐑕!

[𐑞 ·𐑒𐑨𐑐𐑑𐑦𐑯, 𐑩 𐑐𐑩𐑑𐑮𐑦𐑖𐑩𐑯, 𐑣𐑨𐑯𐑕𐑩𐑥, 𐑩𐑚𐑬𐑑 𐑔𐑻𐑑𐑦-𐑓𐑲𐑝, 𐑝𐑧𐑮𐑦 𐑒𐑴𐑤𐑛 𐑯 𐑛𐑦𐑕𐑑𐑦𐑙𐑜𐑢𐑦𐑖𐑑, 𐑝𐑧𐑮𐑦 𐑕𐑵𐑐𐑽𐑮𐑾𐑮 𐑯 𐑷𐑔𐑪𐑮𐑦𐑑𐑱𐑑𐑦𐑝, 𐑕𐑑𐑧𐑐𐑕 𐑳𐑐 𐑪𐑯 𐑩 𐑕𐑑𐑴𐑯 𐑕𐑰𐑑 𐑨𐑑 𐑞 𐑢𐑧𐑕𐑑 𐑕𐑲𐑛 𐑝 𐑞 𐑕𐑒𐑢𐑺, 𐑚𐑦𐑣𐑲𐑯𐑛 𐑞 𐑕𐑧𐑯𐑑𐑿𐑼𐑾𐑯, 𐑕𐑴 𐑨𐑟 𐑑 𐑛𐑪𐑥𐑦𐑯𐑱𐑑 𐑞 𐑳𐑞𐑼𐑟 𐑥𐑹 𐑦𐑓𐑧𐑒𐑗𐑵𐑩𐑤𐑦].

𐑞 𐑒𐑨𐑐𐑑𐑦𐑯. 𐑕𐑧𐑯𐑑𐑿𐑼𐑾𐑯.

𐑕𐑧𐑯𐑑𐑿𐑼𐑾𐑯 [𐑕𐑑𐑨𐑯𐑛𐑦𐑙 𐑨𐑑 𐑩𐑑𐑧𐑯𐑖𐑩𐑯 𐑯 𐑕𐑩𐑤𐑵𐑑𐑦𐑙] 𐑕𐑻?

𐑞 𐑒𐑨𐑐𐑑𐑦𐑯 [𐑕𐑐𐑰𐑒𐑦𐑙 𐑕𐑑𐑦𐑓𐑤𐑦 𐑯 𐑩𐑓𐑦𐑖𐑩𐑤𐑦] 𐑿 𐑢𐑦𐑤 𐑮𐑦𐑥𐑲𐑯𐑛 𐑘𐑹 𐑥𐑧𐑯, 𐑕𐑧𐑯𐑑𐑿𐑼𐑾𐑯, 𐑞𐑨𐑑 𐑢𐑰 𐑸 𐑯𐑬 𐑧𐑯𐑑𐑼𐑦𐑙 ·𐑮𐑴𐑥. 𐑿 𐑢𐑦𐑤 𐑦𐑯𐑕𐑑𐑮𐑳𐑒𐑑 𐑞𐑧𐑥 𐑞𐑨𐑑 𐑢𐑳𐑯𐑕 𐑦𐑯𐑕𐑲𐑛 𐑞 𐑜𐑱𐑑𐑕 𐑝 ·𐑮𐑴𐑥 𐑞𐑱 𐑸 𐑦𐑯 𐑞 𐑐𐑮𐑧𐑟𐑩𐑯𐑕 𐑝 𐑞 ·𐑧𐑥𐑐𐑼𐑼. 𐑿 𐑢𐑦𐑤 𐑥𐑱𐑒 𐑞𐑧𐑥 𐑳𐑯𐑛𐑼𐑕𐑑𐑨𐑯𐑛 𐑞𐑨𐑑 𐑞 𐑤𐑨𐑒𐑕 𐑛𐑦𐑕𐑦𐑐𐑤𐑦𐑯 𐑝 𐑞 𐑥𐑸𐑗 𐑒𐑨𐑯𐑪𐑑 𐑚𐑰 𐑐𐑼𐑥𐑦𐑑𐑩𐑛 𐑣𐑽. 𐑿 𐑢𐑦𐑤 𐑦𐑯𐑕𐑑𐑮𐑳𐑒𐑑 𐑞𐑧𐑥 𐑑 𐑖𐑱𐑝 𐑧𐑝𐑮𐑦 𐑛𐑱, 𐑯𐑪𐑑 𐑧𐑝𐑮𐑦 𐑢𐑰𐑒. 𐑿 𐑢𐑦𐑤 𐑦𐑥𐑐𐑮𐑧𐑕 𐑪𐑯 𐑞𐑧𐑥 𐑐𐑼𐑑𐑦𐑒𐑿𐑤𐑼𐑤𐑦 𐑞𐑨𐑑 𐑞𐑺 𐑥𐑳𐑕𐑑 𐑚𐑰 𐑩𐑯 𐑧𐑯𐑛 𐑑 𐑞 𐑐𐑮𐑩𐑓𐑨𐑯𐑦𐑑𐑦 𐑯 𐑚𐑤𐑨𐑕𐑓𐑩𐑥𐑦 𐑝 𐑕𐑦𐑙𐑦𐑙 𐑒𐑮𐑦𐑕𐑗𐑩𐑯 𐑣𐑦𐑥𐑟 𐑪𐑯 𐑞 𐑥𐑸𐑗. 𐑲 𐑣𐑨𐑝 𐑑 𐑮𐑧𐑐𐑮𐑦𐑥𐑭𐑯𐑛 𐑿, 𐑕𐑧𐑯𐑑𐑿𐑼𐑾𐑯, 𐑓𐑹 𐑯𐑪𐑑 𐑴𐑯𐑤𐑦 𐑩𐑤𐑬𐑦𐑙 𐑞𐑦𐑕, 𐑚𐑳𐑑 𐑨𐑒𐑗𐑵𐑩𐑤𐑦 𐑛𐑵𐑦𐑙 𐑦𐑑 𐑘𐑹𐑕𐑧𐑤𐑓.

𐑕𐑧𐑯𐑑𐑿𐑼𐑾𐑯 [𐑩𐑐𐑪𐑤𐑩𐑡𐑧𐑑𐑦𐑒𐑤𐑦] 𐑞 𐑥𐑧𐑯 𐑥𐑸𐑗 𐑚𐑧𐑑𐑼, 𐑒𐑨𐑐𐑑𐑦𐑯.

𐑞 𐑒𐑨𐑐𐑑𐑦𐑯. 𐑯𐑴 𐑛𐑬𐑑. 𐑓𐑹 𐑞𐑨𐑑 𐑮𐑰𐑟𐑩𐑯 𐑩𐑯 𐑦𐑒𐑕𐑧𐑐𐑖𐑩𐑯 𐑥𐑱 𐑚𐑰 𐑥𐑱𐑛 𐑦𐑯 𐑞 𐑒𐑱𐑕 𐑝 𐑞 𐑥𐑸𐑗 𐑒𐑷𐑤𐑛 ·𐑪𐑯𐑢𐑼𐑛 ·𐑒𐑮𐑦𐑕𐑗𐑩𐑯 ·𐑕𐑴𐑤𐑡𐑼𐑟. 𐑞𐑦𐑕 𐑥𐑱 𐑚𐑰 𐑕𐑳𐑙, 𐑦𐑒𐑕𐑧𐑐𐑑 𐑢𐑧𐑯 𐑥𐑸𐑗𐑦𐑙 𐑔𐑮𐑵 𐑞 𐑓𐑹𐑩𐑥 𐑹

the captain. [*The Captain arrives*]. Attention! Salute! [*The soldiers salute*].

A CHRISTIAN [*cheerfully*] God bless you, Captain!

CENTURION [*scandalized*] Silence!

The Captain, a patrician, handsome, about thirty-five, very cold and distinguished, very superior and authoritative, steps up on a stone seat at the west side of the square, behind the centurion, so as to dominate the others more effectually.

THE CAPTAIN. Centurion.

CENTURION [*standing at attention and saluting*] Sir?

THE CAPTAIN [*speaking stiffly and officially*] You will remind your men, Centurion, that we are now entering Rome. You will instruct them that once inside the gates of Rome they are in the presence of the Emperor. You will make them understand that the lax discipline of the march cannot be permitted here. You will instruct them to shave every day, not every week. You will impress on them particularly that there must be an end to the profanity and blasphemy of singing Christian hymns on the march. I have to reprimand you, Centurion, for not only allowing this, but actually doing it yourself.

CENTURION [*apologetic*] The men march better, Captain.

THE CAPTAIN. No doubt. For that reason an exception is made in the case of the march called Onward Christian Soldiers. This may be sung, except when marching through the forum or

𐑢𐑦𐑞𐑦𐑯 𐑣𐑽𐑦𐑙 𐑝 𐑞 𐑧𐑥𐑐𐑼𐑼'𐑟 𐑐𐑨𐑤𐑩𐑕; 𐑚𐑳𐑑 𐑞 𐑢𐑻𐑛𐑟 𐑥𐑳𐑕𐑑 𐑚𐑰 𐑗𐑱𐑯𐑡𐑛 𐑑 '𐑔𐑮𐑴 𐑞𐑧𐑥 𐑑 𐑞 𐑤𐑲𐑩𐑯𐑟.'

[𐑞 𐑒𐑮𐑦𐑕𐑗𐑩𐑯𐑟 𐑚𐑻𐑕𐑑 𐑦𐑯𐑑𐑵 𐑖𐑮𐑰𐑒𐑕 𐑝 𐑳𐑯𐑒𐑩𐑯𐑑𐑮𐑴𐑤𐑩𐑚𐑩𐑤 𐑤𐑭𐑓𐑑𐑼, 𐑑 𐑞 𐑜𐑮𐑱𐑑 𐑕𐑒𐑨𐑯𐑛𐑩𐑤 𐑝 𐑞 𐑕𐑧𐑯𐑑𐑘𐑫𐑼𐑾𐑯].

𐑕𐑧𐑯𐑑𐑘𐑫𐑼𐑾𐑯. 𐑕𐑲𐑤𐑩𐑯𐑕! 𐑕𐑲𐑤𐑩𐑯𐑕! 𐑢𐑺'𐑟 𐑿𐑼 𐑚𐑦𐑣𐑱𐑝𐑘𐑼? 𐑦𐑟 𐑞𐑨𐑑 𐑞 𐑢𐑱 𐑑 𐑤𐑦𐑕𐑩𐑯 𐑑 𐑩𐑯 𐑪𐑓𐑦𐑕𐑼? [𐑑 𐑞 𐑒𐑨𐑐𐑑𐑩𐑯] 𐑞𐑨𐑑'𐑕 𐑢𐑪𐑑 𐑢𐑰 𐑣𐑨𐑝 𐑑 𐑐𐑫𐑑 𐑳𐑐 𐑢𐑦𐑞 𐑓𐑮𐑪𐑥 𐑞𐑰𐑟 𐑒𐑮𐑦𐑕𐑗𐑩𐑯𐑟 𐑧𐑝𐑮𐑦 𐑛𐑱, 𐑕𐑻. 𐑞𐑺'𐑮 𐑷𐑤𐑢𐑱𐑟 𐑤𐑭𐑓𐑦𐑙 𐑯 𐑡𐑴𐑒𐑦𐑙 𐑕𐑳𐑥𐑔𐑦𐑙 𐑕𐑒𐑨𐑯𐑛𐑩𐑤𐑩𐑕. 𐑞𐑱'𐑝 𐑯𐑴 𐑮𐑦𐑤𐑦𐑡𐑩𐑯: 𐑞𐑨𐑑'𐑕 𐑣𐑬 𐑦𐑑 𐑦𐑟.

𐑤𐑩𐑝𐑦𐑯𐑾. 𐑚𐑳𐑑 𐑲 𐑔𐑦𐑙𐑒 𐑞 𐑒𐑨𐑐𐑑𐑩𐑯 𐑥𐑧𐑯𐑑 𐑳𐑕 𐑑 𐑤𐑭𐑓, 𐑕𐑧𐑯𐑑𐑘𐑫𐑼𐑾𐑯. 𐑦𐑑 𐑢𐑪𐑟 𐑕𐑴 𐑓𐑳𐑯𐑦.

𐑕𐑧𐑯𐑑𐑘𐑫𐑼𐑾𐑯. 𐑿'𐑤 𐑓𐑲𐑯𐑛 𐑬𐑑 𐑣𐑬 𐑓𐑳𐑯𐑦 𐑦𐑑 𐑦𐑟 𐑢𐑧𐑯 𐑿'𐑮 𐑔𐑮𐑴𐑯 𐑑 𐑞 𐑤𐑲𐑩𐑯𐑟 𐑑𐑩𐑥𐑪𐑮𐑴. [𐑑 𐑞 𐑒𐑨𐑐𐑑𐑩𐑯, 𐑣𐑵 𐑤𐑫𐑒𐑕 𐑛𐑦𐑕𐑜𐑳𐑕𐑑𐑦𐑛] 𐑚𐑧𐑜 𐑐𐑸𐑛𐑩𐑯, 𐑕𐑻. [𐑑 𐑞 𐑒𐑮𐑦𐑕𐑗𐑩𐑯𐑟] 𐑕𐑲𐑤𐑩𐑯𐑕!

𐑞 𐑒𐑨𐑐𐑑𐑩𐑯. 𐑿 𐑸 𐑑 𐑦𐑯𐑕𐑑𐑮𐑳𐑒𐑑 𐑿𐑼 𐑥𐑧𐑯 𐑞𐑨𐑑 𐑷𐑤 𐑦𐑯𐑑𐑼𐑒𐑹𐑕 𐑢𐑦𐑞 𐑒𐑮𐑦𐑕𐑗𐑩𐑯 𐑐𐑮𐑦𐑟𐑩𐑯𐑼𐑟 𐑥𐑳𐑕𐑑 𐑯𐑬 𐑕𐑰𐑕. [illegible]

within hearing of the Emperor's palace; but the words must be altered to 'Throw them to the Lions.'

The Christians burst into shrieks of uncontrollable laughter, to the great scandal of the Centurion.

CENTURION. Silence! Silen-n-n-n-nce! Wheres your behavior? Is that the way to listen to an officer? [*To the Captain*] Thats what we have to put up with from these Christians every day, sir. Theyre always laughing and joking something scandalous. Theyve no religion: thats how it is.

LAVINIA. But I think the Captain meant us to laugh, Centurion. It was so funny.

CENTURION. Youll find out how funny it is when youre thrown to the lions tomorrow. [*To the Captain, who looks displeased*] Beg pardon, sir. [*To the Christians*] Silennnnce!

THE CAPTAIN. You are to instruct your men that all intimacy with Christian prisoners must now cease. The men have fallen into habits of dependence upon the prisoners, especially the female prisoners, for cooking, repairs to uniforms, writing letters, and advice in their private affairs. In a Roman soldier such dependence is inadmissible. Let me see no more of it whilst we are in the city. Further, your orders are that in addressing Christian prisoners, the manners and tone of your men must express abhorrence and contempt. Any shortcoming in this respect will be regarded as a breach of discipline. [*He turns to the prisoners*] Prisoners.

𐑕𐑧𐑯𐑑𐑘𐑫𐑼𐑦𐑩𐑯 [𐑚𐑳𐑕𐑤𐑦𐑙] 𐑐𐑮𐑦𐑟𐑩𐑯𐑼𐑟! '𐑑𐑧𐑯𐑖𐑩𐑯! 𐑕𐑲𐑤𐑩𐑯𐑕!

𐑞 𐑒𐑨𐑐𐑑𐑩𐑯. 𐑲 𐑒𐑷𐑤 𐑿𐑼 𐑩𐑑𐑧𐑯𐑖𐑩𐑯, 𐑐𐑮𐑦𐑟𐑩𐑯𐑼𐑟, 𐑑 𐑞 𐑓𐑨𐑒𐑑 𐑞𐑨𐑑 𐑿 𐑥𐑱 𐑚𐑰 𐑒𐑷𐑤𐑛 𐑪𐑯 𐑑 𐑩𐑐𐑽 𐑦𐑯 𐑞 𐑦𐑥𐑐𐑽𐑾𐑤 𐑕𐑻𐑒𐑩𐑕 𐑨𐑑 𐑧𐑯𐑦 𐑑𐑲𐑥 𐑓𐑮𐑪𐑥 𐑑𐑩𐑥𐑪𐑮𐑴 𐑪𐑯𐑢𐑼𐑛𐑟 𐑩𐑒𐑹𐑛𐑦𐑙 𐑑 𐑞 𐑮𐑦𐑒𐑢𐑲𐑼𐑥𐑩𐑯𐑑𐑕 𐑝 𐑞 𐑥𐑨𐑯𐑦𐑡𐑼𐑟. 𐑲 𐑥𐑱 𐑦𐑯𐑓𐑹𐑥 𐑿 𐑞𐑨𐑑 𐑨𐑟 𐑞𐑺 𐑦𐑟 𐑩 𐑖𐑹𐑑𐑦𐑡 𐑝 𐑒𐑮𐑦𐑕𐑗𐑩𐑯𐑟 𐑡𐑳𐑕𐑑 𐑯𐑬, 𐑿 𐑥𐑱 𐑦𐑒𐑕𐑐𐑧𐑒𐑑 𐑑 𐑚𐑰 𐑒𐑷𐑤𐑛 𐑪𐑯 𐑝𐑧𐑮𐑦 𐑕𐑵𐑯.

𐑤𐑨𐑝𐑦𐑯𐑾. 𐑢𐑪𐑑 𐑢𐑦𐑤 𐑞𐑱 𐑛𐑵 𐑑 𐑳𐑕, 𐑒𐑨𐑐𐑑𐑩𐑯?

𐑕𐑧𐑯𐑑𐑘𐑫𐑼𐑦𐑩𐑯. 𐑕𐑲𐑤𐑩𐑯𐑕!

𐑞 𐑒𐑨𐑐𐑑𐑩𐑯. 𐑞 𐑢𐑦𐑥𐑦𐑯 𐑢𐑦𐑤 𐑚𐑰 𐑒𐑩𐑯𐑛𐑳𐑒𐑑𐑦𐑛 𐑦𐑯𐑑𐑫 𐑞 𐑼𐑰𐑯𐑩 𐑢𐑦𐑞 𐑞 𐑢𐑲𐑤𐑛 𐑚𐑰𐑕𐑑𐑕 𐑝 𐑞 𐑦𐑥𐑐𐑽𐑾𐑤 𐑥𐑩𐑯𐑨𐑡𐑼𐑦, 𐑯 𐑢𐑦𐑤 𐑕𐑳𐑓𐑼 𐑞 𐑒𐑪𐑯𐑕𐑦𐑒𐑢𐑩𐑯𐑕𐑦𐑟. 𐑞 𐑥𐑧𐑯, 𐑦𐑓 𐑝 𐑩𐑯 𐑱𐑡 𐑑 𐑚𐑺 𐑸𐑥𐑟, 𐑢𐑦𐑤 𐑚𐑰 𐑜𐑦𐑝𐑩𐑯 𐑢𐑧𐑐𐑩𐑯𐑟 𐑑 𐑛𐑦𐑓𐑧𐑯𐑛 𐑞𐑧𐑥𐑕𐑧𐑤𐑝𐑟, 𐑦𐑓 𐑞𐑱 𐑗𐑵𐑟, 𐑩𐑜𐑱𐑯𐑕𐑑 𐑞 𐑦𐑥𐑐𐑽𐑾𐑤 𐑜𐑤𐑨𐑛𐑦𐑱𐑑𐑼𐑟.

𐑤𐑨𐑝𐑦𐑯𐑾. 𐑒𐑨𐑐𐑑𐑩𐑯: 𐑦𐑟 𐑞𐑺 𐑯𐑴 𐑣𐑴𐑐 𐑞𐑨𐑑 𐑞𐑦𐑕 𐑒𐑮𐑵𐑩𐑤 𐑐𐑻𐑕𐑦𐑒𐑿𐑖𐑩𐑯—

𐑕𐑧𐑯𐑑𐑘𐑫𐑼𐑦𐑩𐑯 [𐑖𐑪𐑒𐑑] 𐑕𐑲𐑤𐑩𐑯𐑕! 𐑣𐑴𐑤𐑛 𐑿𐑼 𐑑𐑳𐑙, 𐑞𐑺. 𐑐𐑻𐑕𐑦𐑒𐑿𐑖𐑩𐑯, 𐑦𐑯𐑛𐑰𐑛!

𐑞 𐑒𐑨𐑐𐑑𐑩𐑯 [𐑳𐑯𐑥𐑵𐑝𐑛 𐑯 𐑕𐑳𐑥𐑢𐑪𐑑 𐑕𐑸𐑛𐑪𐑯𐑦𐑒] 𐑐𐑻𐑕𐑦𐑒𐑿𐑖𐑩𐑯 𐑦𐑟 𐑯𐑪𐑑 𐑩 𐑑𐑻𐑥 𐑨𐑐𐑤𐑦𐑒𐑩𐑚𐑩𐑤 𐑑 𐑞 𐑨𐑒𐑑𐑕 𐑝 𐑞 𐑧𐑥𐑐𐑼𐑼. 𐑞 𐑧𐑥𐑐𐑼𐑼 𐑦𐑟 𐑞 ·𐑛𐑦𐑓𐑧𐑯𐑛𐑼 𐑝 𐑞 ·𐑓𐑱𐑔. 𐑦𐑯 𐑔𐑮𐑴𐑦𐑙 𐑿 𐑑 𐑞 𐑤𐑲𐑩𐑯𐑟 𐑣𐑰 𐑢𐑦𐑤 𐑚𐑰 𐑳𐑐𐑣𐑴𐑤𐑛𐑦𐑙 𐑞 𐑦𐑯𐑑𐑼𐑧𐑕𐑑𐑕 𐑝 𐑮𐑦𐑤𐑦𐑡𐑩𐑯 𐑦𐑯 ·𐑮𐑴𐑥. 𐑦𐑓 𐑿 𐑢𐑻 𐑑 𐑔𐑮𐑴 𐑣𐑦𐑥 𐑑 𐑞 𐑤𐑲𐑩𐑯𐑟, 𐑞𐑨𐑑 𐑢𐑫𐑛 𐑯𐑴 𐑛𐑬𐑑 𐑚𐑰 𐑐𐑻𐑕𐑦𐑒𐑿𐑖𐑩𐑯.

[𐑞 𐑒𐑮𐑦𐑕𐑗𐑩𐑯𐑟 𐑩𐑜𐑱𐑯 𐑤𐑭𐑓 𐑣𐑸𐑑𐑦𐑤𐑦].

𐑕𐑧𐑯𐑑𐑘𐑫𐑼𐑦𐑩𐑯 [𐑣𐑪𐑮𐑦𐑓𐑲𐑛] 𐑕𐑲𐑤𐑩𐑯𐑕, 𐑲 𐑑𐑧𐑤 𐑿! 𐑒𐑰𐑐 𐑕𐑲𐑤𐑩𐑯𐑕 𐑞𐑺. 𐑛𐑦𐑛 𐑧𐑯𐑦𐑢𐑳𐑯 𐑧𐑝𐑼 𐑣𐑽 𐑞 𐑤𐑲𐑒 𐑝 𐑞𐑦𐑕?

CENTURION [*fiercely*] Prisonerrrrrs! Tention! Silence!

THE CAPTAIN. I call your attention, prisoners, to the fact that you may be called on to appear in the Imperial Circus at any time from tomorrow onwards according to the requirements of the managers. I may inform you that as there is a shortage of Christians just now, you may expect to be called on very soon.

LAVINIA. What will they do to us, Captain?

CENTURION. Silence!

THE CAPTAIN. The women will be conducted into the arena with the wild beasts of the Imperial Menagerie, and will suffer the consequences. The men, if of an age to bear arms, will be given weapons to defend themselves, if they choose, against the Imperial Gladiators.

LAVINIA. Captain: is there no hope that this cruel persecution –

CENTURION [*shocked*] Silence! Hold your tongue, there. Persecution, indeed!

THE CAPTAIN [*unmoved and somewhat sardonic*] Persecution is not a term applicable to the acts of the Emperor. The Emperor is the Defender of the Faith. In throwing you to the lions he will be upholding the interests of religion in Rome. If you were to throw him to the lions, that would no doubt be persecution.

The Christians again laugh heartily.

CENTURION [*horrified*] Silence, I tell you! Keep silence there. Did anyone ever hear the like of this?

𐑤𐑩𐑝𐑦𐑯𐑾. 𐑒𐑨𐑐𐑑𐑩𐑯: 𐑞𐑺 𐑢𐑦𐑤 𐑚𐑰 𐑯𐑴𐑚𐑪𐑛𐑦 𐑑 𐑩𐑐𐑮𐑰𐑖𐑦𐑱𐑑 𐑿𐑼 𐑡𐑴𐑒𐑕 𐑢𐑧𐑯 𐑢𐑰 𐑸 𐑛𐑧𐑛.

𐑞 𐑒𐑨𐑐𐑑𐑩𐑯 [*𐑳𐑯𐑖𐑱𐑒𐑩𐑯 𐑦𐑯 𐑣𐑦𐑟 𐑩𐑓𐑦𐑖𐑩𐑤 𐑛𐑦𐑤𐑦𐑝𐑼𐑦*] 𐑲 𐑒𐑷𐑤 𐑞 𐑩𐑑𐑧𐑯𐑖𐑩𐑯 𐑝 𐑞 𐑓𐑰𐑥𐑱𐑤 𐑐𐑮𐑦𐑟𐑩𐑯𐑼 ·𐑤𐑩𐑝𐑦𐑯𐑾 𐑑 𐑞 𐑓𐑨𐑒𐑑 𐑞𐑨𐑑 𐑨𐑟 𐑞 𐑧𐑥𐑐𐑼𐑼 𐑦𐑟 𐑩 𐑛𐑦𐑝𐑲𐑯 𐑐𐑻𐑕𐑩𐑯𐑦𐑡, 𐑣𐑻 𐑦𐑥𐑐𐑿𐑑𐑱𐑖𐑩𐑯 𐑝 𐑒𐑮𐑵𐑩𐑤𐑑𐑦 𐑦𐑟 𐑯𐑪𐑑 𐑴𐑯𐑤𐑦 𐑑𐑮𐑰𐑟𐑩𐑯, 𐑚𐑳𐑑 𐑕𐑨𐑒𐑮𐑦𐑤𐑦𐑡. 𐑲 𐑐𐑶𐑯𐑑 𐑬𐑑 𐑑 𐑣𐑻 𐑓𐑻𐑞𐑼 𐑞𐑨𐑑 𐑞𐑺 𐑦𐑟 𐑯𐑴 𐑓𐑬𐑯𐑛𐑱𐑖𐑩𐑯 𐑓𐑹 𐑞 𐑗𐑸𐑡, 𐑨𐑟 𐑞 𐑧𐑥𐑐𐑼𐑼 𐑛𐑳𐑟 𐑯𐑪𐑑 𐑛𐑦𐑟𐑲𐑼 𐑞𐑨𐑑 𐑧𐑯𐑦 𐑐𐑮𐑦𐑟𐑩𐑯𐑼 𐑖𐑫𐑛 𐑕𐑳𐑓𐑼; 𐑯𐑹 𐑒𐑨𐑯 𐑧𐑯𐑦 𐑒𐑮𐑦𐑕𐑗𐑩𐑯 𐑚𐑰 𐑣𐑸𐑥𐑛 𐑕𐑱𐑝 𐑔𐑮𐑵 𐑣𐑦𐑟 𐑹 𐑣𐑻 𐑴𐑯 𐑪𐑚𐑕𐑑𐑦𐑯𐑩𐑕𐑦. 𐑷𐑤 𐑞𐑨𐑑 𐑦𐑟 𐑯𐑧𐑕𐑩𐑕𐑼𐑦 𐑦𐑟 𐑑 𐑕𐑨𐑒𐑮𐑦𐑓𐑲𐑕 𐑑 𐑞 𐑜𐑪𐑛𐑟: 𐑩 𐑕𐑦𐑥𐑐𐑩𐑤 𐑯 𐑒𐑩𐑯𐑝𐑰𐑯𐑾𐑯𐑑 𐑕𐑧𐑮𐑩𐑥𐑩𐑯𐑦 𐑦𐑓𐑧𐑒𐑑𐑩𐑛 𐑚𐑲 𐑛𐑮𐑪𐑐𐑦𐑙 𐑩 𐑐𐑦𐑯𐑗 𐑝 𐑦𐑯𐑕𐑧𐑯𐑕 𐑪𐑯 𐑞 𐑷𐑤𐑑𐑼, 𐑭𐑓𐑑𐑼 𐑢𐑦𐑗 𐑞 𐑐𐑮𐑦𐑟𐑩𐑯𐑼 𐑦𐑟 𐑨𐑑 𐑢𐑳𐑯𐑕 𐑕𐑧𐑑 𐑓𐑮𐑰. 𐑳𐑯𐑛𐑼 𐑕𐑳𐑗 𐑕𐑻𐑒𐑩𐑥𐑕𐑑𐑨𐑯𐑕𐑩𐑟 𐑿 𐑣𐑨𐑝 𐑴𐑯𐑤𐑦 𐑿𐑼 𐑴𐑯 𐑐𐑼𐑝𐑻𐑕 𐑓𐑪𐑤𐑦 𐑑 𐑚𐑤𐑱𐑥 𐑦𐑓 𐑿 𐑕𐑳𐑓𐑼. 𐑲 𐑕𐑩𐑡𐑧𐑕𐑑 𐑑 𐑿 𐑞𐑨𐑑 𐑦𐑓 𐑿 𐑒𐑨𐑯𐑪𐑑 𐑚𐑻𐑯 𐑩 𐑥𐑹𐑕𐑩𐑤 𐑝 𐑦𐑯𐑕𐑧𐑯𐑕 𐑨𐑟 𐑩 𐑥𐑨𐑑𐑼 𐑝 𐑒𐑩𐑯𐑝𐑦𐑒𐑖𐑩𐑯, 𐑿 𐑥𐑲𐑑 𐑨𐑑 𐑤𐑰𐑕𐑑 𐑛𐑵 𐑕𐑴 𐑨𐑟 𐑩 𐑥𐑨𐑑𐑼 𐑝 𐑜𐑫𐑛 𐑑𐑱𐑕𐑑, 𐑑 𐑩𐑝𐑶𐑛 𐑖𐑪𐑒𐑦𐑙 𐑞 𐑮𐑦𐑤𐑦𐑡𐑩𐑕 𐑒𐑩𐑯𐑝𐑦𐑒𐑖𐑩𐑯𐑟 𐑝 𐑿𐑼 𐑓𐑧𐑤𐑴 𐑕𐑦𐑑𐑦𐑟𐑩𐑯𐑟. 𐑲 𐑨𐑥 𐑩𐑢𐑺 𐑞𐑨𐑑 𐑞𐑰𐑟 𐑒𐑩𐑯𐑕𐑦𐑛𐑼𐑱𐑖𐑩𐑯𐑟 𐑛𐑵 𐑯𐑪𐑑 𐑢𐑱 𐑢𐑦𐑞 𐑒𐑮𐑦𐑕𐑗𐑩𐑯𐑟; 𐑚𐑳𐑑 𐑦𐑑 𐑦𐑟 𐑥𐑲 𐑛𐑿𐑑𐑦 𐑑 𐑒𐑷𐑤 𐑿𐑼 𐑩𐑑𐑧𐑯𐑖𐑩𐑯 𐑑 𐑞𐑧𐑥 𐑦𐑯 𐑹𐑛𐑼 𐑞𐑨𐑑 𐑿 𐑥𐑱 𐑣𐑨𐑝 𐑯𐑴 𐑜𐑮𐑬𐑯𐑛 𐑓𐑹 𐑒𐑩𐑥𐑐𐑤𐑱𐑯𐑦𐑙 𐑝 𐑿𐑼 𐑑𐑮𐑰𐑑𐑥𐑩𐑯𐑑, 𐑹 𐑝 𐑩𐑒𐑿𐑟𐑦𐑙 𐑞 𐑧𐑥𐑐𐑼𐑼 𐑝 𐑒𐑮𐑵𐑩𐑤𐑑𐑦 𐑢𐑧𐑯 𐑣𐑰 𐑦𐑟 𐑖𐑴𐑦𐑙 𐑿 𐑞 𐑥𐑴𐑕𐑑 𐑕𐑦𐑜𐑯𐑩𐑤 𐑒𐑤𐑧𐑥𐑩𐑯𐑕𐑦. 𐑤𐑫𐑒𐑑 𐑨𐑑 𐑓𐑮𐑪𐑥 𐑞𐑦𐑕 𐑐𐑶𐑯𐑑 𐑝 𐑝𐑿, 𐑧𐑝𐑮𐑦 𐑒𐑮𐑦𐑕𐑗𐑩𐑯 𐑣𐑵 𐑣𐑨𐑟 𐑐𐑧𐑮𐑦𐑖𐑑 𐑦𐑯 𐑞 𐑼𐑰𐑯𐑩 𐑣𐑨𐑟 𐑮𐑾𐑤𐑦 𐑒𐑩𐑥𐑦𐑑𐑩𐑛 𐑕𐑵𐑦𐑕𐑲𐑛.

𐑤𐑩𐑝𐑦𐑯𐑾. 𐑒𐑨𐑐𐑑𐑩𐑯: 𐑿𐑼 𐑡𐑴𐑒𐑕 𐑸 𐑑𐑵 𐑜𐑮𐑦𐑥. 𐑛𐑵 𐑯𐑪𐑑 𐑔𐑦𐑙𐑒 𐑦𐑑 𐑦𐑟 𐑰𐑟𐑦 𐑓𐑹 𐑳𐑕 𐑑 𐑛𐑲. 𐑬𐑼 𐑓𐑱𐑔 𐑥𐑱𐑒𐑕 𐑤𐑲𐑓 𐑓𐑸 𐑕𐑑𐑮𐑪𐑙𐑜𐑼 𐑯 𐑥𐑹 𐑢𐑳𐑯𐑛𐑼𐑓𐑩𐑤 𐑦𐑯 𐑳𐑕 𐑞𐑨𐑯 𐑢𐑧𐑯

LAVINIA. Captain: there will be nobody to appreciate your jokes when we are gone.

THE CAPTAIN [*unshaken in his official delivery*] I call the attention of the female prisoner Lavinia to the fact that as the Emperor is a divine personage, her imputation of cruelty is not only treason, but sacrilege. I point out to her further that there is no foundation for the charge, as the Emperor does not desire that any prisoner should suffer; nor can any Christian be harmed save through his or her own obstinacy. All that is necessary is to sacrifice to the gods: a simple and convenient ceremony effected by dropping a pinch of incense on the altar, after which the prisoner is at once set free. Under such circumstances you have only your own perverse folly to blame if you suffer. I suggest to you that if you cannot burn a morsel of incense as a matter of conviction, you might at least do so as a matter of good taste, to avoid shocking the religious convictions of your fellow citizens. I am aware that these considerations do not weigh with Christians; but it is my duty to call your attention to them in order that you may have no ground for complaining of your treatment, or of accusing the Emperor of cruelty when he is shewing you the most signal clemency. Looked at from this point of view, every Christian who has perished in the arena has really committed suicide.

LAVINIA. Captain: your jokes are too grim. Do not think it is easy for us to die. Our faith makes life far stronger and more wonderful in us than when

𐑢𐑰 𐑢𐑩𐑒𐑑 𐑦𐑯 𐑐𐑕𐑒𐑯𐑤𐑕 𐑯 𐑘𐑳𐑐 𐑯𐑲𐑛𐑦𐑤 𐑑 𐑤𐑦𐑩 𐑓𐑹. 𐑐𐑯𐑛 𐑦𐑟 𐑘𐑮𐑐𐑥 𐑓𐑹 𐑲𐑕 𐑞𐑯 𐑓𐑹 𐑣: 𐑞 𐑩𐑮𐑑𐑥'𐑟 𐑨𐑐𐑥𐑦 𐑦𐑟 𐑨𐑟 𐑩𐑦𐑑𐑥 𐑨𐑟 𐑘𐑦𐑟 𐑚𐑲𐑩𐑯𐑛 𐑦𐑟 𐑐𐑒𐑫𐑦𐑩𐑕.

𐑞 𐑒𐑨𐑐𐑑𐑦𐑯 [𐑮𐑕𐑞𐑥 𐑚𐑮𐑲𐑤𐑩𐑤𐑐, 𐑩𐑐𐑮𐑤𐑕𐑦𐑤 𐑘𐑫 𐑓𐑫𐑕𐑩𐑯𐑤𐑦 𐑯 𐑐𐑮𐑧𐑩𐑤𐑦] 𐑩 𐑩𐑮𐑑𐑥, ·𐑤𐑩𐑝𐑦𐑯𐑾, 𐑦𐑟 𐑩 𐑓𐑳𐑤. 𐑣𐑥 𐑐𐑯𐑛 𐑢𐑦𐑤 𐑓𐑳𐑩 𐑯𐑲𐑛𐑦𐑤.

𐑤𐑩𐑝𐑦𐑯𐑾. 𐑞𐑦𐑯 𐑢𐑲 𐑒𐑦𐑤 𐑩𐑰?

𐑞 𐑒𐑨𐑐𐑑𐑦𐑯. 𐑲 𐑩𐑰𐑯 𐑞𐑨𐑑 𐑚𐑳𐑛, 𐑦𐑓 𐑞𐑮 𐑝𐑰 𐑦𐑯𐑦 𐑚𐑳𐑛, 𐑦𐑟𐑰𐑟 𐑯𐑪 𐑩𐑮𐑑𐑥𐑟.

𐑤𐑩𐑝𐑦𐑯𐑾. 𐑯𐑪; 𐑝𐑲𐑑 𐑩𐑲 𐑓𐑧𐑛, 𐑤𐑲𐑒 𐑣𐑥 𐑕𐑫𐑐, 𐑦𐑟𐑰𐑟 𐑑𐑦𐑕𐑑𐑦𐑤. 𐑒𐑨𐑯 𐑣 𐑑𐑦𐑕𐑑 𐑣𐑥 𐑕𐑫𐑐 𐑦𐑒𐑕𐑧𐑐𐑑 𐑝𐑲 𐑕𐑑𐑧𐑒𐑦𐑤 𐑣𐑥 𐑤𐑲𐑓 𐑯𐑯 𐑦𐑑?

𐑞 𐑒𐑨𐑐𐑑𐑦𐑯 [𐑕𐑲𐑐𐑩𐑯𐑤 𐑮𐑦𐑟𐑣𐑩𐑦𐑤 𐑘𐑦𐑟 𐑩𐑓𐑦𐑤𐑩𐑤 𐑑𐑪𐑯] 𐑲 𐑒𐑷𐑤 𐑞 𐑩𐑑𐑧𐑯𐑖𐑩𐑯 𐑝 𐑞 𐑓𐑰𐑥𐑱𐑤 𐑐𐑮𐑦𐑟𐑩𐑯𐑼 𐑑 𐑞 𐑓𐑨𐑒𐑑 𐑞𐑨𐑑 𐑒𐑮𐑦𐑕𐑗𐑩𐑯𐑟 𐑸 𐑯𐑪𐑑 𐑩𐑤𐑬𐑛 𐑑 𐑐𐑮𐑱 𐑞 𐑧𐑥𐑐𐑼𐑼'𐑟 𐑕𐑑𐑨𐑗𐑵𐑟 𐑦𐑯𐑑𐑵 𐑛𐑦𐑕𐑣𐑩𐑯𐑩𐑕 𐑯 𐑛𐑧𐑑 𐑒𐑩𐑕𐑑𐑩𐑥𐑟 𐑑 𐑞𐑧𐑥 𐑓𐑹 𐑢𐑦𐑤 𐑞 𐑕𐑦𐑤𐑑𐑩𐑕 𐑮𐑦𐑐𐑣𐑧𐑯𐑕𐑦𐑚𐑩𐑤𐑦𐑑𐑦𐑟 𐑚𐑦𐑤𐑪𐑙 𐑯𐑪 𐑥𐑩𐑕𐑩𐑯. [𐑞 𐑒𐑮𐑦𐑕𐑗𐑩𐑯𐑟 𐑑𐑦𐑑𐑼].

𐑤𐑩𐑝𐑦𐑯𐑾. 𐑒𐑨𐑐𐑑𐑦𐑯: 𐑣𐑬 𐑒𐑨𐑯 𐑣?

𐑞 𐑒𐑨𐑐𐑑𐑦𐑯. 𐑲 𐑒𐑷𐑤 𐑞 𐑓𐑰𐑥𐑱𐑤 𐑐𐑮𐑦𐑟𐑩𐑯𐑼'𐑟 𐑩𐑑𐑧𐑯𐑖𐑩𐑯 𐑕𐑐𐑧𐑖𐑩𐑤𐑦 𐑑 𐑞 𐑓𐑨𐑒𐑑 𐑞𐑨𐑑 𐑓𐑹 𐑒𐑪𐑥𐑐𐑦𐑑𐑩𐑯𐑑 𐑢𐑦𐑑𐑯𐑩𐑕𐑩𐑟 𐑣𐑨𐑝 𐑚𐑰𐑯 𐑩𐑯𐑜𐑱𐑡𐑛 𐑚𐑲 𐑞 𐑤𐑦𐑜𐑩𐑤 𐑩𐑛𐑝𐑲𐑟𐑼 𐑝 𐑞𐑦𐑕 𐑩𐑛𐑥𐑦𐑯𐑦𐑕𐑑𐑮𐑱𐑖𐑩𐑯, 𐑯 𐑢𐑦𐑤 𐑚𐑰 𐑒𐑨𐑯 𐑣𐑨𐑝 𐑘𐑹 𐑚𐑨𐑒 𐑞 𐑕𐑪𐑤𐑩𐑯𐑑 𐑚𐑰 𐑚𐑦𐑓𐑹 𐑑 𐑕𐑧𐑛𐑦𐑖𐑩𐑕 𐑨𐑟 𐑢𐑧𐑤 𐑨𐑟 𐑛𐑦𐑕𐑴𐑚𐑰𐑛𐑾𐑯𐑕 𐑑𐑵 𐑞𐑧𐑥. 𐑲 𐑣𐑨𐑝 𐑯𐑪 𐑢𐑰𐑤 𐑑 𐑕𐑦 𐑑 𐑞 𐑐𐑮𐑦𐑟𐑩𐑯𐑼𐑟.

𐑕𐑐𐑦𐑯𐑔𐑴. 𐑓𐑩𐑤𐑦𐑕! 𐑢𐑲𐑑 𐑕𐑧𐑛 𐑢𐑰 𐑣 𐑞𐑧𐑥.

𐑞 𐑒𐑨𐑐𐑑𐑦𐑯. 𐑕𐑐𐑦𐑯𐑔𐑴: 𐑣 𐑢𐑦𐑤 𐑮𐑦𐑕𐑧𐑯 𐑘𐑹 𐑢𐑦𐑞 𐑣𐑥 𐑦𐑯 𐑦𐑯 𐑐𐑷𐑟 𐑝 𐑞 𐑐𐑮𐑦𐑟𐑩𐑯𐑼𐑟 𐑲𐑯𐑑𐑦𐑤 𐑞 𐑮𐑲𐑩𐑤 𐑝 𐑛𐑲𐑰 𐑒𐑮𐑦𐑕𐑗𐑩𐑯 𐑐𐑮𐑦𐑟𐑩𐑯𐑼𐑟 𐑦𐑯 𐑞 𐑒𐑲𐑕𐑑𐑩𐑤 𐑝 𐑩 𐑒𐑪𐑘𐑫𐑑 𐑝 𐑞 𐑑𐑦𐑯𐑛 𐑤𐑰𐑟𐑩𐑯. 𐑩𐑤𐑲𐑛 𐑞𐑰𐑟 𐑐𐑮𐑦𐑟𐑩𐑯𐑼𐑟 𐑣 𐑢𐑦𐑤 𐑐𐑩𐑑𐑦𐑒𐑴𐑤𐑩𐑤𐑦 𐑲𐑯𐑝𐑦𐑑𐑦𐑛𐑲 𐑩𐑯

we walked in darkness and had nothing to live for. Death is harder for us than for you: the martyr's agony is as bitter as his triumph is glorious.

THE CAPTAIN [*rather troubled, addressing her personally and gravely*] A martyr, Lavinia, is a fool. Your death will prove nothing.

LAVINIA. Then why kill me?

THE CAPTAIN. I mean that truth, if there be any truth, needs no martyrs.

LAVINIA. No; but my faith, like your sword, needs testing. Can you test your sword except by staking your life on it?

THE CAPTAIN [*suddenly resuming his official tone*] I call the attention of the female prisoner to the fact that Christians are not allowed to draw the Emperor's officers into arguments and put questions to them for which the military regulations provide no answer. [*The Christians titter*].

LAVINIA. Captain: how can you?

THE CAPTAIN. I call the female prisoner's attention specially to the fact that four comfortable homes have been offered her by officers of this regiment, of which she can have her choice the moment she chooses to sacrifice as all wellbred Roman ladies do. I have no more to say to the prisoners.

CENTURION. Dismiss! But stay where you are.

THE CAPTAIN. Centurion: you will remain here with your men in charge of the prisoners until the arrival of three Christian prisoners in the custody of a cohort of the tenth legion. Among these prisoners you will particularly identify an

𐑸𐑥𐑼𐑼 𐑯𐑱𐑥𐑛 ·𐑓𐑧𐑮𐑴𐑝𐑾𐑕, 𐑝 𐑛𐑱𐑯𐑡𐑼𐑩𐑕 𐑒𐑨𐑮𐑩𐑒𐑑𐑼 𐑯 𐑜𐑮𐑱𐑑 𐑐𐑻𐑕𐑩𐑯𐑩𐑤 𐑕𐑑𐑮𐑧𐑙𐑔, 𐑯 𐑩 𐑜𐑮𐑰𐑒 𐑑𐑱𐑤𐑼 𐑮𐑦𐑐𐑿𐑑𐑩𐑛 𐑑 𐑚𐑰 𐑩 𐑕𐑹𐑕𐑼𐑼, 𐑚𐑲 𐑯𐑱𐑥 ·𐑨𐑯𐑛𐑮𐑩𐑒𐑤𐑰𐑟. 𐑿 𐑢𐑦𐑤 𐑨𐑛 𐑞 𐑐𐑺 𐑑 𐑿𐑼 𐑗𐑱𐑯 𐑜𐑨𐑙 𐑯 𐑥𐑸𐑗 𐑞𐑧𐑥 𐑷𐑤 𐑑 𐑞 𐑒𐑩𐑤𐑦𐑕𐑾𐑥, 𐑢𐑺 𐑿 𐑢𐑦𐑤 𐑛𐑦𐑤𐑦𐑝𐑼 𐑞𐑧𐑥 𐑦𐑯𐑑𐑵 𐑞 𐑒𐑳𐑕𐑑𐑩𐑛𐑦 𐑝 𐑞 𐑥𐑭𐑕𐑑𐑼 𐑝 𐑞 𐑜𐑤𐑨𐑛𐑦𐑱𐑑𐑼𐑟 𐑯 𐑑𐑱𐑒 𐑣𐑦𐑟 𐑮𐑦𐑕𐑰𐑑, 𐑒𐑬𐑯𐑑𐑼𐑕𐑲𐑯𐑛 𐑚𐑲 𐑞 𐑒𐑰𐑐𐑼 𐑝 𐑞 𐑚𐑰𐑕𐑑𐑕 𐑯 𐑞 𐑨𐑒𐑑𐑦𐑙 𐑥𐑨𐑯𐑦𐑡𐑼. 𐑿 𐑳𐑯𐑛𐑼𐑕𐑑𐑨𐑯𐑛 𐑿𐑼 𐑦𐑯𐑕𐑑𐑮𐑳𐑒𐑖𐑩𐑯𐑟?

𐑕𐑧𐑯𐑑𐑘𐑫𐑼𐑾𐑯. 𐑘𐑧𐑕, 𐑕𐑻.

𐑞 𐑒𐑨𐑐𐑑𐑩𐑯. 𐑛𐑦𐑕𐑥𐑦𐑕. [𐑣𐑰 𐑔𐑮𐑴𐑟 𐑪𐑓 𐑣𐑦𐑟 𐑺 𐑝 𐑐𐑼𐑱𐑛, 𐑯 𐑛𐑦𐑕𐑧𐑯𐑛𐑟 𐑓𐑮𐑪𐑥 𐑣𐑦𐑟 𐑐𐑴𐑕𐑑. 𐑞 𐑕𐑧𐑯𐑑𐑘𐑫𐑼𐑾𐑯 𐑕𐑰𐑑𐑕 𐑣𐑦𐑥𐑕𐑧𐑤𐑓 𐑪𐑯 𐑦𐑑 𐑯 𐑐𐑮𐑦𐑐𐑺𐑟 𐑓𐑹 𐑩 [illegible], 𐑢𐑲𐑤𐑕𐑑 𐑣𐑦𐑟 𐑥𐑧𐑯 𐑕𐑑𐑨𐑯𐑛 𐑨𐑑 𐑰𐑟. 𐑞 𐑒𐑮𐑦𐑕𐑑𐑘𐑩𐑯𐑟 𐑕𐑦𐑑 𐑛𐑬𐑯 𐑪𐑯 𐑞 𐑢𐑧𐑕𐑑 𐑕𐑲𐑛 𐑝 𐑞 𐑕𐑒𐑢𐑺, 𐑜𐑤𐑨𐑛 𐑑 𐑮𐑧𐑕𐑑. ·𐑤𐑩𐑝𐑦𐑯𐑾 𐑩𐑤𐑴𐑯 𐑮𐑦𐑥𐑱𐑯𐑟 𐑕𐑑𐑨𐑯𐑛𐑦𐑙 𐑑 𐑕𐑐𐑰𐑒 𐑑 𐑞 𐑒𐑨𐑐𐑑𐑩𐑯].

𐑤𐑩𐑝𐑦𐑯𐑾. 𐑒𐑨𐑐𐑑𐑩𐑯: 𐑦𐑟 𐑞𐑦𐑕 𐑥𐑨𐑯 𐑣𐑵 𐑦𐑟 𐑑 𐑜𐑸𐑛 𐑳𐑕 𐑞 𐑓𐑱𐑥𐑩𐑕 ·𐑓𐑧𐑮𐑴𐑝𐑾𐑕, 𐑣𐑵 𐑣𐑨𐑟 𐑥𐑱𐑛 𐑕𐑳𐑗 𐑢𐑳𐑯𐑛𐑼𐑓𐑩𐑤 𐑒𐑩𐑯𐑝𐑻𐑠𐑩𐑯𐑟 𐑦𐑯 𐑞 𐑯𐑹𐑞𐑼𐑯 𐑕𐑦𐑑𐑦𐑟?

𐑞 𐑒𐑨𐑐𐑑𐑩𐑯. 𐑘𐑧𐑕. 𐑢𐑰 𐑸 𐑢𐑹𐑯𐑛 𐑞𐑨𐑑 𐑣𐑰 𐑣𐑨𐑟 𐑞 𐑕𐑑𐑮𐑧𐑙𐑔 𐑝 𐑩𐑯 𐑧𐑤𐑩𐑓𐑩𐑯𐑑 𐑯 𐑞 𐑑𐑧𐑥𐑐𐑼 𐑝 𐑩 𐑥𐑨𐑛 𐑚𐑫𐑤. 𐑷𐑤𐑕𐑴 𐑞𐑨𐑑 𐑣𐑰 𐑦𐑟 𐑕𐑑𐑸𐑒 𐑥𐑨𐑛. 𐑯𐑪𐑑 𐑩 𐑥𐑪𐑛𐑩𐑤 𐑒𐑮𐑦𐑕𐑑𐑘𐑩𐑯, 𐑦𐑑 𐑢𐑫𐑛 𐑕𐑰𐑥.

𐑤𐑩𐑝𐑦𐑯𐑾. 𐑿 𐑯𐑰𐑛 𐑯𐑪𐑑 𐑓𐑽 𐑣𐑦𐑥 𐑦𐑓 𐑣𐑰 𐑦𐑟 𐑩 𐑒𐑮𐑦𐑕𐑑𐑘𐑩𐑯, 𐑒𐑨𐑐𐑑𐑩𐑯.

𐑞 𐑒𐑨𐑐𐑑𐑩𐑯 [𐑒𐑴𐑤𐑛𐑤𐑦] 𐑲 𐑖𐑨𐑤 𐑯𐑪𐑑 𐑓𐑽 𐑣𐑦𐑥 𐑦𐑯 𐑧𐑯𐑦 𐑒𐑱𐑕, ·𐑤𐑩𐑝𐑦𐑯𐑾.

𐑤𐑩𐑝𐑦𐑯𐑾 [𐑣𐑻 𐑲𐑟 𐑛𐑭𐑯𐑕𐑦𐑙] 𐑣𐑬 𐑚𐑮𐑱𐑝 𐑝 𐑿, 𐑒𐑨𐑐𐑑𐑩𐑯!

𐑞 𐑒𐑨𐑐𐑑𐑩𐑯. 𐑿 𐑸 𐑮𐑲𐑑: 𐑦𐑑 𐑢𐑪𐑟 𐑩 𐑕𐑦𐑤𐑦 𐑔𐑦𐑙 𐑑

armorer named Ferrovius, of dangerous character and great personal strength, and a Greek tailor reputed to be a sorcerer, by name Androcles. You will add the three to your charge here and march them all to the Coliseum, where you will deliver them into the custody of the master of the gladiators and take his receipt, countersigned by the keeper of the beasts and the acting manager. You understand your instructions?

CENTURION. Yes, sir.

THE CAPTAIN. Dismiss. [*He throws off his air of parade, and descends from his perch. The Centurion seats himself on it and prepares for a nap, whilst his men stand at ease. The Christians sit down on the west side of the square, glad to rest. Lavinia alone remains standing to speak to the Captain*].

LAVINIA. Captain: is this man who is to join us the famous Ferrovius, who has made such wonderful conversions in the northern cities?

THE CAPTAIN. Yes. We are warned that he has the strength of an elephant and the temper of a mad bull. Also that he is stark mad. Not a model Christian, it would seem.

LAVINIA. You need not fear him if he is a Christian, Captain.

THE CAPTAIN [*coldly*] I shall not fear him in any case, Lavinia.

LAVINIA [*her eyes dancing*] How brave of you, Captain!

THE CAPTAIN. You are right: it was a silly thing to

𐑕𐑱. [𐑦𐑯 𐑩 𐑤𐑴𐑼 𐑑𐑴𐑯, 𐑣𐑿𐑥𐑱𐑯 𐑯 𐑻𐑡𐑩𐑯𐑑] ·𐑤𐑩𐑝𐑦𐑯𐑾: 𐑛𐑵 𐑒𐑮𐑦𐑕𐑗𐑩𐑯𐑟 𐑯𐑴 𐑣𐑬 𐑑 𐑤𐑳𐑝?

𐑤𐑩𐑝𐑦𐑯𐑾 [𐑒𐑩𐑥𐑐𐑴𐑟𐑦𐑛𐑤𐑦] 𐑘𐑧𐑕, 𐑒𐑨𐑐𐑑𐑩𐑯: 𐑞𐑱 𐑤𐑳𐑝 𐑰𐑝𐑩𐑯 𐑞𐑺 𐑧𐑯𐑩𐑥𐑦𐑟.

𐑞 𐑒𐑨𐑐𐑑𐑩𐑯. 𐑦𐑟 𐑞𐑨𐑑 𐑰𐑟𐑦?

𐑤𐑩𐑝𐑦𐑯𐑾. 𐑝𐑧𐑮𐑦 𐑰𐑟𐑦, 𐑒𐑨𐑐𐑑𐑩𐑯, 𐑢𐑧𐑯 𐑞𐑺 𐑧𐑯𐑩𐑥𐑦𐑟 𐑸 𐑨𐑟 𐑣𐑨𐑯𐑕𐑩𐑥 𐑨𐑟 𐑿.

𐑞 𐑒𐑨𐑐𐑑𐑩𐑯. ·𐑤𐑩𐑝𐑦𐑯𐑾: 𐑿 𐑸 𐑤𐑭𐑓𐑦𐑙 𐑨𐑑 𐑥𐑰.

𐑤𐑩𐑝𐑦𐑯𐑾. 𐑨𐑑 𐑿, 𐑒𐑨𐑐𐑑𐑩𐑯! 𐑦𐑥𐑐𐑪𐑕𐑦𐑚𐑩𐑤.

𐑞 𐑒𐑨𐑐𐑑𐑩𐑯. 𐑞𐑧𐑯 𐑿 𐑸 𐑓𐑤𐑻𐑑𐑦𐑙 𐑢𐑦𐑞 𐑥𐑰, 𐑢𐑦𐑗 𐑦𐑟 𐑢𐑻𐑕. 𐑛𐑴𐑯𐑑 𐑚𐑰 𐑓𐑵𐑤𐑦𐑖.

𐑤𐑩𐑝𐑦𐑯𐑾. 𐑚𐑳𐑑 𐑕𐑳𐑗 𐑩 𐑝𐑧𐑮𐑦 𐑣𐑨𐑯𐑕𐑩𐑥 𐑒𐑨𐑐𐑑𐑩𐑯.

𐑞 𐑒𐑨𐑐𐑑𐑩𐑯. 𐑦𐑯𐑒𐑪𐑮𐑦𐑡𐑩𐑚𐑩𐑤! [𐑻𐑡𐑩𐑯𐑑𐑤𐑦] 𐑤𐑦𐑕𐑩𐑯 𐑑 𐑥𐑰. 𐑞 𐑥𐑧𐑯 𐑦𐑯 𐑞𐑨𐑑 𐑷𐑛𐑦𐑩𐑯𐑕 𐑑𐑩𐑥𐑪𐑮𐑴 𐑢𐑦𐑤 𐑚𐑰 𐑞 𐑝𐑲𐑤𐑩𐑕𐑑 𐑝 𐑝𐑩𐑤𐑳𐑐𐑗𐑵𐑼𐑦𐑟: 𐑥𐑧𐑯 𐑦𐑯 𐑣𐑵𐑥 𐑞 𐑴𐑯𐑤𐑦 𐑐𐑨𐑖𐑩𐑯 𐑦𐑒𐑕𐑲𐑑𐑩𐑛 𐑚𐑲 𐑩 𐑚𐑿𐑑𐑦𐑓𐑩𐑤 𐑢𐑫𐑥𐑩𐑯 𐑦𐑟 𐑩 𐑤𐑳𐑕𐑑 𐑑 𐑕𐑰 𐑣𐑻 𐑑𐑹𐑗𐑼𐑛 𐑯 𐑑𐑹𐑯 𐑖𐑮𐑰𐑒𐑦𐑙 𐑤𐑦𐑥 𐑓𐑮𐑪𐑥 𐑤𐑦𐑥. 𐑦𐑑 𐑦𐑟 𐑩 𐑒𐑮𐑲𐑥 𐑑 𐑜𐑮𐑨𐑑𐑦𐑓𐑲 𐑞𐑨𐑑 𐑐𐑨𐑖𐑩𐑯. 𐑦𐑑 𐑦𐑟 𐑪𐑓𐑼𐑦𐑙 𐑘𐑹𐑕𐑧𐑤𐑓 𐑓𐑹 𐑝𐑲𐑩𐑤𐑱𐑖𐑩𐑯 𐑚𐑲 𐑞 𐑣𐑴𐑤 𐑮𐑨𐑚𐑩𐑤 𐑝 𐑞 𐑕𐑑𐑮𐑰𐑑𐑕 𐑯 𐑞 𐑮𐑦𐑓-𐑮𐑨𐑓 𐑝 𐑞 𐑒𐑹𐑑 𐑨𐑑 𐑞 𐑕𐑱𐑥 𐑑𐑲𐑥. 𐑢𐑲 𐑢𐑦𐑤 𐑿 𐑯𐑪𐑑 𐑗𐑵𐑟 𐑮𐑭𐑞𐑼 𐑩 𐑒𐑲𐑯𐑛𐑤𐑦 𐑤𐑳𐑝 𐑯 𐑩𐑯 𐑪𐑯𐑼𐑩𐑚𐑩𐑤 𐑩𐑤𐑲𐑩𐑯𐑕?

𐑤𐑩𐑝𐑦𐑯𐑾. 𐑞𐑱 𐑒𐑨𐑯𐑪𐑑 𐑝𐑲𐑩𐑤𐑱𐑑 𐑥𐑲 𐑕𐑴𐑤. 𐑲 𐑩𐑤𐑴𐑯 𐑒𐑨𐑯 𐑛𐑵 𐑞𐑨𐑑 𐑚𐑲 𐑕𐑨𐑒𐑮𐑦𐑓𐑲𐑕𐑦𐑙 𐑑 𐑓𐑷𐑤𐑕 𐑜𐑪𐑛𐑟.

𐑞 𐑒𐑨𐑐𐑑𐑩𐑯. 𐑕𐑨𐑒𐑮𐑦𐑓𐑲𐑕 𐑞𐑧𐑯 𐑑 𐑞 𐑑𐑮𐑵 𐑜𐑪𐑛. 𐑢𐑪𐑑 𐑛𐑳𐑟 𐑣𐑦𐑟 𐑯𐑱𐑥 𐑥𐑨𐑑𐑼? 𐑢𐑰 𐑒𐑷𐑤 𐑣𐑦𐑥 ·𐑡𐑵𐑐𐑦𐑑𐑼. 𐑞 𐑜𐑮𐑰𐑒𐑕 𐑒𐑷𐑤 𐑣𐑦𐑥 ·𐑟𐑿𐑕. 𐑒𐑷𐑤 𐑣𐑦𐑥 𐑢𐑪𐑑 𐑿 𐑢𐑦𐑤 𐑨𐑟 𐑿 𐑛𐑮𐑪𐑐 𐑞 𐑦𐑯𐑕𐑧𐑯𐑕 𐑪𐑯 𐑞 𐑷𐑤𐑑𐑼 𐑓𐑤𐑱𐑥: 𐑣𐑰 𐑢𐑦𐑤 𐑳𐑯𐑛𐑼𐑕𐑑𐑨𐑯𐑛.

𐑤𐑩𐑝𐑦𐑯𐑾. 𐑯𐑴. 𐑲 𐑒𐑫𐑛𐑩𐑯𐑑. 𐑞𐑨𐑑 𐑦𐑟 𐑞 𐑕𐑑𐑮𐑱𐑯𐑡 𐑔𐑦𐑙, 𐑒𐑨𐑐𐑑𐑩𐑯, 𐑞𐑨𐑑 𐑩 𐑤𐑦𐑑𐑩𐑤 𐑐𐑦𐑯𐑗 𐑝 𐑦𐑯𐑕𐑧𐑯𐑕 𐑖𐑫𐑛 𐑥𐑱𐑒 𐑷𐑤 𐑞𐑨𐑑 𐑛𐑦𐑓𐑼𐑩𐑯𐑕. 𐑮𐑦𐑤𐑦𐑡𐑩𐑯 𐑦𐑟 𐑕𐑳𐑗 𐑩 𐑜𐑮𐑱𐑑

say. [*In a lower tone, humane and urgent*] Lavinia: do Christians know how to love?

LAVINIA [*composedly*] Yes, Captain: they love even their enemies.

THE CAPTAIN. Is that easy?

LAVINIA. Very easy, Captain, when their enemies are as handsome as you.

THE CAPTAIN. Lavinia: you are laughing at me.

LAVINIA. At you, Captain! Impossible.

THE CAPTAIN. Then you are flirting with me, which is worse. Dont be foolish.

LAVINIA. But such a very handsome captain.

THE CAPTAIN. Incorrigible! [*Urgently*] Listen to me. The men in that audience tomorrow will be the vilest of voluptuaries: men in whom the only passion excited by a beautiful woman is a lust to see her tortured and torn shrieking limb from limb. It is a crime to gratify that passion. It is offering yourself for violation by the whole rabble of the streets and the riff-raff of the court at the same time. Why will you not choose rather a kindly love and an honorable alliance?

LAVINIA. They cannot violate my soul. I alone can do that by sacrificing to false gods.

THE CAPTAIN. Sacrifice then to the true God. What does his name matter? We call him Jupiter. The Greeks call him Zeus. Call him what you will as you drop the incense on the altar flame; He will understand.

LAVINIA. No. I couldnt. That is the strange thing, Captain, that a little pinch of incense should make all that difference. Religion is such a great

𐑔𐑦𐑙 𐑞𐑨𐑑 𐑢𐑧𐑯 𐑲 𐑥𐑰𐑑 𐑮𐑾𐑤𐑦 𐑮𐑦𐑤𐑦𐑡𐑩𐑕 𐑐𐑰𐑐𐑩𐑤 𐑢𐑰 𐑸 𐑓𐑮𐑧𐑯𐑛𐑟 𐑨𐑑 𐑢𐑳𐑯𐑕, 𐑯𐑴 𐑥𐑨𐑑𐑼 𐑢𐑪𐑑 𐑯𐑱𐑥 𐑢𐑰 𐑜𐑦𐑝 𐑑 𐑞 𐑛𐑦𐑝𐑲𐑯 𐑢𐑦𐑤 𐑞𐑨𐑑 𐑥𐑱𐑛 𐑳𐑕 𐑯 𐑥𐑵𐑝𐑟 𐑳𐑕. 𐑴, 𐑛𐑵 𐑿 𐑔𐑦𐑙𐑒 𐑞𐑨𐑑 𐑲, 𐑩 𐑢𐑫𐑥𐑩𐑯, 𐑢𐑫𐑛 𐑒𐑢𐑪𐑮𐑩𐑤 𐑢𐑦𐑞 𐑿 𐑓𐑹 𐑕𐑨𐑒𐑮𐑦𐑓𐑲𐑕𐑦𐑙 𐑑 𐑩 𐑢𐑫𐑥𐑩𐑯 𐑜𐑪𐑛 𐑤𐑲𐑒 ·𐑛𐑲𐑨𐑯𐑩, 𐑦𐑓 ·𐑛𐑲𐑨𐑯𐑩 𐑥𐑧𐑯𐑑 𐑑 𐑿 𐑢𐑪𐑑 ·𐑒𐑮𐑲𐑕𐑑 𐑥𐑰𐑯𐑟 𐑑 𐑥𐑰? 𐑯𐑴: 𐑢𐑰 𐑖𐑫𐑛 𐑯𐑰𐑤 𐑕𐑲𐑛 𐑚𐑲 𐑕𐑲𐑛 𐑚𐑦𐑓𐑹 𐑣𐑻 𐑷𐑤𐑑𐑼 𐑤𐑲𐑒 𐑑𐑵 𐑗𐑦𐑤𐑛𐑮𐑩𐑯. 𐑚𐑳𐑑 𐑢𐑧𐑯 𐑥𐑧𐑯 𐑣𐑵 𐑚𐑦𐑤𐑰𐑝 𐑯𐑲𐑞𐑼 𐑦𐑯 𐑥𐑲 𐑜𐑪𐑛 𐑯𐑹 𐑦𐑯 𐑞𐑺 𐑴𐑯—𐑥𐑧𐑯 𐑣𐑵 𐑛𐑵 𐑯𐑪𐑑 𐑯𐑴 𐑞 𐑥𐑰𐑯𐑦𐑙 𐑝 𐑞 𐑢𐑻𐑛 𐑮𐑦𐑤𐑦𐑡𐑩𐑯—𐑢𐑧𐑯 𐑞𐑰𐑟 𐑥𐑧𐑯 𐑛𐑮𐑨𐑜 𐑥𐑰 𐑑 𐑞 𐑓𐑫𐑑 𐑝 𐑩𐑯 𐑲𐑼𐑯 𐑕𐑑𐑨𐑗𐑵 𐑞𐑨𐑑 𐑣𐑨𐑟 𐑚𐑦𐑒𐑳𐑥 𐑞 𐑕𐑦𐑥𐑚𐑩𐑤 𐑝 𐑞 𐑑𐑧𐑮𐑼 𐑯 𐑛𐑸𐑒𐑯𐑩𐑕 𐑔𐑮𐑵 𐑢𐑦𐑗 𐑞𐑱 𐑢𐑷𐑒, 𐑝 𐑞𐑺 𐑒𐑮𐑵𐑩𐑤𐑑𐑦 𐑯 𐑜𐑮𐑰𐑛, 𐑝 𐑞𐑺 𐑣𐑱𐑑𐑮𐑩𐑛 𐑝 ·𐑜𐑪𐑛 𐑯 𐑞𐑺 𐑩𐑐𐑮𐑧𐑖𐑩𐑯 𐑝 𐑥𐑨𐑯—𐑢𐑧𐑯 𐑞𐑱 𐑭𐑕𐑒 𐑥𐑰 𐑑 𐑐𐑤𐑧𐑡 𐑥𐑲 𐑕𐑴𐑤 𐑚𐑦𐑓𐑹 𐑞 𐑐𐑰𐑐𐑩𐑤 𐑞𐑨𐑑 𐑞𐑦𐑕 𐑣𐑦𐑛𐑾𐑕 𐑲𐑛𐑩𐑤 𐑦𐑟 ·𐑜𐑪𐑛, 𐑯 𐑞𐑨𐑑 𐑷𐑤 𐑞𐑦𐑕 𐑢𐑦𐑒𐑩𐑛𐑯𐑩𐑕 𐑯 𐑓𐑷𐑤𐑕𐑣𐑫𐑛 𐑦𐑟 𐑛𐑦𐑝𐑲𐑯 𐑑𐑮𐑵𐑔, 𐑲 𐑒𐑨𐑯𐑪𐑑 𐑛𐑵 𐑦𐑑, 𐑯𐑪𐑑 𐑦𐑓 𐑞𐑱 𐑒𐑫𐑛 𐑐𐑫𐑑 𐑩 𐑔𐑬𐑟𐑩𐑯𐑛 𐑒𐑮𐑵𐑩𐑤 𐑛𐑧𐑔𐑕 𐑪𐑯 𐑥𐑰. 𐑲 𐑑𐑧𐑤 𐑿, 𐑦𐑑 𐑦𐑟 𐑓𐑦𐑟𐑦𐑒𐑤𐑦 𐑦𐑥𐑐𐑪𐑕𐑦𐑚𐑩𐑤. 𐑤𐑦𐑕𐑩𐑯, 𐑒𐑨𐑐𐑑𐑩𐑯: 𐑛𐑦𐑛 𐑿 𐑧𐑝𐑼 𐑑𐑮𐑲 𐑑 𐑒𐑨𐑗 𐑩 𐑥𐑬𐑕 𐑦𐑯 𐑿𐑼 𐑣𐑨𐑯𐑛? 𐑢𐑳𐑯𐑕 𐑞𐑺 𐑢𐑪𐑟 𐑩 𐑛𐑽 𐑤𐑦𐑑𐑩𐑤 𐑥𐑬𐑕 𐑞𐑨𐑑 𐑿𐑕𐑑 𐑑 𐑒𐑳𐑥 𐑬𐑑 𐑯 𐑐𐑤𐑱 𐑪𐑯 𐑥𐑲 𐑑𐑱𐑚𐑩𐑤 𐑨𐑟 𐑲 𐑢𐑪𐑟 𐑮𐑰𐑛𐑦𐑙. 𐑲 𐑢𐑪𐑯𐑑𐑩𐑛 𐑑 𐑑𐑱𐑒 𐑣𐑦𐑥 𐑦𐑯 𐑥𐑲 𐑣𐑨𐑯𐑛 𐑯 𐑒𐑩𐑮𐑧𐑕 𐑣𐑦𐑥; 𐑯 𐑕𐑳𐑥𐑑𐑲𐑥𐑟 𐑣𐑰 𐑜𐑪𐑑 𐑩𐑥𐑳𐑙 𐑥𐑲 𐑚𐑫𐑒𐑕 𐑕𐑴 𐑞𐑨𐑑 𐑣𐑰 𐑒𐑫𐑛 𐑯𐑪𐑑 𐑦𐑕𐑒𐑱𐑐 𐑥𐑰 𐑢𐑧𐑯 𐑲 𐑕𐑑𐑮𐑧𐑗𐑑 𐑬𐑑 𐑥𐑲 𐑣𐑨𐑯𐑛. 𐑯 𐑲 𐑛𐑦𐑛 𐑕𐑑𐑮𐑧𐑗 𐑬𐑑 𐑥𐑲 𐑣𐑨𐑯𐑛; 𐑚𐑳𐑑 𐑦𐑑 𐑷𐑤𐑢𐑱𐑟 𐑒𐑱𐑥 𐑚𐑨𐑒 𐑦𐑯 𐑕𐑐𐑲𐑑 𐑝 𐑥𐑰. 𐑲 𐑢𐑪𐑟 𐑯𐑪𐑑 𐑩𐑓𐑮𐑱𐑛 𐑝 𐑣𐑦𐑥 𐑦𐑯 𐑥𐑲 𐑣𐑸𐑑; 𐑚𐑳𐑑 𐑥𐑲 𐑣𐑨𐑯𐑛 𐑮𐑦𐑓𐑿𐑟𐑛: 𐑦𐑑 𐑦𐑟 𐑯𐑪𐑑 𐑦𐑯 𐑞 𐑯𐑱𐑗𐑼 𐑝 𐑥𐑲 𐑣𐑨𐑯𐑛 𐑑 𐑑𐑳𐑗 𐑩 𐑥𐑬𐑕. 𐑢𐑧𐑤, 𐑒𐑨𐑐𐑑𐑩𐑯, 𐑦𐑓 𐑲 𐑑𐑫𐑒 𐑩 𐑐𐑦𐑯𐑗 𐑝 𐑦𐑯𐑕𐑧𐑯𐑕 𐑦𐑯 𐑥𐑲 𐑣𐑨𐑯𐑛 𐑯 𐑕𐑑𐑮𐑧𐑗𐑑 𐑦𐑑 𐑬𐑑 𐑴𐑝𐑼 𐑞

thing that when I meet really religious people we are friends at once, no matter what name we give to the divine will that made us and moves us. Oh, do you think that I, a woman, would quarrel with you for sacrificing to a woman god like Diana, if Diana meant to you what Christ means to me? No: we should kneel side by side before her altar like two children. But when men who believe neither in my god nor in their own – men who do not know the meaning of the word religion – when these men drag me to the foot of an iron statue that has become the symbol of the terror and darkness through which they walk, of their cruelty and greed, of their hatred of God and their oppression of man – when they ask me to pledge my soul before the people that this hideous idol is God, and that all this wickedness and falsehood is divine truth, I cannot do it, not if they could put a thousand cruel deaths on me. I tell you, it is physically impossible. Listen, Captain: did you ever try to catch a mouse in your hand? Once there was a dear little mouse that used to come out and play on my table as I was reading. I wanted to take him in my hand and caress him; and sometimes he got among my books so that he could not escape me when I stretched out my hand. And I did stretch out my hand; but it always came back in spite of me. I was not afraid of him in my heart; but my hand refused: it is not in the nature of my hand to touch a mouse. Well, Captain, if I took a pinch of incense in my hand and stretched it out over the

altar fire, my hand would come back. My body would be true to my faith even if you could corrupt my mind. And all the time I should believe more in Diana than my persecutors have ever believed in anything. Can you understand that?

THE CAPTAIN [*simply*] Yes; I understand that. But my hand would not come back. The hand that holds the sword has been trained not to come back from anything but victory.

LAVINIA. Not even from death?

THE CAPTAIN. Least of all from death.

LAVINIA. Then I must not come back from death either. A woman has to be braver than a soldier.

THE CAPTAIN. Prouder, you mean.

LAVINIA [*startled*] Prouder! You call our courage pride!

THE CAPTAIN. There is no such thing as courage: there is only pride. You Christians are the proudest devils on earth.

LAVINIA [*hurt*] Pray God then my pride may never become a false pride. [*She turns away as if she did not wish to continue the conversation, but softens and says to him with a smile*] Thank you for trying to save me.

THE CAPTAIN. I knew it was no use; but one tries in spite of one's knowledge.

LAVINIA. Something stirs, even in the iron breast of a Roman soldier?

THE CAPTAIN. I will soon be iron again. I have seen many women die, and forgotten them in a week.

LAVINIA. Remember me for a fortnight, handsome Captain. I shall be watching you, perhaps.

THE CAPTAIN. From the skies? Do not deceive yourself, Lavinia. There is no future for you beyond the grave.

LAVINIA. What does that matter? Do you think I am only running away from the terrors of life into the comfort of heaven? If there were no future, or if the future were one of torment, I should have to go just the same. The hand of God is upon me.

THE CAPTAIN. Yes: when all is said, we are both patricians, Lavinia, and must die for our beliefs. Farewell. [*He offers her his hand. She takes it and presses it. He walks away, trim and calm. She looks after him for a moment, and cries a little as he disappears through the eastern arch. A trumpet-call is heard from the road through the western arch*].

CENTURION [*waking up and rising*] Cohort of the tenth with prisoners. Two file out with me to receive them. [*He goes out through the western arch, followed by four soldiers in two files*].

Lentulus and Metellus come into the square from the west side with a little retinue of servants. Both are young courtiers, dressed in the extremity of fashion. Lentulus is slender, fair-haired, epicene. Metellus is manly, compactly built, olive skinned, not a talker.

LENTULUS. Christians, by Jove! Lets chaff them.

METELLUS. Awful brutes. If you knew as much

𐑮𐑦𐑕𐑑 𐑞𐑧𐑥 𐑥𐑰 𐑲 𐑛𐑵 𐑿 𐑥𐑳𐑕𐑑 𐑢𐑪𐑯𐑑 𐑑 𐑕𐑱𐑝 𐑞𐑧𐑥. 𐑤𐑰𐑝 𐑞𐑧𐑥 𐑑 𐑞 𐑤𐑲𐑩𐑯𐑟.

𐑤𐑧𐑯𐑑𐑿𐑤𐑩𐑕 [𐑩𐑐𐑮𐑴𐑗𐑦𐑙 ·𐑤𐑩𐑝𐑦𐑯𐑾, 𐑣𐑵 𐑦𐑟 𐑕𐑑𐑦𐑤 𐑤𐑫𐑒𐑦𐑙 𐑑𐑩𐑢𐑹𐑛𐑟 𐑞 𐑸𐑗𐑩𐑟 𐑭𐑓𐑑𐑼 𐑞 𐑒𐑨𐑐𐑑𐑦𐑯] 𐑞𐑨𐑑 𐑓𐑧𐑤𐑴'𐑟 𐑜𐑪𐑑 𐑩 𐑑𐑧𐑥𐑐𐑼. [𐑣𐑰 𐑤𐑫𐑒𐑕 𐑐𐑭𐑕𐑑 𐑣𐑼, 𐑕𐑑𐑺𐑦𐑙 𐑨𐑑 𐑣𐑼 𐑦𐑥𐑐𐑿𐑛𐑩𐑯𐑑𐑤𐑦; 𐑚𐑳𐑑 𐑖𐑰 𐑦𐑟 𐑳𐑯𐑒𐑩𐑯𐑕𐑻𐑯𐑛 𐑯 𐑦𐑟 𐑯𐑪𐑑 𐑒𐑪𐑯𐑖𐑩𐑕 𐑝 𐑣𐑦𐑥]. 𐑛𐑵 𐑿 𐑑𐑻𐑯 𐑞 𐑳𐑞𐑼 𐑗𐑰𐑒 𐑢𐑧𐑯 𐑞𐑱 𐑒𐑦𐑕 𐑿?

𐑤𐑩𐑝𐑦𐑯𐑾 [𐑕𐑑𐑸𐑑𐑩𐑤𐑛] 𐑢𐑪𐑑?

𐑤𐑧𐑯𐑑𐑿𐑤𐑩𐑕. 𐑛𐑵 𐑿 𐑑𐑻𐑯 𐑞 𐑳𐑞𐑼 𐑗𐑰𐑒 𐑢𐑧𐑯 𐑞𐑱 𐑒𐑦𐑕 𐑿, 𐑓𐑨𐑕𐑦𐑯𐑱𐑑𐑦𐑙 𐑒𐑮𐑦𐑕𐑗𐑩𐑯?

𐑤𐑩𐑝𐑦𐑯𐑾. 𐑛𐑴𐑯𐑑 𐑚𐑰 𐑓𐑵𐑤𐑦𐑖. [𐑑 ·𐑥𐑧𐑑𐑧𐑤𐑩𐑕, 𐑣𐑵 𐑣𐑨𐑟 𐑕𐑑𐑱𐑛 𐑪𐑯 𐑣𐑼 𐑮𐑲𐑑, 𐑕𐑴 𐑞𐑨𐑑 𐑖𐑰 𐑦𐑟 𐑚𐑦𐑑𐑢𐑰𐑯 𐑞𐑧𐑥] 𐑐𐑤𐑰𐑟 𐑛𐑴𐑯𐑑 𐑤𐑧𐑑 𐑿𐑼 𐑓𐑮𐑧𐑯𐑛 𐑚𐑦𐑣𐑱𐑝 𐑤𐑲𐑒 𐑩 𐑒𐑨𐑛 𐑚𐑦𐑓𐑹 𐑞 𐑕𐑴𐑤𐑡𐑼𐑟. 𐑣𐑬 𐑸 𐑞𐑱 𐑑 𐑮𐑦𐑕𐑐𐑧𐑒𐑑 𐑯 𐑴𐑚𐑱 𐑐𐑩𐑑𐑮𐑦𐑖𐑩𐑯𐑟 𐑦𐑓 𐑞𐑱 𐑕𐑰 𐑞𐑧𐑥 𐑚𐑦𐑣𐑱𐑝𐑦𐑙 𐑤𐑲𐑒 𐑕𐑑𐑮𐑰𐑑 𐑚𐑶𐑟? [𐑖𐑸𐑐𐑤𐑦 𐑑 ·𐑤𐑧𐑯𐑑𐑿𐑤𐑩𐑕] 𐑐𐑫𐑤 𐑿𐑼𐑕𐑧𐑤𐑓 𐑑𐑩𐑜𐑧𐑞𐑼, 𐑥𐑨𐑯. 𐑣𐑴𐑤𐑛 𐑿𐑼 𐑣𐑧𐑛 𐑳𐑐. 𐑒𐑰𐑐 𐑞 𐑒𐑹𐑯𐑼𐑟 𐑝 𐑿𐑼 𐑥𐑬𐑔 𐑓𐑻𐑥; 𐑯 𐑑𐑮𐑰𐑑 𐑥𐑰 𐑮𐑦𐑕𐑐𐑧𐑒𐑑𐑓𐑫𐑤𐑦. 𐑢𐑪𐑑 𐑛𐑵 𐑿 𐑑𐑱𐑒 𐑥𐑰 𐑓𐑹?

𐑤𐑧𐑯𐑑𐑿𐑤𐑩𐑕 [𐑦𐑮𐑧𐑟𐑩𐑤𐑵𐑑𐑤𐑦] 𐑤𐑫𐑒 𐑣𐑽, 𐑿 𐑯𐑴: 𐑲 — 𐑿 — 𐑲 —

𐑤𐑩𐑝𐑦𐑯𐑾. 𐑕𐑑𐑳𐑓! 𐑜𐑴 𐑩𐑚𐑬𐑑 𐑿𐑼 𐑚𐑦𐑟𐑯𐑩𐑕. [𐑖𐑰 𐑑𐑻𐑯𐑟 𐑛𐑦𐑕𐑲𐑕𐑦𐑝𐑤𐑦 𐑩𐑢𐑱 𐑯 𐑕𐑦𐑑𐑕 𐑛𐑬𐑯 𐑢𐑦𐑞 𐑣𐑼 𐑒𐑪𐑥𐑮𐑱𐑛𐑟, 𐑤𐑰𐑝𐑦𐑙 𐑣𐑦𐑥 𐑛𐑦𐑕𐑒𐑩𐑯𐑕𐑻𐑑𐑩𐑛].

𐑥𐑧𐑑𐑧𐑤𐑩𐑕. 𐑿 𐑛𐑦𐑛𐑯𐑑 𐑜𐑧𐑑 𐑥𐑳𐑗 𐑬𐑑 𐑝 𐑞𐑨𐑑. 𐑲 𐑑𐑴𐑤𐑛 𐑿 𐑞𐑱 𐑢𐑻 𐑚𐑮𐑵𐑑𐑕.

𐑤𐑧𐑯𐑑𐑿𐑤𐑩𐑕. 𐑐𐑤𐑳𐑒𐑦 𐑤𐑦𐑑𐑩𐑤 𐑓𐑦𐑤𐑦! 𐑲 𐑕𐑩𐑐𐑴𐑟 𐑖𐑰 𐑔𐑦𐑙𐑒𐑕 𐑲 𐑒𐑺. [𐑢𐑦𐑞 𐑩𐑯 𐑺 𐑝 𐑦𐑯𐑛𐑦𐑓𐑼𐑩𐑯𐑕 𐑣𐑰 𐑕𐑑𐑮𐑴𐑤𐑟 𐑢𐑦𐑞 ·𐑥𐑧𐑑𐑧𐑤𐑩𐑕 𐑑 𐑞 𐑰𐑕𐑑 𐑕𐑲𐑛 𐑝 𐑞 𐑕𐑒𐑢𐑺, 𐑢𐑺 𐑞𐑱 𐑕𐑑𐑨𐑯𐑛 𐑢𐑪𐑗𐑦𐑙 𐑞 𐑮𐑦𐑑𐑻𐑯 𐑝 𐑞 𐑕𐑧𐑯𐑑𐑿𐑼𐑾𐑯 𐑔𐑮𐑵 𐑞 𐑢𐑧𐑕𐑑𐑼𐑯 𐑸𐑗, 𐑧𐑕𐑒𐑹𐑑𐑦𐑙 𐑔𐑮𐑰

about them as I do you wouldnt want to chaff them. Leave them to the lions.

LENTULUS [*indicating Lavinia, who is still looking towards the arches after the Captain*] That woman's got a figure. [*He walks past her, staring at her invitingly; but she is preoccupied and is not conscious of him*]. Do you turn the other cheek when they kiss you?

LAVINIA [*starting*] What?

LENTULUS. Do you turn the other cheek when they kiss you, fascinating Christian?

LAVINIA. Dont be foolish. [*To Metellus, who has remained on her right, so that she is between them*] Please dont let your friend behave like a cad before the soldiers. How are they to respect and obey patricians if they see them behaving like street boys? [*Sharply to Lentulus*] Pull yourself together, man. Hold your head up. Keep the corners of your mouth firm; and treat me respectfully. What do you take me for?

LENTULUS [*irresolutely*] Look here, you know: I – you – I –

LAVINIA. Stuff! Go about your business. [*She turns decisively away and sits down with her comrades, leaving him disconcerted*].

METELLUS. You didnt get much out of that. I told you they were brutes.

LENTULUS. Plucky little filly! I suppose she thinks I care. [*With an air of indifference he strolls with Metellus to the east side of the square, where they stand watching the return of the Centurion through the western arch with his men, escorting three* [illegible]: ·𐑓𐑧𐑮𐑴𐑝𐑾𐑕, ·𐑨𐑯𐑛𐑮𐑩𐑒𐑤𐑰𐑟, 𐑯 ·𐑕𐑐𐑦𐑯𐑔𐑴. ·𐑓𐑧𐑮𐑴𐑝𐑾𐑕 𐑦𐑟 𐑩 𐑐𐑬𐑼𐑓𐑩𐑤, 𐑒𐑪𐑤𐑼𐑦𐑒 𐑥𐑨𐑯 𐑦𐑯 𐑞 𐑐𐑮𐑲𐑥 𐑝 𐑤𐑲𐑓, 𐑢𐑦𐑞 𐑤𐑸𐑡 𐑯𐑪𐑕𐑑𐑮𐑦𐑤𐑟, 𐑕𐑑𐑺𐑮𐑦𐑙 𐑲𐑟, 𐑯 𐑩 𐑔𐑦𐑒 𐑯𐑧𐑒: 𐑩 𐑥𐑨𐑯 𐑣𐑵𐑟 𐑕𐑧𐑯𐑕𐑦𐑚𐑦𐑤𐑦𐑑𐑦𐑟 𐑸 𐑒𐑰𐑯 𐑯 𐑝𐑲𐑩𐑤𐑩𐑯𐑑 𐑑 𐑞 𐑝𐑻𐑡 𐑝 𐑥𐑨𐑛𐑯𐑩𐑕. ·𐑕𐑐𐑦𐑯𐑔𐑴 𐑦𐑟 𐑩 𐑛𐑧𐑚𐑷𐑗𐑰, 𐑞 𐑮𐑧𐑒 𐑝 𐑩 𐑜𐑫𐑛-𐑤𐑫𐑒𐑦𐑙 𐑥𐑨𐑯 𐑜𐑪𐑯 𐑣𐑴𐑐𐑤𐑩𐑕𐑤𐑦 𐑑 𐑞 𐑚𐑨𐑛. ·𐑨𐑯𐑛𐑮𐑩𐑒𐑤𐑰𐑟 𐑦𐑟 𐑴𐑝𐑼𐑢𐑧𐑤𐑥𐑛 𐑢𐑦𐑞 𐑜𐑮𐑰𐑓, 𐑯 𐑦𐑟 𐑮𐑦𐑕𐑑𐑮𐑱𐑯𐑦𐑙 𐑣𐑦𐑟 𐑑𐑽𐑟 𐑢𐑦𐑞 𐑜𐑮𐑱𐑑 𐑛𐑦𐑓𐑦𐑒𐑩𐑤𐑑𐑦].

𐑕𐑧𐑯𐑑𐑿𐑼𐑾𐑯 [𐑑 ·𐑤𐑩𐑝𐑦𐑯𐑾] 𐑣𐑽 𐑸 𐑕𐑳𐑥 𐑐𐑨𐑤𐑟 𐑓𐑹 𐑿. 𐑞𐑦𐑕 𐑤𐑦𐑑𐑩𐑤 𐑚𐑦𐑑 𐑦𐑟 ·𐑓𐑧𐑮𐑴𐑝𐑾𐑕 𐑞𐑨𐑑 𐑿 𐑑𐑷𐑒 𐑕𐑴 𐑥𐑳𐑗 𐑩𐑚𐑬𐑑. [·𐑓𐑧𐑮𐑴𐑝𐑾𐑕 𐑑𐑻𐑯𐑟 𐑪𐑯 𐑣𐑦𐑥 𐑔𐑮𐑧𐑑𐑩𐑯𐑦𐑙𐑤𐑦. 𐑞 𐑕𐑧𐑯𐑑𐑿𐑼𐑾𐑯 𐑣𐑴𐑤𐑛𐑟 𐑳𐑐 𐑣𐑦𐑟 𐑤𐑧𐑓𐑑 𐑓𐑹𐑓𐑦𐑙𐑜𐑼 𐑦𐑯 𐑩𐑛𐑥𐑩𐑯𐑦𐑖𐑩𐑯]. 𐑯𐑬 𐑮𐑦𐑥𐑧𐑥𐑚𐑼 𐑞𐑨𐑑 𐑿𐑼 𐑩 𐑒𐑮𐑦𐑕𐑗𐑩𐑯, 𐑯 𐑞𐑨𐑑 𐑿𐑝 𐑜𐑪𐑑 𐑑 𐑮𐑦𐑑𐑻𐑯 𐑜𐑫𐑛 𐑓 𐑰𐑝𐑩𐑤. [·𐑓𐑧𐑮𐑴𐑝𐑾𐑕 𐑒𐑩𐑯𐑑𐑮𐑴𐑤𐑟 𐑣𐑦𐑥𐑕𐑧𐑤𐑓 𐑒𐑩𐑯𐑝𐑳𐑤𐑕𐑦𐑝𐑤𐑦; 𐑥𐑵𐑝𐑟 𐑩𐑢𐑱 𐑓𐑮𐑪𐑥 𐑑𐑧𐑥𐑑𐑱𐑖𐑩𐑯 𐑑 𐑞 𐑰𐑕𐑑 𐑕𐑲𐑛 𐑯𐑽 ·𐑤𐑧𐑯𐑑𐑿𐑤𐑩𐑕; 𐑒𐑤𐑭𐑕𐑐𐑕 𐑣𐑦𐑟 𐑣𐑨𐑯𐑛𐑟 𐑦𐑯 𐑕𐑲𐑤𐑩𐑯𐑑 𐑐𐑮𐑺; 𐑯 𐑔𐑮𐑴𐑟 𐑣𐑦𐑥𐑕𐑧𐑤𐑓 𐑪𐑯 𐑣𐑦𐑟 𐑯𐑰𐑟]. 𐑞𐑨𐑑𐑕 𐑞 𐑢𐑱 𐑑 𐑥𐑨𐑯𐑦𐑡 𐑞𐑧𐑥, 𐑱! 𐑞𐑦𐑕 𐑓𐑲𐑯 𐑓𐑧𐑤𐑴 [𐑦𐑯𐑛𐑦𐑒𐑱𐑑𐑦𐑙 ·𐑨𐑯𐑛𐑮𐑩𐑒𐑤𐑰𐑟, 𐑣𐑵 𐑒𐑳𐑥𐑟 𐑑 𐑣𐑦𐑟 𐑤𐑧𐑓𐑑, 𐑯 𐑥𐑱𐑒𐑕 ·𐑤𐑩𐑝𐑦𐑯𐑾 𐑩 𐑣𐑸𐑑-𐑚𐑮𐑴𐑒𐑩𐑯 𐑕𐑨𐑤𐑿𐑑𐑱𐑖𐑩𐑯] 𐑦𐑟 𐑩 𐑕𐑹𐑕𐑼𐑼. 𐑩 𐑜𐑮𐑰𐑒 𐑑𐑱𐑤𐑼, 𐑣𐑰 𐑦𐑟. 𐑩 𐑮𐑾𐑤 𐑕𐑹𐑕𐑼𐑼, 𐑑𐑵: 𐑯𐑴 𐑥𐑦𐑕𐑑𐑱𐑒 𐑩𐑚𐑬𐑑 𐑦𐑑. 𐑞 𐑑𐑧𐑯𐑔 [illegible] [illegible] 𐑩 𐑤𐑧𐑐𐑼𐑛 𐑨𐑑 𐑞 𐑣𐑧𐑛 𐑝 𐑞 𐑒𐑪𐑤𐑩𐑥. 𐑣𐑰 𐑥𐑱𐑛 𐑩 𐑐𐑧𐑑 𐑝 𐑞 𐑤𐑧𐑐𐑼𐑛; 𐑯 𐑯𐑬 𐑣𐑰𐑟 𐑒𐑮𐑲𐑦𐑙 𐑨𐑑 𐑚𐑰𐑦𐑙 𐑐𐑸𐑑𐑩𐑛 𐑓𐑮𐑪𐑥 𐑦𐑑. [·𐑨𐑯𐑛𐑮𐑩𐑒𐑤𐑰𐑟 [illegible] [illegible]]. [illegible] 𐑿, [illegible]? [illegible], [illegible], [illegible] [illegible] 𐑢𐑦𐑞 𐑩 [illegible] [illegible] [·𐑨𐑯𐑛𐑮𐑩𐑒𐑤𐑰𐑟 [illegible] [illegible]] 𐑞𐑨𐑑𐑕 [illegible] [illegible] [illegible] 𐑯 [illegible] 𐑩 [illegible]. 𐑣𐑰 [illegible] [illegible] [illegible] [illegible] 𐑩 [illegible] [illegible] 𐑣𐑰 [illegible]. [·𐑨𐑯𐑛𐑮𐑩𐑒𐑤𐑰𐑟, [illegible] [illegible], [illegible] [illegible] 𐑞 𐑕𐑧𐑯𐑑𐑿𐑼𐑾𐑯 𐑑 ·𐑤𐑩𐑝𐑦𐑯𐑾,

prisoners: Ferrovius, Androcles, and Spintho. Ferrovius is a powerful, choleric man in the prime of life, with large nostrils, staring eyes, and a thick neck: a man whose sensibilities are keen and violent to the verge of madness. Spintho is a debauchee, the wreck of a good-looking man gone hopelessly to the bad. Androcles is overwhelmed with grief, and is restraining his tears with great difficulty].

CENTURION [*to Lavinia*] Here are some pals for you. This little bit is Ferrovius that you talk so much about. [*Ferrovius turns on him threateningly. The Centurion holds up his left forefinger in admonition*]. Now remember that youre a Christian, and that youve got to return good for evil. [*Ferrovius controls himself convulsively; moves away from temptation to the east side near Lentulus; clasps his hands in silent prayer; and throws himself on his knees*]. Thats the way to manage them, eh! This fine fellow [*indicating Androcles, who comes to his left, and makes Lavinia a heart-broken salutation*] is a sorcerer. A Greek tailor, he is. A real sorcerer, too: no mistake about it. The tenth marches with a leopard at the head of the column. He made a pet of the leopard; and now he's crying at being parted from it. [*Androcles sniffs lamentably*]. Aint you, old chap? Well, cheer up, we march with a Billy goat [*Androcles brightens up*] thats killed two leopards and ate a turkey-cock. You can have him for a pet if you like. [*Androcles, quite consoled, goes past the Centurion to Lavinia,*

𐑯 𐑕𐑦𐑑𐑕 𐑛𐑬𐑯 𐑒𐑩𐑯𐑑𐑧𐑯𐑑𐑦𐑛𐑤𐑦 𐑪𐑯 𐑞 𐑜𐑮𐑬𐑯𐑛 𐑪𐑯 𐑣𐑦𐑟 𐑤𐑧𐑓𐑑]. 𐑞𐑦𐑕 𐑛𐑻𐑑𐑦 𐑛𐑪𐑜 [𐑒𐑪𐑤𐑼𐑦𐑙 ·𐑕𐑐𐑦𐑯𐑔𐑴] 𐑦𐑟 𐑩 𐑮𐑾𐑤 𐑒𐑮𐑦𐑕𐑗𐑩𐑯. 𐑣𐑰 𐑥𐑪𐑚𐑟 𐑞 𐑑𐑧𐑥𐑐𐑩𐑤𐑟, 𐑣𐑰 𐑛𐑳𐑟 [𐑨𐑑 𐑰𐑗 𐑮𐑧𐑐𐑩𐑑𐑦𐑖𐑩𐑯 𐑣𐑰 𐑜𐑦𐑝𐑟 𐑞 𐑯𐑧𐑒 𐑝 ·𐑕𐑐𐑦𐑯𐑔𐑴𐑟 𐑑𐑿𐑯𐑦𐑒 𐑩 𐑑𐑢𐑦𐑕𐑑]; 𐑣𐑰 𐑜𐑴𐑟 𐑕𐑥𐑨𐑖𐑦𐑙 𐑔𐑦𐑙𐑟 𐑥𐑨𐑛 𐑛𐑮𐑳𐑙𐑒, 𐑣𐑰 𐑛𐑳𐑟; 𐑣𐑰 𐑕𐑑𐑰𐑤𐑟 𐑞 𐑜𐑴𐑤𐑛 𐑝𐑧𐑕𐑩𐑤𐑟, 𐑣𐑰 𐑛𐑳𐑟; 𐑣𐑰 𐑩𐑕𐑷𐑤𐑑𐑕 𐑞 𐑐𐑮𐑰𐑕𐑑𐑩𐑕𐑩𐑟, 𐑣𐑰 𐑛𐑳𐑟 — 𐑐𐑭! [𐑣𐑰 𐑓𐑤𐑦𐑙𐑟 ·𐑕𐑐𐑦𐑯𐑔𐑴 𐑦𐑯𐑑𐑵 𐑞 𐑥𐑦𐑛𐑩𐑤 𐑝 𐑞 𐑤𐑲𐑯 𐑝 𐑐𐑮𐑦𐑟𐑩𐑯𐑼𐑟]. 𐑿𐑼 𐑞 𐑕𐑹𐑑 𐑞𐑨𐑑 𐑥𐑱𐑒𐑕 𐑛𐑿𐑑𐑦 𐑩 𐑐𐑤𐑧𐑠𐑼, 𐑿 𐑸.

𐑕𐑐𐑦𐑯𐑔𐑴 [𐑜𐑨𐑕𐑐𐑦𐑙] 𐑞𐑨𐑑𐑕 𐑦𐑑: 𐑕𐑑𐑮𐑨𐑙𐑜𐑩𐑤 𐑥𐑰. 𐑒𐑦𐑒 𐑥𐑰. 𐑚𐑰𐑑 𐑥𐑰. 𐑮𐑦𐑝𐑲𐑤 𐑥𐑰. 𐑬𐑼 ·𐑤𐑹𐑛 𐑢𐑪𐑟 𐑚𐑰𐑑𐑩𐑯 𐑯 𐑮𐑦𐑝𐑲𐑤𐑛. 𐑞𐑨𐑑𐑕 𐑥𐑲 𐑢𐑱 𐑑 𐑣𐑧𐑝𐑩𐑯. 𐑧𐑝𐑮𐑦 𐑥𐑸𐑑𐑼 𐑜𐑴𐑟 𐑑 𐑣𐑧𐑝𐑩𐑯, 𐑯𐑴 𐑥𐑨𐑑𐑼 𐑢𐑪𐑑 𐑣𐑰𐑟 𐑛𐑳𐑯. 𐑞𐑨𐑑 𐑦𐑟 𐑕𐑴, 𐑦𐑟𐑩𐑯𐑑 𐑦𐑑, 𐑚𐑮𐑳𐑞𐑼?

𐑕𐑧𐑯𐑑𐑘𐑫𐑼𐑾𐑯. 𐑘𐑧𐑕, 𐑦𐑓 𐑿𐑼 𐑜𐑴𐑦𐑙 𐑑 𐑣𐑧𐑝𐑩𐑯, 𐑲 𐑛𐑴𐑯𐑑 𐑢𐑪𐑯𐑑 𐑑 𐑜𐑴 𐑞𐑺. 𐑲 𐑢𐑫𐑛𐑩𐑯𐑑 𐑚𐑰 𐑕𐑰𐑯 𐑢𐑦𐑞 𐑿.

𐑤𐑧𐑯𐑑𐑿𐑤𐑩𐑕. 𐑣𐑷! 𐑜𐑫𐑛! [𐑯𐑴𐑑𐑦𐑕𐑦𐑙 𐑞 𐑯𐑰𐑤𐑦𐑙 ·𐑓𐑧𐑮𐑴𐑝𐑾𐑕]. 𐑦𐑟 𐑞𐑦𐑕 𐑢𐑳𐑯 𐑝 𐑞 𐑑𐑻𐑯-𐑞-𐑳𐑞𐑼-𐑗𐑰𐑒 𐑡𐑧𐑯𐑑𐑩𐑤𐑥𐑧𐑯, 𐑕𐑧𐑯𐑑𐑘𐑫𐑼𐑾𐑯?

𐑕𐑧𐑯𐑑𐑘𐑫𐑼𐑾𐑯. 𐑘𐑧𐑕, 𐑕𐑻. 𐑤𐑳𐑒𐑦 𐑓 𐑿 𐑑𐑵, 𐑕𐑻, 𐑦𐑓 𐑿 𐑢𐑪𐑯𐑑 𐑑 𐑑𐑱𐑒 𐑧𐑯𐑦 𐑤𐑦𐑚𐑼𐑑𐑦𐑟 𐑢𐑦𐑞 𐑣𐑦𐑥.

𐑤𐑧𐑯𐑑𐑿𐑤𐑩𐑕 [𐑑 ·𐑓𐑧𐑮𐑴𐑝𐑾𐑕] 𐑿 𐑑𐑻𐑯 𐑞 𐑳𐑞𐑼 𐑗𐑰𐑒 𐑢𐑧𐑯 𐑿𐑼 𐑕𐑑𐑮𐑳𐑒, 𐑲𐑥 𐑑𐑴𐑤𐑛.

𐑓𐑧𐑮𐑴𐑝𐑾𐑕 [𐑕𐑤𐑴𐑤𐑦 𐑑𐑻𐑯𐑦𐑙 𐑣𐑦𐑟 𐑜𐑮𐑱𐑑 𐑲𐑟 𐑪𐑯 𐑣𐑦𐑥] 𐑘𐑧𐑕, 𐑚𐑲 𐑞 𐑜𐑮𐑱𐑕 𐑝 ·𐑜𐑪𐑛, 𐑲 𐑛𐑵, 𐑯𐑬.

𐑤𐑧𐑯𐑑𐑿𐑤𐑩𐑕. 𐑯𐑪𐑑 𐑞𐑨𐑑 𐑿𐑼 𐑩 𐑒𐑬𐑼𐑛, 𐑝 𐑒𐑹𐑕; 𐑚𐑳𐑑 𐑬𐑑 𐑝 𐑐𐑿𐑼 𐑐𐑲𐑩𐑑𐑦.

𐑓𐑧𐑮𐑴𐑝𐑾𐑕. 𐑲 𐑓𐑽 ·𐑜𐑪𐑛 𐑥𐑹 𐑞𐑨𐑯 𐑥𐑨𐑯; 𐑨𐑑 𐑤𐑰𐑕𐑑 𐑲 𐑑𐑮𐑲 𐑑.

𐑤𐑧𐑯𐑑𐑿𐑤𐑩𐑕. 𐑤𐑧𐑑𐑕 𐑕𐑰. [𐑣𐑰 𐑕𐑑𐑮𐑲𐑒𐑕 𐑣𐑦𐑥 𐑪𐑯 𐑞 𐑗𐑰𐑒. ·𐑨𐑯𐑛𐑮𐑩𐑒𐑤𐑰𐑟 𐑥𐑱𐑒𐑕 𐑩 𐑢𐑲𐑤𐑛 𐑥𐑵𐑝𐑥𐑩𐑯𐑑 𐑑 𐑮𐑲𐑟 𐑯

and sits down contentedly on the ground on her left]. This dirty dog [*collaring Spintho*] is a real Christian. He mobs the temples, he does [*at each accusation he gives the neck of Spintho's tunic a twist*]; he goes smashing things mad drunk, he does; he steals the gold vessels, he does; he assaults the priestesses, he does – yah! [*He flings Spintho into the middle of the group of prisoners*]. Youre the sort that makes duty a pleasure, you are.

SPINTHO [*gasping*] Thats it: strangle me. Kick me. Beat me. Revile me. Our Lord was beaten and reviled. Thats my way to heaven. Every martyr goes to heaven, no matter what he's done. That is so, isnt it, brother?

CENTURION. Well, if youre going to heaven, *I* dont want to go there. I wouldnt be seen with you.

LENTULUS. Haw! Good! [*Indicating the kneeling Ferrovius*]. Is this one of the turn-the-other-cheek gentlemen, Centurion?

CENTURION. Yes, sir. Lucky for you too, sir, if you want to take any liberties with him.

LENTULUS [*to Ferrovius*] You turn the other cheek when youre struck, I'm told.

FERROVIUS [*slowly turning his great eyes on him*] Yes, by the grace of God, I do, now.

LENTULUS. Not that youre a coward, of course; but out of pure piety.

FERROVIUS. I fear God more than man; at least I try to.

LENTULUS. Lets see. [*He strikes him on the cheek. Androcles makes a wild movement to rise and*

𐑦𐑯𐑑𐑼𐑓𐑽; 𐑚𐑳𐑑 ·𐑤𐑩𐑝𐑦𐑯𐑾 𐑣𐑴𐑤𐑛𐑟 𐑣𐑦𐑥 𐑛𐑬𐑯, 𐑢𐑪𐑗𐑦𐑙 ·𐑓𐑧𐑮𐑴𐑝𐑾𐑕 𐑦𐑯𐑑𐑧𐑯𐑑𐑤𐑦. ·𐑓𐑧𐑮𐑴𐑝𐑾𐑕, 𐑢𐑦𐑞𐑬𐑑 𐑓𐑤𐑦𐑯𐑗𐑦𐑙, 𐑑𐑻𐑯𐑟 𐑞 𐑳𐑞𐑼 𐑗𐑰𐑒. ·𐑤𐑧𐑯𐑑𐑿𐑤𐑩𐑕, 𐑮𐑭𐑞𐑼 𐑬𐑑 𐑝 𐑒𐑬𐑯𐑑𐑩𐑯𐑩𐑯𐑕, 𐑤𐑭𐑓𐑕 𐑓𐑵𐑤𐑦𐑖𐑤𐑦, 𐑯 𐑕𐑑𐑮𐑲𐑒𐑕 𐑣𐑦𐑥 𐑩𐑜𐑧𐑯 𐑓𐑰𐑚𐑤𐑦]. 𐑿 𐑯𐑴, 𐑲 𐑖𐑫𐑛 𐑓𐑰𐑤 𐑩𐑖𐑱𐑥𐑛 𐑦𐑓 𐑲 𐑤𐑧𐑑 𐑥𐑲𐑕𐑧𐑤𐑓 𐑚𐑰 𐑕𐑑𐑮𐑳𐑒 𐑤𐑲𐑒 𐑞𐑨𐑑, 𐑯 𐑑𐑫𐑒 𐑦𐑑 𐑤𐑲𐑦𐑙 𐑛𐑬𐑯. 𐑚𐑳𐑑 𐑞𐑧𐑯 𐑲'𐑥 𐑯𐑪𐑑 𐑩 𐑒𐑮𐑦𐑕𐑗𐑩𐑯: 𐑲'𐑥 𐑩 𐑥𐑨𐑯. [·𐑓𐑧𐑮𐑴𐑝𐑾𐑕 𐑮𐑲𐑟𐑩𐑟 𐑦𐑥𐑐𐑮𐑧𐑕𐑦𐑝𐑤𐑦 𐑯 𐑑𐑬𐑼𐑟 𐑴𐑝𐑼 𐑣𐑦𐑥. ·𐑤𐑧𐑯𐑑𐑿𐑤𐑩𐑕 𐑚𐑦𐑒𐑳𐑥𐑟 𐑢𐑲𐑑 𐑢𐑦𐑞 𐑑𐑧𐑮𐑼; 𐑯 𐑩 𐑖𐑱𐑛 𐑝 𐑜𐑮𐑰𐑯 𐑓𐑤𐑦𐑒𐑼𐑟 𐑦𐑯 𐑣𐑦𐑟 𐑗𐑰𐑒 𐑓𐑹 𐑩 𐑥𐑴𐑥𐑩𐑯𐑑].

·𐑓𐑧𐑮𐑴𐑝𐑾𐑕 [𐑢𐑦𐑞 𐑞 𐑒𐑭𐑥 𐑝 𐑩 𐑜𐑮𐑨𐑯𐑦𐑑 𐑐𐑦𐑤𐑼] 𐑲 𐑣𐑨𐑝 𐑯𐑪𐑑 𐑷𐑤𐑢𐑱𐑟 𐑚𐑰𐑯 𐑓𐑱𐑔𐑓𐑫𐑤. 𐑞 𐑓𐑻𐑕𐑑 𐑥𐑨𐑯 𐑣𐑵 𐑕𐑑𐑮𐑳𐑒 𐑥𐑰 𐑨𐑟 𐑿 𐑣𐑨𐑝 𐑡𐑳𐑕𐑑 𐑕𐑑𐑮𐑳𐑒 𐑥𐑰 𐑢𐑪𐑟 𐑩 𐑕𐑑𐑮𐑪𐑙𐑜𐑼 𐑥𐑨𐑯 𐑞𐑨𐑯 𐑿; 𐑣𐑰 𐑣𐑦𐑑 𐑥𐑰 𐑣𐑸𐑛𐑼 𐑞𐑨𐑯 𐑲 𐑦𐑒𐑕𐑐𐑧𐑒𐑑𐑩𐑛. 𐑲 𐑢𐑪𐑟 𐑑𐑧𐑥𐑐𐑑𐑩𐑛 𐑯 𐑓𐑧𐑤; 𐑯 𐑦𐑑 𐑢𐑪𐑟 𐑞𐑧𐑯 𐑞𐑨𐑑 𐑲 𐑓𐑻𐑕𐑑 𐑑𐑱𐑕𐑑𐑩𐑛 𐑚𐑦𐑑𐑼 𐑖𐑱𐑥. 𐑲 𐑯𐑧𐑝𐑼 𐑣𐑨𐑛 𐑩 𐑣𐑨𐑐𐑦 𐑥𐑴𐑥𐑩𐑯𐑑 𐑭𐑓𐑑𐑼 𐑞𐑨𐑑 𐑳𐑯𐑑𐑦𐑤 𐑲 𐑣𐑨𐑛 𐑯𐑧𐑤𐑑 𐑯 𐑭𐑕𐑒𐑑 𐑣𐑦𐑟 𐑐𐑸𐑛𐑩𐑯 𐑚𐑲 𐑣𐑦𐑟 𐑚𐑧𐑛𐑕𐑲𐑛 𐑦𐑯 𐑞 𐑣𐑪𐑕𐑐𐑦𐑑𐑩𐑤. [𐑐𐑫𐑑𐑦𐑙 𐑣𐑦𐑟 𐑣𐑨𐑯𐑛𐑟 𐑪𐑯 ·𐑤𐑧𐑯𐑑𐑿𐑤𐑩𐑕'𐑩𐑟 𐑖𐑴𐑤𐑛𐑼𐑟 𐑢𐑦𐑞 𐑐𐑩𐑑𐑻𐑯𐑩𐑤 𐑢𐑱𐑑]. 𐑚𐑳𐑑 𐑯𐑬 𐑲 𐑣𐑨𐑝 𐑤𐑻𐑯𐑑 𐑑 𐑮𐑦𐑟𐑦𐑕𐑑 𐑢𐑦𐑞 𐑩 𐑕𐑑𐑮𐑧𐑙𐑔 𐑞𐑨𐑑 𐑦𐑟 𐑯𐑪𐑑 𐑥𐑲 𐑴𐑯. 𐑲 𐑨𐑥 𐑯𐑪𐑑 𐑩𐑖𐑱𐑥𐑛 𐑯𐑬, 𐑯𐑹 𐑨𐑙𐑜𐑮𐑦.

·𐑤𐑧𐑯𐑑𐑿𐑤𐑩𐑕 [𐑳𐑯𐑰𐑟𐑦𐑤𐑦] 𐑻—𐑜𐑫𐑛 𐑰𐑝𐑯𐑦𐑙. [𐑣𐑰 𐑑𐑮𐑲𐑟 𐑑 𐑥𐑵𐑝 𐑩𐑢𐑱].

·𐑓𐑧𐑮𐑴𐑝𐑾𐑕 [𐑜𐑮𐑦𐑐𐑦𐑙 𐑣𐑦𐑟 𐑖𐑴𐑤𐑛𐑼𐑟] 𐑴, 𐑛𐑵 𐑯𐑪𐑑 𐑣𐑸𐑛𐑩𐑯 𐑿𐑼 𐑣𐑸𐑑, 𐑘𐑳𐑙 𐑥𐑨𐑯. 𐑒𐑳𐑥: 𐑑𐑮𐑲 𐑓𐑹 𐑿𐑼𐑕𐑧𐑤𐑓 𐑢𐑧𐑞𐑼 𐑬𐑼 𐑢𐑱 𐑦𐑟 𐑯𐑪𐑑 𐑚𐑧𐑑𐑼 𐑞𐑨𐑯 𐑿𐑼𐑟. 𐑲 𐑢𐑦𐑤 𐑯𐑬 𐑕𐑑𐑮𐑲𐑒 𐑿 𐑪𐑯 𐑢𐑳𐑯 𐑗𐑰𐑒; 𐑯 𐑿 𐑢𐑦𐑤 𐑑𐑻𐑯 𐑞 𐑳𐑞𐑼 𐑯 𐑤𐑻𐑯 𐑣𐑬 𐑥𐑳𐑗 𐑚𐑧𐑑𐑼 𐑿 𐑢𐑦𐑤 𐑓𐑰𐑤 𐑞𐑨𐑯 𐑦𐑓 𐑿 𐑜𐑱𐑝 𐑢𐑱 𐑑 𐑞

interfere; but Lavinia holds him down, watching Ferrovius intently. Ferrovius, without flinching, turns the other cheek. Lentulus, rather out of countenance, titters foolishly, and strikes him again feebly]. You know, I should feel ashamed if I let myself be struck like that, and took it lying down. But then I'm not a Christian: I'm a man. [*Ferrovius rises impressively and towers over him. Lentulus becomes white with terror; and a shade of green flickers in his cheek for a moment*].

FERROVIUS [*with the calm of a steam hammer*] I have not always been faithful. The first man who struck me as you have just struck me was a stronger man than you: he hit me harder than I expected. I was tempted and fell; and it was then that I first tasted bitter shame. I never had a happy moment after that until I had knelt and asked his forgiveness by his bedside in the hospital. [*Putting his hands on Lentulus's shoulders with paternal weight*]. But now I have learnt to resist with a strength that is not my own. I am not ashamed now, nor angry.

LENTULUS [*uneasily*] Er – good evening. [*He tries to move away*].

FERROVIUS [*gripping his shoulders*] Oh, do not harden your heart, young man. Come: try for yourself whether our way is not better than yours. I will now strike you on one cheek; and you will turn the other and learn how much better you will feel than if you gave way to the

𐑚𐑮𐑵𐑑𐑩𐑤𐑦𐑟 𐑦𐑯 𐑞𐑧𐑥. [𐑣𐑰 𐑣𐑴𐑤𐑛𐑟 𐑣𐑦𐑟 𐑮𐑦𐑥 𐑮𐑲𐑑 𐑣𐑨𐑯𐑛 𐑯 𐑒𐑤𐑧𐑯𐑗𐑩𐑟 𐑞 𐑳𐑞𐑼 𐑓𐑦𐑕𐑑].

𐑤𐑧𐑯𐑑𐑿𐑤𐑩𐑕. 𐑕𐑧𐑯𐑑𐑿𐑼𐑾𐑯: 𐑲 𐑖𐑨𐑤 𐑭𐑕𐑒 𐑿 𐑑 𐑐𐑮𐑩𐑑𐑧𐑒𐑑 𐑥𐑰.

𐑕𐑧𐑯𐑑𐑿𐑼𐑾𐑯. 𐑿 𐑭𐑕𐑒𐑑 𐑓𐑹 𐑦𐑑, 𐑕𐑻. 𐑦𐑑𐑕 𐑯𐑴 𐑚𐑦𐑟𐑯𐑩𐑕 𐑝 𐑬𐑼𐑟. 𐑿𐑝 𐑣𐑨𐑛 𐑞 𐑓𐑻𐑕𐑑 𐑚𐑤𐑴 𐑨𐑑 𐑣𐑦𐑥. 𐑢𐑧𐑯 𐑣𐑰 𐑣𐑦𐑟 𐑩 𐑚𐑨𐑛𐑤𐑦 𐑯 𐑕𐑥𐑲𐑤𐑟 𐑦𐑑 𐑞𐑨𐑑 𐑢𐑱.

𐑤𐑧𐑯𐑑𐑿𐑤𐑩𐑕. 𐑢𐑧𐑤, 𐑦𐑯 𐑒𐑱𐑕. [𐑑 ·𐑓𐑧𐑮𐑴𐑝𐑾𐑕] 𐑦𐑑 𐑮𐑦𐑟 𐑴𐑝𐑼 𐑩 𐑦𐑑 𐑦𐑯 𐑛𐑲𐑯, 𐑲 𐑩𐑤𐑬𐑯 𐑿: 𐑲 𐑥𐑧𐑯𐑑 𐑯𐑴 𐑣𐑸𐑥. 𐑣𐑩𐑥. [𐑣𐑰 𐑚𐑩𐑜𐑦𐑯𐑟 𐑣𐑦𐑟 𐑩 𐑐𐑴𐑤 𐑒𐑲𐑩].

𐑓𐑧𐑮𐑴𐑝𐑾𐑕 [𐑑𐑧𐑮𐑦𐑚𐑩𐑤 𐑦𐑑 𐑯 𐑛𐑱𐑥𐑦𐑚𐑩𐑤 𐑦𐑑 𐑑 𐑞 𐑴𐑤𐑛 𐑦𐑯𐑐𐑩𐑯, 𐑣𐑨𐑟 𐑕𐑳𐑛𐑩𐑯𐑤𐑦 𐑦𐑑 𐑑𐑲 𐑰𐑐𐑾𐑤, 𐑯 𐑣𐑨𐑮𐑦𐑟𐑛 𐑛𐑴 𐑑 𐑕𐑑𐑮𐑦𐑒 𐑦𐑑] 𐑐𐑦𐑟 𐑟𐑧 𐑞𐑧 𐑣𐑨𐑕𐑑 𐑑 𐑞 𐑚𐑦𐑩𐑯. 𐑒𐑲𐑩,

𐑚𐑳𐑒𐑩: 𐑒𐑲𐑩𐑛! 𐑲 𐑟𐑧 𐑣𐑭𐑑 𐑿𐑩 𐑦𐑯𐑦 𐑛𐑵 𐑩 𐑥𐑪𐑮𐑩𐑑; 𐑦𐑑 𐑿𐑩 𐑚𐑪𐑒 𐑮𐑦𐑒 𐑛𐑦𐑟𐑑 𐑦𐑯 𐑞 𐑦𐑯𐑒𐑩𐑯 𐑦𐑯 𐑞 𐑕𐑑𐑮𐑦𐑑 𐑴𐑝𐑩 𐑞 𐑛𐑧𐑒. [𐑣𐑰 𐑚𐑳𐑟𐑤𐑟 𐑑 𐑕𐑑𐑮𐑲𐑒].

𐑨𐑯𐑛𐑮𐑩𐑒𐑤𐑰𐑟. 𐑘𐑧𐑕, ·𐑓𐑧𐑮𐑴𐑝𐑾𐑕, 𐑘𐑧𐑕: 𐑿 𐑚𐑴𐑒 𐑞 𐑒𐑻𐑕𐑑 𐑥𐑨𐑯𐑟 𐑕𐑴𐑤.

[·𐑤𐑧𐑯𐑑𐑿𐑤𐑩𐑕, 𐑮𐑦𐑞 𐑩 𐑥𐑪𐑮 𐑦𐑯 𐑑𐑧𐑮𐑼, 𐑩𐑕𐑑𐑩𐑑𐑕 𐑑 𐑛𐑧𐑒; 𐑦𐑑 ·𐑓𐑧𐑮𐑴𐑝𐑾𐑕 𐑣𐑴𐑤𐑛𐑟 𐑣𐑦𐑥 𐑦𐑯𐑧𐑒𐑕𐑼𐑕𐑦𐑚𐑤𐑦].

𐑓𐑧𐑮𐑴𐑝𐑾𐑕. 𐑢𐑧𐑤; 𐑦𐑑 𐑲 𐑕𐑑𐑦𐑤 𐑣𐑨𐑟 𐑕𐑴𐑤. 𐑮𐑦𐑑 𐑥𐑧𐑯𐑟 𐑩 𐑚𐑴𐑛𐑦 𐑛𐑧𐑟?

𐑤𐑧𐑯𐑑𐑿𐑤𐑩𐑕. 𐑚𐑴𐑑 𐑑𐑳𐑗 𐑥𐑰, 𐑦𐑯 𐑿 𐑣𐑦𐑩? 𐑞 𐑤𐑷 —

𐑓𐑧𐑮𐑴𐑝𐑾𐑕. 𐑞 𐑤𐑷 𐑮𐑦𐑒 𐑛𐑴𐑛 𐑥𐑰 𐑑 𐑞 𐑤𐑲𐑩𐑯𐑟 𐑑𐑳𐑥𐑪𐑮𐑴; 𐑮𐑦𐑑 𐑮𐑴𐑕 𐑒𐑧𐑮 𐑦𐑑 𐑦𐑯 𐑮𐑵 𐑲 𐑑 𐑕𐑧𐑑 𐑿? 𐑚𐑧𐑑 𐑛𐑵 𐑕𐑚𐑦𐑤𐑛; 𐑯 𐑦𐑑 𐑢𐑧𐑤 𐑦𐑯 𐑐𐑦𐑮𐑩𐑯 𐑑 𐑿.

𐑤𐑧𐑯𐑑𐑿𐑤𐑩𐑕. 𐑤𐑧𐑑 𐑥𐑰 𐑜𐑴. 𐑿𐑩 𐑛𐑦𐑯𐑒𐑩𐑯 𐑛𐑴𐑦𐑙𐑟 𐑿 𐑑 𐑕𐑚𐑲𐑛 𐑥𐑰.

𐑓𐑧𐑮𐑴𐑝𐑾𐑕. 𐑦𐑯 𐑞 𐑒𐑮𐑦𐑕𐑗𐑩𐑯, 𐑦𐑑 𐑒𐑮𐑦𐑥𐑦𐑙𐑟 𐑥𐑰 𐑑

promptings of anger. [*He holds him with one hand and clenches the other fist*].

LENTULUS. Centurion: I call on you to protect me.

CENTURION. You asked for it, sir. It's no business of ours. Youve had two whacks at him. Better pay him a trifle and square it that way.

LENTULUS. Yes, of course. [*To Ferrovius*] It was only a bit of fun, I assure you: I meant no harm. Here. [*He proffers a gold coin*].

FERROVIUS [*taking it and throwing it to the old beggar, who snatches it up eagerly, and hobbles off to spend it*] Give all thou hast to the poor. Come, friend: courage! I may hurt your body for a moment; but your soul will rejoice in the victory of the spirit over the flesh. [*He prepares to strike*].

ANDROCLES. Easy, Ferrovius, easy: you broke the last man's jaw.

Lentulus, with a moan of terror, attempts to fly; but Ferrovius holds him ruthlessly.

FERROVIUS. Yes; but I saved his soul. What matters a broken jaw?

LENTULUS. Dont touch me, do you hear? The law –

FERROVIUS. The law will throw me to the lions tomorrow; what worse could it do were I to slay you? Pray for strength; and it shall be given to you.

LENTULUS. Let me go. Your religion forbids you to strike me.

FERROVIUS. On the contrary, it commands me to

𐑕𐑑𐑮𐑲𐑒 𐑿. 𐑣𐑬 𐑒𐑨𐑯 𐑿 𐑑𐑻𐑯 𐑞 𐑳𐑞𐑼 𐑗𐑰𐑒, 𐑦𐑓 𐑿 𐑛𐑵 𐑯𐑪𐑑 𐑓𐑻𐑕𐑑 𐑕𐑑𐑮𐑲𐑒 𐑪𐑯 𐑞 𐑢𐑳𐑯 𐑗𐑰𐑒?

𐑤𐑧𐑯𐑑𐑿𐑤𐑩𐑕 [*𐑷𐑤𐑥𐑴𐑕𐑑 𐑦𐑯 𐑑𐑽𐑟*] 𐑚𐑳𐑑 𐑲'𐑥 𐑒𐑩𐑯𐑝𐑦𐑯𐑕𐑑 𐑷𐑤𐑮𐑧𐑛𐑦 𐑞𐑨𐑑 𐑢𐑪𐑑 𐑿 𐑕𐑧𐑛 𐑦𐑟 𐑒𐑢𐑲𐑑 𐑮𐑲𐑑. 𐑲 𐑩𐑐𐑪𐑤𐑩-𐑡𐑲𐑟 𐑓𐑹 𐑕𐑑𐑮𐑲𐑒𐑦𐑙 𐑿.

𐑓𐑧𐑮𐑴𐑝𐑾𐑕 [*𐑜𐑮𐑱𐑑𐑤𐑦 𐑐𐑤𐑰𐑟𐑛*] 𐑥𐑲 𐑕𐑳𐑯: 𐑣𐑨𐑝 𐑲 𐑕𐑪𐑓𐑩𐑯𐑛 𐑿𐑼 𐑣𐑸𐑑? 𐑣𐑨𐑟 𐑞 𐑜𐑫𐑛 𐑕𐑰𐑛 𐑓𐑷𐑤𐑩𐑯 𐑦𐑯 𐑩 𐑓𐑮𐑵𐑑𐑓𐑩𐑤 𐑐𐑤𐑱𐑕? 𐑸 𐑿𐑼 𐑓𐑰𐑑 𐑑𐑻𐑯𐑦𐑙 𐑑𐑫𐑢𐑹𐑛𐑟 𐑩 𐑚𐑧𐑑𐑼 𐑤𐑲𐑓?

𐑤𐑧𐑯𐑑𐑿𐑤𐑩𐑕 [*𐑨𐑚𐑡𐑧𐑒𐑑𐑤𐑦*] 𐑘𐑧𐑕, 𐑘𐑧𐑕. 𐑞𐑺'𐑟 𐑩 𐑜𐑮𐑱𐑑 𐑛𐑰𐑤 𐑦𐑯 𐑢𐑪𐑑 𐑿 𐑕𐑱.

𐑓𐑧𐑮𐑴𐑝𐑾𐑕 [*𐑮𐑱𐑛𐑾𐑯𐑑*] 𐑡𐑶𐑯 𐑳𐑕. 𐑒𐑳𐑥 𐑑 𐑞 𐑤𐑲𐑩𐑯𐑟. 𐑒𐑳𐑥 𐑑 𐑕𐑳𐑓𐑼𐑦𐑙 𐑯 𐑛𐑧𐑔.

𐑤𐑧𐑯𐑑𐑿𐑤𐑩𐑕 [*𐑓𐑷𐑤𐑦𐑙 𐑪𐑯 𐑣𐑦𐑟 𐑯𐑰𐑟 𐑯 𐑚𐑻𐑕𐑑𐑦𐑙 𐑦𐑯𐑑𐑵 𐑑𐑽𐑟*] 𐑴, 𐑣𐑧𐑤𐑐 𐑥𐑰. 𐑥𐑳𐑞𐑼! 𐑥𐑳𐑞𐑼!

𐑓𐑧𐑮𐑴𐑝𐑾𐑕. 𐑞𐑰𐑟 𐑑𐑽𐑟 𐑢𐑦𐑤 𐑢𐑷𐑑𐑼 𐑿𐑼 𐑕𐑴𐑤 𐑯 𐑥𐑱𐑒 𐑦𐑑 𐑚𐑮𐑦𐑙 𐑓𐑹𐑔 𐑜𐑫𐑛 𐑓𐑮𐑵𐑑, 𐑥𐑲 𐑕𐑳𐑯. ·𐑜𐑪𐑛 𐑣𐑨𐑟 𐑜𐑮𐑱𐑑𐑤𐑦 𐑚𐑤𐑧𐑕𐑑 𐑥𐑲 𐑧𐑓𐑼𐑑𐑕 𐑨𐑑 𐑒𐑩𐑯𐑝𐑻𐑠𐑩𐑯. 𐑖𐑨𐑤 𐑲 𐑑𐑧𐑤 𐑿 𐑩 𐑥𐑦𐑮𐑩𐑒𐑩𐑤 — 𐑘𐑧𐑕, 𐑩 𐑥𐑦𐑮𐑩𐑒𐑩𐑤 — 𐑮𐑷𐑑 𐑚𐑲 𐑥𐑰 𐑦𐑯 ·𐑒𐑨𐑐𐑩𐑛𐑴𐑖𐑾? 𐑩 𐑘𐑳𐑙 𐑥𐑨𐑯 — 𐑡𐑳𐑕𐑑 𐑕𐑳𐑗 𐑩 𐑢𐑳𐑯 𐑨𐑟 𐑿, 𐑢𐑦𐑞 𐑜𐑴𐑤𐑛𐑩𐑯 𐑣𐑺 𐑤𐑲𐑒 𐑿𐑼𐑟 — 𐑕𐑒𐑪𐑓𐑑 𐑨𐑑 𐑯 𐑕𐑑𐑮𐑳𐑒 𐑥𐑰 𐑨𐑟 𐑿 𐑕𐑒𐑪𐑓𐑑 𐑨𐑑 𐑯 𐑕𐑑𐑮𐑳𐑒 𐑥𐑰. 𐑲 𐑕𐑨𐑑 𐑳𐑐 𐑷𐑤 𐑯𐑲𐑑 𐑢𐑦𐑞 𐑞𐑨𐑑 𐑿𐑔 𐑮𐑧𐑕𐑤𐑦𐑙 𐑓𐑹 𐑣𐑦𐑟 𐑕𐑴𐑤; 𐑯 𐑦𐑯 𐑞 𐑥𐑹𐑯𐑦𐑙 𐑯𐑪𐑑 𐑴𐑯𐑤𐑦 𐑢𐑪𐑟 𐑣𐑰 𐑩 𐑒𐑮𐑦𐑕𐑗𐑩𐑯, 𐑚𐑳𐑑 𐑣𐑦𐑟 𐑣𐑺 𐑢𐑪𐑟 𐑨𐑟 𐑢𐑲𐑑 𐑨𐑟 𐑕𐑯𐑴. [*·𐑤𐑧𐑯𐑑𐑿𐑤𐑩𐑕 𐑓𐑷𐑤𐑟 𐑦𐑯 𐑩 𐑛𐑧𐑛 𐑓𐑱𐑯𐑑*]. 𐑞𐑺, 𐑞𐑺; 𐑑𐑱𐑒 𐑣𐑦𐑥 𐑩𐑢𐑱. 𐑞 𐑕𐑐𐑦𐑮𐑦𐑑 𐑣𐑨𐑟 𐑴𐑝𐑼𐑐𐑬𐑼𐑛 𐑣𐑦𐑥, 𐑐𐑫𐑼 𐑤𐑨𐑥. 𐑒𐑨𐑮𐑦 𐑣𐑦𐑥 𐑡𐑧𐑯𐑑𐑤𐑦 𐑑 𐑣𐑦𐑟 𐑣𐑬𐑕; 𐑯 𐑤𐑰𐑝 𐑞 𐑮𐑧𐑕𐑑 𐑑 𐑣𐑧𐑝𐑩𐑯.

𐑕𐑧𐑯𐑑𐑿𐑮𐑾𐑯. 𐑑𐑱𐑒 𐑣𐑦𐑥 𐑣𐑴𐑥. [*𐑞 𐑕𐑻𐑝𐑩𐑯𐑑𐑕, 𐑐𐑨𐑯𐑦𐑒𐑕𐑑𐑮𐑦𐑒𐑩𐑯, 𐑣𐑱𐑕𐑑𐑦𐑤𐑦 𐑒𐑨𐑮𐑦 𐑣𐑦𐑥 𐑬𐑑. ·𐑥𐑩𐑑𐑧𐑤𐑩𐑕 𐑦𐑟*

strike you. How can you turn the other cheek, if you are not first struck on the one cheek?

LENTULUS [*almost in tears*] But I'm convinced already that what you said is quite right. I apologize for striking you.

FERROVIUS [*greatly pleased*] My son: have I softened your heart? Has the good seed fallen in a fruitful place? Are your feet turning towards a better path?

LENTULUS [*abjectly*] Yes, yes. Theres a great deal in what you say.

FERROVIUS [*radiant*] Join us. Come to the lions. Come to suffering and death.

LENTULUS [*falling on his knees and bursting into tears*] Oh, help me. Mother! mother!

FERROVIUS. These tears will water your soul and make it bring forth good fruit, my son. God has greatly blessed my efforts at conversion. Shall I tell you a miracle – yes, a miracle – wrought by me in Cappadocia? A young man – just such a one as you, with golden hair like yours – scoffed at and struck me as you scoffed at and struck me. I sat up all night with that youth wrestling for his soul; and in the morning not only was he a Christian, but his hair was as white as snow. [*Lentulus falls in a dead faint*]. There, there: take him away. The spirit has overwrought him, poor lad. Carry him gently to his house; and leave the rest to heaven.

CENTURION. Take him home. [*The servants, intimidated, hastily carry him out. Metellus is*

𐑩𐑚𐑬𐑑 𐑑 𐑓𐑪𐑤𐑴 𐑢𐑧𐑯 ·𐑓𐑧𐑮𐑴𐑝𐑦𐑩𐑕 𐑤𐑱𐑟 𐑣𐑦𐑟 𐑣𐑨𐑯𐑛 𐑪𐑯 𐑣𐑦𐑟 𐑖𐑴𐑤𐑛𐑼].

𐑓𐑧𐑮𐑴𐑝𐑦𐑩𐑕. 𐑿 𐑸 𐑣𐑦𐑟 𐑓𐑮𐑧𐑯𐑛, 𐑘𐑳𐑙 𐑥𐑨𐑯. 𐑿 𐑢𐑦𐑤 𐑕𐑰 𐑞𐑨𐑑 𐑣𐑰 𐑦𐑟 𐑑𐑱𐑒𐑩𐑯 𐑕𐑱𐑓𐑤𐑦 𐑣𐑴𐑥.

𐑥𐑩𐑑𐑧𐑤𐑩𐑕 [𐑢𐑦𐑞 𐑦𐑒𐑕𐑑𐑮𐑰𐑥 𐑕𐑦𐑝𐑦𐑤𐑦𐑑𐑦] 𐑕𐑻𐑑𐑩𐑯𐑤𐑦, 𐑕𐑻. 𐑲 𐑖𐑨𐑤 𐑛𐑵 𐑢𐑪𐑑𐑧𐑝𐑼 𐑿 𐑔𐑦𐑙𐑒 𐑚𐑧𐑕𐑑. 𐑥𐑴𐑕𐑑 𐑣𐑨𐑐𐑦 𐑑 𐑣𐑨𐑝 𐑥𐑱𐑛 𐑿𐑼 𐑩𐑒𐑢𐑱𐑯𐑑𐑩𐑯𐑕, 𐑲'𐑥 𐑖𐑫𐑼. 𐑿 𐑥𐑱 𐑛𐑦𐑐𐑧𐑯𐑛 𐑪𐑯 𐑥𐑰. 𐑜𐑫𐑛 𐑰𐑝𐑯𐑦𐑙, 𐑕𐑻.

𐑓𐑧𐑮𐑴𐑝𐑦𐑩𐑕 [𐑢𐑦𐑞 𐑦𐑥𐑴𐑖𐑩𐑯] 𐑞 𐑚𐑤𐑧𐑕𐑦𐑙 𐑝 𐑣𐑧𐑝𐑩𐑯 𐑩𐑐𐑪𐑯 𐑿 𐑯 𐑣𐑦𐑥.

[·𐑥𐑩𐑑𐑧𐑤𐑩𐑕 𐑓𐑪𐑤𐑴𐑟 ·𐑤𐑧𐑯𐑑𐑿𐑤𐑩𐑕. 𐑞 𐑕𐑧𐑯𐑑𐑿𐑼𐑾𐑯 𐑮𐑦𐑑𐑻𐑯𐑟 𐑑 𐑣𐑦𐑟 𐑕𐑰𐑑 𐑑 𐑮𐑦𐑟𐑿𐑥 𐑣𐑦𐑟 𐑦𐑯𐑑𐑼𐑳𐑐𐑑𐑦𐑛 𐑯𐑨𐑐. 𐑞 𐑛𐑰𐑐𐑩𐑕𐑑 𐑷 𐑣𐑨𐑟 𐑕𐑧𐑑𐑩𐑤𐑛 𐑪𐑯 𐑞 𐑕𐑐𐑧𐑒𐑑𐑱𐑑𐑼𐑟. ·𐑓𐑧𐑮𐑴𐑝𐑦𐑩𐑕, 𐑢𐑦𐑞 𐑩 𐑤𐑪𐑙 𐑕𐑲 𐑝 𐑣𐑨𐑐𐑦𐑯𐑩𐑕, 𐑜𐑴𐑟 𐑑 ·𐑤𐑩𐑝𐑦𐑯𐑦𐑩, 𐑯 𐑪𐑓𐑼𐑟 𐑣𐑻 𐑣𐑦𐑟 𐑣𐑨𐑯𐑛].

𐑤𐑩𐑝𐑦𐑯𐑦𐑩 [𐑑𐑱𐑒𐑦𐑙 𐑦𐑑] 𐑕𐑴 𐑞𐑨𐑑 𐑦𐑟 𐑣𐑬 𐑿 𐑒𐑩𐑯𐑝𐑻𐑑 𐑐𐑰𐑐𐑩𐑤, ·𐑓𐑧𐑮𐑴𐑝𐑦𐑩𐑕.

𐑓𐑧𐑮𐑴𐑝𐑦𐑩𐑕. 𐑘𐑧𐑕: 𐑞𐑺 𐑣𐑨𐑟 𐑚𐑰𐑯 𐑩 𐑚𐑤𐑧𐑕𐑦𐑙 𐑪𐑯 𐑥𐑲 𐑢𐑻𐑒 𐑦𐑯 𐑕𐑐𐑲𐑑 𐑝 𐑥𐑲 𐑳𐑯𐑢𐑻𐑞𐑦𐑯𐑩𐑕 𐑯 𐑥𐑲 𐑚𐑨𐑒𐑕𐑤𐑲𐑛𐑦𐑙𐑟 — 𐑷𐑤 𐑔𐑮𐑵 𐑥𐑲 𐑢𐑦𐑒𐑦𐑛, 𐑛𐑧𐑝𐑦𐑤𐑦𐑖 𐑑𐑧𐑥𐑐𐑼. 𐑞𐑦𐑕 𐑥𐑨𐑯 —

𐑨𐑯𐑛𐑮𐑩𐑒𐑤𐑰𐑟 [𐑣𐑱𐑕𐑑𐑦𐑤𐑦] 𐑛𐑴𐑯𐑑 𐑕𐑤𐑨𐑐 𐑥𐑰 𐑪𐑯 𐑞 𐑚𐑨𐑒, 𐑚𐑮𐑳𐑞𐑼. 𐑖𐑰 𐑯𐑴𐑟 𐑿 𐑥𐑧𐑯𐑑 𐑥𐑰.

𐑓𐑧𐑮𐑴𐑝𐑦𐑩𐑕. 𐑣𐑬 𐑲 𐑢𐑦𐑖 𐑲 𐑢𐑻 𐑢𐑰𐑒 𐑤𐑲𐑒 𐑬𐑼 𐑚𐑮𐑳𐑞𐑼 𐑣𐑽! 𐑓 𐑞𐑧𐑯 𐑲 𐑖𐑫𐑛 𐑐𐑼𐑣𐑨𐑐𐑕 𐑚𐑰 𐑥𐑰𐑒 𐑯 𐑡𐑧𐑯𐑑𐑩𐑤 𐑤𐑲𐑒 𐑣𐑦𐑥. 𐑯 𐑘𐑧𐑑 𐑞𐑺 𐑕𐑰𐑥𐑟 𐑑 𐑚𐑰 𐑩 𐑕𐑐𐑧𐑖𐑩𐑤 𐑐𐑮𐑪𐑝𐑦𐑛𐑩𐑯𐑕 𐑞𐑨𐑑 𐑥𐑱𐑒𐑕 𐑥𐑲 𐑑𐑮𐑲𐑩𐑤𐑟 𐑤𐑧𐑕 𐑞𐑨𐑯 𐑣𐑦𐑟. 𐑲 𐑣𐑽 𐑑𐑱𐑤𐑟 𐑝 𐑞 𐑒𐑮𐑬𐑛 𐑕𐑒𐑪𐑓𐑦𐑙 𐑯 𐑒𐑭𐑕𐑑𐑦𐑙 𐑕𐑑𐑴𐑯𐑟 𐑯 𐑮𐑦𐑝𐑲𐑤𐑦𐑙 𐑞 𐑚𐑮𐑧𐑞𐑮𐑩𐑯; 𐑚𐑳𐑑 𐑢𐑧𐑯 𐑲 𐑒𐑳𐑥, 𐑷𐑤 𐑞𐑦𐑕 𐑕𐑑𐑪𐑐𐑕: 𐑥𐑲 𐑦𐑯𐑓𐑤𐑵𐑩𐑯𐑕 𐑒𐑭𐑥𐑟 𐑞 𐑐𐑨𐑖𐑩𐑯𐑟 𐑝 𐑞 𐑥𐑪𐑚: 𐑞𐑱 𐑤𐑦𐑕𐑩𐑯 𐑑 𐑥𐑰 𐑦𐑯 𐑕𐑲𐑤𐑩𐑯𐑕; 𐑯 𐑦𐑯𐑓𐑦𐑛𐑩𐑤𐑟 𐑸 𐑪𐑓𐑩𐑯 𐑒𐑩𐑯𐑝𐑻𐑑𐑩𐑛 𐑚𐑲 𐑩 𐑕𐑑𐑮𐑱𐑑 𐑣𐑸𐑑-𐑑-𐑣𐑸𐑑

about to follow when Ferrovius lays his hand on his shoulder].

FERROVIUS. You are his friend, young man. You will see that he is taken safely home.

METELLUS [*with awestruck civility*] Certainly, sir. I shall do whatever you think best. Most happy to have made your acquaintance, I'm sure. You may depend on me. Good evening, sir.

FERROVIUS [*with unction*] The blessing of heaven upon you and him.

Metellus follows Lentulus. The Centurion returns to his seat to resume his interrupted nap. The deepest awe has settled on the spectators. Ferrovius, with a long sigh of happiness, goes to Lavinia, and offers her his hand.

LAVINIA [*taking it*] So that is how you convert people, Ferrovius.

FERROVIUS. Yes: there has been a blessing on my work in spite of my unworthiness and my backslidings – all through my wicked, devilish temper. This man –

ANDROCLES [*hastily*] Dont slap me on the back, brother. She knows you mean me.

FERROVIUS. How I wish I were weak like our brother here! for then I should perhaps be meek and gentle like him. And yet there seems to be a special providence that makes my trials less than his. I hear tales of the crowd scoffing and casting stones and reviling the brethren; but when I come, all this stops: my influence calms the passions of the mob: they listen to me in silence; and infidels are often converted by a straight heart-to-heart

𐑑𐑷𐑒 𐑢𐑦𐑞 𐑥𐑰. 𐑐𐑮𐑱 𐑞𐑨𐑑 𐑲 𐑥𐑱 𐑓𐑰𐑤 𐑣𐑳𐑥𐑚𐑩𐑤, 𐑕𐑴 𐑒𐑪𐑯𐑓𐑦𐑛𐑩𐑯𐑑. 𐑐𐑮𐑱 𐑞𐑨𐑑 𐑲 𐑥𐑱 𐑤𐑦𐑕𐑩𐑯 𐑞 𐑒𐑷𐑤 𐑝 𐑞 𐑚𐑮𐑱𐑟𐑩𐑯 𐑑𐑿𐑚.

𐑤𐑩𐑝𐑦𐑯𐑾. 𐑞 𐑚𐑮𐑱𐑟𐑩𐑯 𐑑𐑿𐑚? 𐑢𐑪𐑑 𐑦𐑟 𐑞𐑨𐑑?

[·𐑓𐑧𐑮𐑴𐑝𐑾𐑕 𐑖𐑱𐑒𐑕 𐑣𐑦𐑟 𐑣𐑧𐑛 𐑯 𐑛𐑳𐑟 𐑯𐑪𐑑 𐑭𐑯𐑕𐑼. 𐑣𐑰 𐑕𐑦𐑙𐑒𐑕 𐑛𐑬𐑯 𐑛𐑦𐑕𐑥𐑩𐑤𐑦 𐑩𐑯 𐑞 𐑕𐑑𐑧𐑐𐑕 𐑩𐑟 𐑦𐑓 𐑣𐑰 𐑒𐑫𐑛 𐑯𐑪𐑑 𐑕𐑑𐑨𐑯𐑛, 𐑯 𐑚𐑧𐑮𐑦𐑟 𐑣𐑦𐑟 𐑓𐑱𐑕 𐑦𐑯 𐑣𐑦𐑟 𐑣𐑨𐑯𐑛𐑟 𐑦𐑯 𐑚𐑦𐑑𐑼 𐑕𐑧𐑤𐑓𐑮𐑦𐑐𐑮𐑴𐑗].

𐑨𐑯𐑛𐑮𐑩𐑒𐑤𐑰𐑟. 𐑢𐑧𐑤, 𐑲 𐑕𐑰, 𐑕𐑦𐑕𐑑𐑼, 𐑣𐑰'𐑟 𐑯𐑧𐑝𐑼 𐑒𐑢𐑲𐑑 𐑖𐑫𐑼 𐑝 𐑣𐑦𐑥𐑕𐑧𐑤𐑓. 𐑕𐑩𐑐𐑴𐑟 𐑨𐑑 𐑞 𐑤𐑭𐑕𐑑 𐑥𐑴𐑥𐑩𐑯𐑑 𐑦𐑯 𐑞 𐑩𐑮𐑰𐑯𐑩, 𐑢𐑦𐑞 𐑞 𐑜𐑤𐑨𐑛𐑦𐑱𐑑𐑼𐑟 𐑞𐑺 𐑑 𐑓𐑲𐑑 𐑣𐑦𐑥, 𐑢𐑳𐑯 𐑝 𐑞𐑧𐑥 𐑢𐑪𐑟 𐑑 𐑕𐑱 𐑧𐑯𐑦𐑔𐑦𐑙 𐑑 𐑩𐑯𐑶 𐑣𐑦𐑥, 𐑣𐑰 𐑥𐑲𐑑 𐑓𐑼𐑜𐑧𐑑 𐑣𐑦𐑥𐑕𐑧𐑤𐑓 𐑯 𐑤𐑱 𐑞𐑨𐑑 𐑜𐑤𐑨𐑛𐑦𐑱𐑑𐑼 𐑬𐑑.

𐑤𐑩𐑝𐑦𐑯𐑾. 𐑞𐑨𐑑 𐑢𐑫𐑛 𐑚𐑰 𐑕𐑐𐑤𐑧𐑯𐑛𐑦𐑛.

𐑓𐑧𐑮𐑴𐑝𐑾𐑕 [𐑕𐑐𐑮𐑦𐑙𐑦𐑙 𐑳𐑐 𐑦𐑯 𐑩 𐑓𐑮𐑧𐑯𐑟𐑦] 𐑢𐑪𐑑!

𐑨𐑯𐑛𐑮𐑩𐑒𐑤𐑰𐑟. 𐑴, 𐑕𐑦𐑕𐑑𐑼!

𐑓𐑧𐑮𐑴𐑝𐑾𐑕. 𐑕𐑐𐑤𐑧𐑯𐑛𐑦𐑛 𐑑 𐑚𐑦𐑑𐑮𐑱 𐑥𐑲 ·𐑥𐑭𐑕𐑑𐑼, 𐑤𐑲𐑒 ·𐑐𐑰𐑑𐑼! 𐑕𐑐𐑤𐑧𐑯𐑛𐑦𐑛 𐑑 𐑨𐑒𐑑 𐑤𐑲𐑒 𐑧𐑯𐑦 𐑒𐑪𐑥𐑩𐑯 𐑚𐑤𐑨𐑜𐑸𐑛 𐑦𐑯 𐑞 𐑛𐑱 𐑝 𐑥𐑲 𐑐𐑮𐑵𐑝𐑦𐑙! 𐑢𐑫𐑥𐑩𐑯: 𐑲 𐑨𐑥 𐑯𐑴 𐑒𐑮𐑦𐑕𐑗𐑩𐑯. [𐑣𐑰 𐑥𐑵𐑝𐑟 𐑩𐑢𐑱 𐑓𐑮𐑪𐑥 𐑞𐑧𐑥 𐑑 𐑞 𐑥𐑦𐑛𐑩𐑤 𐑝 𐑞 𐑕𐑒𐑢𐑺, 𐑩𐑟 𐑦𐑓 𐑣𐑰 𐑯𐑴 𐑤𐑪𐑙𐑜𐑼 𐑛𐑺𐑛 𐑑𐑮𐑳𐑕𐑑 𐑣𐑦𐑥𐑕𐑧𐑤𐑓].

𐑤𐑩𐑝𐑦𐑯𐑾 [𐑒𐑭𐑤𐑥𐑦] 𐑲 𐑯𐑴, ·𐑓𐑧𐑮𐑴𐑝𐑾𐑕. 𐑲 𐑨𐑥 𐑯𐑪𐑑 𐑷𐑤𐑢𐑱𐑟 𐑩 𐑒𐑮𐑦𐑕𐑗𐑩𐑯. 𐑲 𐑛𐑴𐑯𐑑 𐑔𐑦𐑙𐑒 𐑧𐑯𐑦𐑚𐑪𐑛𐑦 𐑦𐑟. 𐑞𐑺 𐑸 𐑥𐑴𐑥𐑩𐑯𐑑𐑕 𐑢𐑧𐑯 𐑲 𐑓𐑼𐑜𐑧𐑑 𐑷𐑤 𐑩𐑚𐑬𐑑 𐑦𐑑, 𐑯 𐑕𐑳𐑥𐑔𐑦𐑙 𐑒𐑳𐑥𐑟 𐑬𐑑 𐑒𐑢𐑲𐑑 𐑯𐑨𐑗𐑼𐑩𐑤𐑦, 𐑨𐑟 𐑦𐑑 𐑛𐑦𐑛 𐑞𐑧𐑯.

𐑕𐑐𐑦𐑯𐑔𐑴. 𐑢𐑪𐑑 𐑛𐑳𐑟 𐑦𐑑 𐑥𐑨𐑑𐑼? 𐑦𐑓 𐑲 𐑛𐑲 𐑦𐑯 𐑞 𐑩𐑮𐑰𐑯𐑩, 𐑲'𐑤 𐑚𐑰 𐑩 𐑥𐑸𐑑𐑼; 𐑯 𐑥𐑸𐑑𐑼𐑟 𐑜𐑴 𐑑 𐑣𐑧𐑝𐑩𐑯, 𐑯𐑴 𐑥𐑨𐑑𐑼 𐑢𐑪𐑑 𐑞𐑱 𐑣𐑨𐑝 𐑛𐑳𐑯. 𐑞𐑨𐑑'𐑕 𐑕𐑴, 𐑦𐑟𐑩𐑯𐑑 𐑦𐑑, ·𐑓𐑧𐑮𐑴𐑝𐑾𐑕?

𐑓𐑧𐑮𐑴𐑝𐑾𐑕. 𐑘𐑧𐑕: 𐑞𐑨𐑑 𐑦𐑟 𐑕𐑴, 𐑦𐑓 𐑢𐑰 𐑸 𐑓𐑱𐑔𐑓𐑩𐑤 𐑑 𐑞 𐑧𐑯𐑛.

talk with me. Every day I feel happier, more confident. Every day lightens the load of the great terror.

LAVINIA. The great terror? What is that?

Ferrovius shakes his head and does not answer. He sits down beside her on her left, and buries his face in his hands in gloomy meditation.

ANDROCLES. Well, you see, sister, he's never quite sure of himself. Suppose at the last moment in the arena, with the gladiators there to fight him, one of them was to say anything to annoy him, he might forget himself and lay that gladiator out.

LAVINIA. That would be splendid.

FERROVIUS [*springing up in horror*] What!

ANDROCLES. Oh, sister!

FERROVIUS. Splendid to betray my master, like Peter! Splendid to act like any common blackguard in the day of my proving! Woman: you are no Christian. [*He moves away from her to the middle of the square, as if her neighborhood contaminated him*].

LAVINIA [*laughing*] You know, Ferrovius, I am not always a Christian. I dont think anybody is. There are moments when I forget all about it, and something comes out quite naturally, as it did then.

SPINTHO. What does it matter? If you die in the arena, youll be a martyr; and all martyrs go to heaven, no matter what they have done. Thats so, isnt it, Ferrovius?

FERROVIUS. Yes: that is so, if we are faithful to the end.

𐑤𐑩𐑝𐑦𐑯𐑦𐑩. 𐑲'𐑥 𐑯𐑪𐑑 𐑕𐑴 𐑖𐑫𐑼.

𐑕𐑐𐑦𐑯𐑔𐑴. 𐑛𐑴𐑯𐑑 𐑕𐑱 𐑞𐑨𐑑. 𐑞𐑨𐑑'𐑕 𐑚𐑤𐑨𐑕𐑓𐑩𐑥𐑩𐑕. 𐑛𐑴𐑯𐑑 𐑕𐑱 𐑞𐑨𐑑, 𐑲 𐑑𐑧𐑤 𐑿. 𐑢𐑰 𐑖𐑨𐑤 𐑚𐑰 𐑕𐑱𐑝𐑛, 𐑯𐑴 𐑥𐑨𐑑𐑼 𐑢𐑪𐑑 𐑢𐑰 𐑛𐑵.

𐑤𐑩𐑝𐑦𐑯𐑦𐑩. 𐑐𐑼𐑣𐑨𐑐𐑕 𐑿 𐑥𐑧𐑯 𐑢𐑦𐑤 𐑷𐑤 𐑜𐑴 𐑦𐑯𐑑𐑫 𐑣𐑧𐑝𐑩𐑯 𐑚𐑮𐑱𐑝𐑤𐑦 𐑯 𐑦𐑯 𐑑𐑮𐑲𐑩𐑥𐑓, 𐑢𐑦𐑞 𐑿𐑼 𐑣𐑧𐑛𐑟 𐑦𐑮𐑧𐑒𐑑 𐑯 𐑜𐑴𐑤𐑛𐑩𐑯 𐑑𐑮𐑳𐑥𐑐𐑩𐑑𐑕 𐑕𐑬𐑯𐑛𐑦𐑙 𐑓𐑹 𐑿. 𐑚𐑳𐑑 𐑲 𐑨𐑥 𐑖𐑫𐑼 𐑲 𐑖𐑨𐑤 𐑴𐑯𐑤𐑦 𐑚𐑰 𐑩𐑤𐑬𐑛 𐑑 𐑕𐑒𐑢𐑰𐑟 𐑥𐑲𐑕𐑧𐑤𐑓 𐑦𐑯 𐑔𐑮𐑵 𐑩 𐑤𐑦𐑑𐑩𐑤 𐑒𐑮𐑨𐑒 𐑦𐑯 𐑞 𐑜𐑱𐑑 𐑭𐑓𐑑𐑼 𐑩 𐑜𐑮𐑱𐑑 𐑛𐑰𐑤 𐑝 𐑚𐑧𐑜𐑦𐑙. 𐑲 𐑨𐑥 𐑯𐑪𐑑 𐑜𐑫𐑛 𐑷𐑤𐑢𐑱𐑟: 𐑲 𐑣𐑨𐑝 𐑥𐑴𐑥𐑩𐑯𐑑𐑕 𐑴𐑯𐑤𐑦.

𐑕𐑐𐑦𐑯𐑔𐑴. 𐑿'𐑼 𐑑𐑷𐑒𐑦𐑙 𐑯𐑪𐑯𐑕𐑩𐑯𐑕, 𐑢𐑫𐑥𐑩𐑯. 𐑲 𐑑𐑧𐑤 𐑿, 𐑥𐑸𐑑𐑼𐑛𐑩𐑥 𐑐𐑱𐑟 𐑷𐑤 𐑕𐑒𐑹𐑟.

𐑨𐑯𐑛𐑮𐑩𐑒𐑤𐑰𐑟. 𐑢𐑧𐑤, 𐑤𐑧𐑑 𐑳𐑕 𐑣𐑴𐑐 𐑕𐑴, 𐑚𐑮𐑳𐑞𐑼, 𐑓𐑹 𐑿𐑼 𐑕𐑱𐑒. 𐑿'𐑝 𐑣𐑨𐑛 𐑩 𐑜𐑱 𐑑𐑲𐑥, 𐑣𐑨𐑝𐑩𐑯𐑑 𐑿? 𐑢𐑦𐑞 𐑿𐑼 𐑮𐑱𐑛𐑟 𐑪𐑯 𐑞 𐑑𐑧𐑥𐑐𐑩𐑤𐑟. 𐑲 𐑒𐑭𐑯𐑑 𐑣𐑧𐑤𐑐 𐑔𐑦𐑙𐑒𐑦𐑙 𐑞𐑨𐑑 𐑣𐑧𐑝𐑩𐑯 𐑢𐑦𐑤 𐑚𐑰 𐑝𐑧𐑮𐑦 𐑛𐑳𐑤 𐑓𐑹 𐑩 𐑥𐑨𐑯 𐑝 𐑿𐑼 𐑑𐑧𐑥𐑐𐑼𐑩𐑥𐑩𐑯𐑑. [·𐑕𐑐𐑦𐑯𐑔𐑴 𐑕𐑒𐑬𐑤𐑟]. 𐑛𐑴𐑯𐑑 𐑚𐑰 𐑨𐑙𐑜𐑮𐑦: 𐑲 𐑕𐑱 𐑦𐑑 𐑴𐑯𐑤𐑦 𐑑 𐑒𐑩𐑯𐑕𐑴𐑤 𐑿 𐑦𐑯 𐑒𐑱𐑕 𐑿 𐑖𐑫𐑛 𐑛𐑲 𐑦𐑯 𐑿𐑼 𐑚𐑧𐑛 𐑑𐑩𐑯𐑲𐑑 𐑦𐑯 𐑞 𐑯𐑨𐑗𐑼𐑩𐑤 𐑢𐑱. 𐑞𐑺'𐑟 𐑩 𐑤𐑪𐑑 𐑝 𐑐𐑤𐑱𐑜 𐑩𐑚𐑬𐑑.

𐑕𐑐𐑦𐑯𐑔𐑴 [𐑮𐑲𐑟𐑦𐑙 𐑯 𐑮𐑳𐑯𐑦𐑙 𐑩𐑚𐑬𐑑 𐑦𐑯 𐑨𐑚𐑡𐑧𐑒𐑑 𐑑𐑧𐑮𐑼] 𐑲 𐑯𐑧𐑝𐑼 𐑔𐑷𐑑 𐑝 𐑞𐑨𐑑. 𐑴 ·𐑤𐑹𐑛, 𐑕𐑐𐑺 𐑥𐑰 𐑑 𐑚𐑰 𐑥𐑸𐑑𐑼𐑛. 𐑴, 𐑢𐑪𐑑 𐑩 𐑔𐑷𐑑 𐑑 𐑐𐑫𐑑 𐑦𐑯𐑑𐑫 𐑞 𐑥𐑲𐑯𐑛 𐑝 𐑩 𐑚𐑮𐑳𐑞𐑼! 𐑴, 𐑤𐑧𐑑 𐑥𐑰 𐑚𐑰 𐑥𐑸𐑑𐑼𐑛 𐑑𐑩𐑛𐑱, 𐑯𐑬. 𐑲 𐑖𐑨𐑤 𐑛𐑲 𐑦𐑯 𐑞 𐑯𐑲𐑑 𐑯 𐑜𐑴 𐑑 𐑣𐑧𐑤. 𐑿'𐑼 𐑩 𐑕𐑹𐑕𐑼𐑼: 𐑿'𐑝 𐑐𐑫𐑑 𐑛𐑧𐑔 𐑦𐑯𐑑𐑫 𐑥𐑲 𐑥𐑲𐑯𐑛. 𐑴, 𐑒𐑻𐑕 𐑿, 𐑒𐑻𐑕 𐑿! [𐑣𐑰 𐑑𐑮𐑲𐑟 𐑑 𐑕𐑰𐑟 ·𐑨𐑯𐑛𐑮𐑩𐑒𐑤𐑰𐑟 𐑚𐑲 𐑞 𐑔𐑮𐑴𐑑].

𐑓𐑼𐑴𐑝𐑦𐑩𐑕 [𐑣𐑴𐑤𐑛𐑦𐑙 𐑣𐑦𐑥 𐑦𐑯 𐑩 𐑜𐑮𐑭𐑕𐑐 𐑝 𐑲𐑼𐑯] 𐑢𐑪𐑑'𐑕 𐑞𐑦𐑕, 𐑚𐑮𐑳𐑞𐑼? 𐑨𐑙𐑜𐑼! 𐑝𐑲𐑩𐑤𐑩𐑯𐑕! 𐑮𐑱𐑟𐑦𐑙 𐑿𐑼 𐑣𐑨𐑯𐑛 𐑑 𐑩 𐑚𐑮𐑳𐑞𐑼 𐑒𐑮𐑦𐑕𐑗𐑩𐑯!

LAVINIA. I'm not so sure.

SPINTHO. Dont say that. Thats blasphemy. Dont say that, I tell you. We shall be saved, no matter what we do.

LAVINIA. Perhaps you men will all go into heaven bravely and in triumph, with your heads erect and golden trumpets sounding for you. But I am sure, I shall only be allowed to squeeze myself in through a little crack in the gate after a great deal of begging. I am not good always: I have moments only.

SPINTHO. Youre talking nonsense, woman. I tell you, martyrdom pays all scores.

ANDROCLES. Well, let us hope so, brother, for your sake. Youve had a gay time, havnt you? with your raids on the temples. I cant help thinking that heaven will be very dull for a man of your temperament. [*Spintho snarls*]. Dont be angry: I say it only to console you in case you should die in your bed tonight in the natural way. There's a lot of plague about.

SPINTHO [*rising and running about in abject terror*] I never thought of that. Oh Lord, spare me to be martyred. Oh, what a thought to put into the mind of a brother! Oh, let me be martyred today, now. I shall die in the night and go to hell. Youre a sorcerer: youve put death into my mind. Oh, curse you, curse you! [*He tries to seize Androcles by the throat*].

FERROVIUS [*holding him in a grasp of iron*] Whats this, brother? Anger! Violence! Raising your hand to a brother Christian!

𐑕𐑐𐑦𐑯𐑔𐑴. 𐑦𐑑'𐑕 𐑰𐑟𐑦 𐑓𐑹 𐑿. 𐑿'𐑼 𐑕𐑑𐑮𐑪𐑙. 𐑿𐑼 𐑯𐑻𐑝𐑟 𐑸 𐑷𐑤 𐑮𐑲𐑑. 𐑚𐑳𐑑 𐑲'𐑥 𐑓𐑫𐑤 𐑝 𐑛𐑦𐑟𐑰𐑟. [·𐑓𐑧𐑮𐑴𐑝𐑾𐑕 𐑑𐑻𐑯𐑟 𐑣𐑦𐑟 𐑣𐑧𐑛 𐑓𐑮𐑪𐑥 𐑣𐑦𐑥 𐑢𐑦𐑞 𐑦𐑯𐑕𐑑𐑦𐑙𐑒𐑑𐑦𐑝 𐑛𐑦𐑕𐑜𐑳𐑕𐑑]. 𐑲'𐑝 𐑛𐑮𐑳𐑙𐑒 𐑷𐑤 𐑥𐑲 𐑯𐑻𐑝𐑟 𐑩𐑢𐑱. 𐑲 𐑖𐑨𐑤 𐑣𐑨𐑝 𐑞 𐑣𐑪𐑮𐑼𐑟 𐑷𐑤 𐑯𐑲𐑑.

𐑨𐑯𐑛𐑮𐑩𐑒𐑤𐑰𐑟 [𐑕𐑦𐑥𐑐𐑩𐑔𐑧𐑑𐑦𐑒𐑩𐑤𐑦] 𐑴, 𐑛𐑴𐑯𐑑 𐑑𐑱𐑒 𐑪𐑯 𐑕𐑴, 𐑚𐑮𐑳𐑞𐑼. 𐑢𐑰'𐑼 𐑷𐑤 𐑕𐑦𐑯𐑼𐑟.

𐑕𐑐𐑦𐑯𐑔𐑴 [𐑕𐑯𐑦𐑝𐑩𐑤𐑦𐑙, 𐑑𐑮𐑲𐑦𐑙 𐑑 𐑓𐑰𐑤 𐑒𐑩𐑯𐑕𐑴𐑤𐑛] 𐑘𐑧𐑕: 𐑲 𐑛𐑺𐑕𐑱 𐑦𐑓 𐑞 𐑑𐑮𐑵𐑔 𐑢𐑻 𐑯𐑴𐑯, 𐑿'𐑼 𐑷𐑤 𐑨𐑟 𐑚𐑨𐑛 𐑨𐑟 𐑲 𐑨𐑥.

𐑤𐑩𐑝𐑦𐑯𐑾 [𐑒𐑩𐑯𐑑𐑧𐑥𐑐𐑗𐑵𐑩𐑕𐑤𐑦] 𐑛𐑳𐑟 𐑞𐑨𐑑 𐑒𐑳𐑥𐑓𐑼𐑑 𐑿?

𐑓𐑧𐑮𐑴𐑝𐑾𐑕 [𐑕𐑑𐑻𐑯𐑤𐑦] 𐑐𐑮𐑱, 𐑥𐑨𐑯, 𐑐𐑮𐑱.

𐑕𐑐𐑦𐑯𐑔𐑴. 𐑢𐑪𐑑'𐑕 𐑞 𐑜𐑫𐑛 𐑝 𐑐𐑮𐑱𐑦𐑙? 𐑦𐑓 𐑢𐑰'𐑼 𐑥𐑸𐑑𐑼𐑛 𐑢𐑰 𐑖𐑨𐑤 𐑜𐑴 𐑑 𐑣𐑧𐑝𐑩𐑯, 𐑖𐑭𐑯𐑑 𐑢𐑰, 𐑢𐑧𐑞𐑼 𐑢𐑰 𐑐𐑮𐑱 𐑹 𐑯𐑪𐑑?

𐑓𐑧𐑮𐑴𐑝𐑾𐑕. 𐑢𐑪𐑑'𐑕 𐑞𐑨𐑑? 𐑯𐑪𐑑 𐑐𐑮𐑱! [𐑕𐑰𐑟𐑦𐑙 𐑣𐑦𐑥 𐑩𐑜𐑧𐑯] 𐑐𐑮𐑱 𐑞𐑦𐑕 𐑦𐑯𐑕𐑑𐑩𐑯𐑑, 𐑿 𐑛𐑪𐑜, 𐑿 𐑮𐑪𐑑𐑩𐑯 𐑣𐑬𐑯𐑛, 𐑿 𐑕𐑤𐑲𐑥𐑦 𐑕𐑯𐑱𐑒, 𐑿 𐑚𐑰𐑕𐑑𐑤𐑦 𐑜𐑴𐑑, 𐑹 –

𐑕𐑐𐑦𐑯𐑔𐑴. 𐑘𐑧𐑕: 𐑚𐑰𐑑 𐑥𐑰: 𐑒𐑦𐑒 𐑥𐑰. 𐑲 𐑓𐑼𐑜𐑦𐑝 𐑿: 𐑥𐑲𐑯𐑛 𐑞𐑨𐑑.

𐑓𐑧𐑮𐑴𐑝𐑾𐑕 [𐑕𐑐𐑻𐑯𐑦𐑙 𐑣𐑦𐑥 𐑢𐑦𐑞 𐑤𐑴𐑞𐑦𐑙] 𐑘𐑭! [𐑕𐑐𐑦𐑯𐑔𐑴 𐑮𐑰𐑤𐑟 𐑩𐑢𐑱 𐑯 𐑓𐑷𐑤𐑟 𐑦𐑯 𐑓𐑮𐑳𐑯𐑑 𐑝 ·𐑓𐑧𐑮𐑴𐑝𐑾𐑕].

𐑨𐑯𐑛𐑮𐑩𐑒𐑤𐑰𐑟 [𐑮𐑰𐑗𐑦𐑙 𐑬𐑑 𐑯 𐑒𐑨𐑗𐑦𐑙 𐑞 𐑕𐑒𐑻𐑑 𐑝 ·𐑓𐑧𐑮𐑴𐑝𐑾𐑕'𐑦𐑟 𐑑𐑴𐑜𐑩] 𐑛𐑽 𐑚𐑮𐑳𐑞𐑼: 𐑦𐑓 𐑿 𐑢𐑫𐑛𐑩𐑯𐑑 𐑥𐑲𐑯𐑛 – 𐑡𐑳𐑕𐑑 𐑓𐑹 𐑥𐑲 𐑕𐑱𐑒 –

𐑓𐑧𐑮𐑴𐑝𐑾𐑕. 𐑢𐑧𐑤?

𐑨𐑯𐑛𐑮𐑩𐑒𐑤𐑰𐑟. 𐑛𐑴𐑯𐑑 𐑒𐑷𐑤 𐑣𐑦𐑥 𐑚𐑲 𐑞 𐑯𐑱𐑥𐑟 𐑝 𐑞 𐑨𐑯𐑦𐑥𐑩𐑤𐑟. 𐑢𐑰'𐑝 𐑯𐑴 𐑮𐑲𐑑 𐑑. 𐑲'𐑝 𐑣𐑨𐑛 𐑕𐑳𐑗 𐑓𐑮𐑧𐑯𐑛𐑟 𐑦𐑯 𐑛𐑪𐑜𐑟. 𐑩 𐑐𐑧𐑑 𐑕𐑯𐑱𐑒 𐑦𐑟 𐑞 𐑚𐑧𐑕𐑑 𐑝 𐑒𐑳𐑥𐑐𐑩𐑯𐑦. 𐑲 𐑢𐑪𐑟 𐑯𐑻𐑕𐑑 𐑪𐑯 𐑜𐑴𐑑'𐑕 𐑥𐑦𐑤𐑒. 𐑦𐑟 𐑦𐑑 𐑓𐑺 𐑑 𐑞𐑧𐑥 𐑑 𐑒𐑷𐑤 𐑞 𐑤𐑲𐑒𐑕 𐑝 𐑣𐑦𐑥 𐑩 𐑛𐑪𐑜 𐑹 𐑩 𐑕𐑯𐑱𐑒 𐑹 𐑩 𐑜𐑴𐑑?

SPINTHO. It's easy for you. Youre strong. Your nerves are all right. But I'm full of disease. [*Ferrovius takes his hand from him with instinctive disgust*]. Ive drunk all my nerves away. I shall have the horrors all night.

ANDROCLES [*sympathetically*] Oh, dont take on so, brother. We're all sinners.

SPINTHO [*snivelling, trying to feel consoled*] Yes: I daresay if the truth were known, youre all as bad as I am.

LAVINIA [*contemptuously*] Does that comfort you?

FERROVIUS [*sternly*] Pray, man, pray.

SPINTHO. Whats the good of praying? If we're martyred we shall go to heaven, shant we, whether we pray or not?

FERROVIUS. Whats that? Not pray! [*Seizing him again*] Pray this instant, you dog, you rotten hound, you slimy snake, you beastly goat, or –

SPINTHO. Yes: beat me: kick me. I forgive you: mind that.

FERROVIUS [*spurning him with loathing*] Yah! [*Spintho reels away and falls in front of Ferrovius*].

ANDROCLES [*reaching out and catching the skirt of Ferrovius's tunic*] Dear brother: if you wouldnt mind – just for my sake –

FERROVIUS. Well?

ANDROCLES. Dont call him by the names of the animals. Weve no right to. Ive had such friends in dogs. A pet snake is the best of company. I was nursed on goat's milk. Is it fair to them to call the like of him a dog or a snake or a goat?

𐑓𐑧𐑮𐑴𐑝𐑾𐑕. 𐑲 𐑴𐑯𐑤𐑦 𐑥𐑧𐑯𐑑 𐑞𐑨𐑑 𐑞𐑱 𐑣𐑨𐑝 𐑯𐑴 𐑕𐑴𐑤𐑟.

𐑨𐑯𐑛𐑮𐑩𐑒𐑤𐑰𐑟 [*𐑨𐑙𐑒𐑖𐑩𐑕𐑤𐑦 𐑐𐑮𐑩𐑑𐑧𐑕𐑑𐑦𐑙*] 𐑴, 𐑚𐑦𐑤𐑰𐑝 𐑥𐑰, 𐑞𐑱 𐑣𐑨𐑝. 𐑡𐑳𐑕𐑑 𐑞 𐑕𐑱𐑥 𐑨𐑟 𐑿 𐑯 𐑥𐑰. 𐑲 𐑮𐑾𐑤𐑦 𐑛𐑴𐑯𐑑 𐑔𐑦𐑙𐑒 𐑲 𐑒𐑫𐑛 𐑒𐑩𐑯𐑕𐑧𐑯𐑑 𐑑 𐑜𐑴 𐑑 𐑣𐑧𐑝𐑩𐑯 𐑦𐑓 𐑲 𐑔𐑷𐑑 𐑞𐑺 𐑢𐑻 𐑑 𐑚𐑰 𐑯𐑴 𐑨𐑯𐑦𐑥𐑩𐑤𐑟 𐑞𐑺. 𐑔𐑦𐑙𐑒 𐑝 𐑢𐑪𐑑 𐑞𐑱 𐑕𐑳𐑓𐑼 𐑣𐑽.

𐑓𐑧𐑮𐑴𐑝𐑾𐑕. 𐑞𐑨𐑑𐑕 𐑑𐑮𐑵. 𐑘𐑧𐑕: 𐑞𐑨𐑑 𐑦𐑟 𐑡𐑳𐑕𐑑. 𐑞𐑱 𐑢𐑦𐑤 𐑣𐑨𐑝 𐑞𐑺 𐑖𐑺 𐑦𐑯 𐑣𐑧𐑝𐑩𐑯.

𐑕𐑐𐑦𐑯𐑔𐑴 [*𐑣𐑵 𐑣𐑨𐑟 𐑐𐑦𐑒𐑑 𐑣𐑦𐑥𐑕𐑧𐑤𐑓 𐑳𐑐 𐑯 𐑦𐑟 𐑕𐑯𐑰𐑒𐑦𐑙 𐑐𐑭𐑕𐑑 ·𐑓𐑧𐑮𐑴𐑝𐑾𐑕 𐑪𐑯 𐑣𐑦𐑟 𐑤𐑧𐑓𐑑, 𐑕𐑳𐑤𐑒𐑦 𐑛𐑦𐑓𐑲𐑩𐑯𐑑𐑤𐑦*].

𐑓𐑧𐑮𐑴𐑝𐑾𐑕 [*𐑑𐑻𐑯𐑦𐑙 𐑪𐑯 𐑣𐑦𐑥 𐑓𐑽𐑕𐑤𐑦*] 𐑢𐑪𐑑𐑕 𐑞𐑨𐑑 𐑿 𐑕𐑱?

𐑕𐑐𐑦𐑯𐑔𐑴 [*𐑒𐑬𐑼𐑦𐑙*] 𐑯𐑳𐑔𐑦𐑙.

𐑓𐑧𐑮𐑴𐑝𐑾𐑕 [*𐑒𐑤𐑧𐑯𐑗𐑦𐑙 𐑣𐑦𐑟 𐑓𐑦𐑕𐑑*] 𐑛𐑵 𐑨𐑯𐑦𐑥𐑩𐑤𐑟 𐑜𐑴 𐑑 𐑣𐑧𐑝𐑩𐑯 𐑹 𐑯𐑪𐑑?

𐑕𐑐𐑦𐑯𐑔𐑴. 𐑲 𐑯𐑧𐑝𐑼 𐑕𐑧𐑛 𐑞𐑱 𐑛𐑦𐑛𐑩𐑯𐑑.

𐑓𐑧𐑮𐑴𐑝𐑾𐑕 [*𐑦𐑥𐑐𐑤𐑨𐑒𐑩𐑚𐑤𐑦*] 𐑛𐑵 𐑞𐑱 𐑹 𐑛𐑵 𐑞𐑱 𐑯𐑪𐑑?

𐑕𐑐𐑦𐑯𐑔𐑴. 𐑞𐑱 𐑛𐑵: 𐑞𐑱 𐑛𐑵. [*𐑕𐑒𐑮𐑨𐑥𐑚𐑤𐑦𐑙 𐑬𐑑 𐑝 ·𐑓𐑧𐑮𐑴𐑝𐑾𐑕𐑦𐑟 𐑮𐑰𐑗*]. 𐑴, 𐑒𐑻𐑕 𐑿 𐑓𐑹 𐑓𐑮𐑲𐑑𐑩𐑯𐑦𐑙 𐑥𐑰!

[*𐑩 𐑚𐑿𐑜𐑩𐑤 𐑒𐑷𐑤 𐑦𐑟 𐑣𐑻𐑛*].

𐑕𐑧𐑯𐑑𐑘𐑫𐑼𐑾𐑯 [*𐑢𐑱𐑒𐑦𐑙 𐑳𐑐*] '𐑑𐑧𐑯𐑖𐑩𐑯! 𐑓𐑹𐑥 𐑩𐑟 𐑚𐑦𐑓𐑹. 𐑯𐑬 𐑞𐑧𐑯, 𐑐𐑮𐑦𐑟𐑩𐑯𐑼𐑟: 𐑳𐑐 𐑢𐑦𐑞 𐑿 𐑯 𐑑𐑮𐑪𐑑 𐑩𐑤𐑪𐑙 𐑕𐑐𐑮𐑲. [*𐑞 𐑕𐑴𐑤𐑡𐑼𐑟 𐑓𐑷𐑤 𐑦𐑯. 𐑞 𐑒𐑮𐑦𐑕𐑗𐑩𐑯𐑟 𐑮𐑲𐑟. 𐑩 𐑥𐑨𐑯 𐑢𐑦𐑞 𐑩𐑯 𐑪𐑒𐑕 𐑜𐑴𐑛 𐑒𐑳𐑥𐑟 𐑮𐑳𐑯𐑦𐑙 𐑔𐑮𐑵 𐑞 𐑕𐑧𐑯𐑑𐑮𐑩𐑤 𐑸𐑗*].

𐑞 𐑪𐑒𐑕 𐑛𐑮𐑲𐑝𐑼. 𐑣𐑽, 𐑿 𐑕𐑴𐑤𐑡𐑼𐑟! 𐑒𐑤𐑽 𐑬𐑑 𐑝 𐑞 𐑢𐑱 𐑓𐑹 𐑞 𐑥𐑩𐑯𐑨𐑡𐑼𐑦.

𐑕𐑧𐑯𐑑𐑘𐑫𐑼𐑾𐑯. 𐑥𐑩𐑯𐑨𐑡𐑼𐑦! 𐑢𐑪𐑑𐑕 𐑞 𐑥𐑩𐑯𐑨𐑡𐑼𐑦? 𐑿 𐑢𐑪𐑯𐑑 𐑞 𐑥𐑩𐑯𐑨𐑡𐑼𐑦, 𐑛𐑵 𐑿?

𐑞 𐑪𐑒𐑕 𐑛𐑮𐑲𐑝𐑼. 𐑦𐑑𐑕 𐑞 𐑥𐑩𐑯𐑨𐑡𐑼𐑦 𐑕𐑻𐑝𐑦𐑕. 𐑥𐑲

FERROVIUS. I only meant that they have no souls.

ANDROCLES [*anxiously protesting*] Oh, believe me, they have. Just the same as you and me. I really dont think I could consent to go to heaven if I thought there were to be no animals there. Think of what they suffer here.

FERROVIUS. Thats true. Yes: that is just. They will have their share in heaven.

SPINTHO [*who has picked himself up and is sneaking past Ferrovius on his left, sneers derisively*]!!

FERROVIUS [*turning on him fiercely*] Whats that you say?

SPINTHO [*cowering*] Nothing.

FERROVIUS [*clenching his fist*] Do animals go to heaven or not?

SPINTHO. I never said they didnt.

FERROVIUS [*implacable*] Do they or do they not?

SPINTHO. They do: they do. [*Scrambling out of Ferrovius's reach*]. Oh, curse you for frightening me!

A bugle call is heard.

CENTURION [*waking up*] Tention! Form as before. Now then, prisoners: up with you and trot along spry. [*The soldiers fall in. The Christians rise*].

A man with an ox goad comes running through the central arch.

THE OX DRIVER. Here, you soldiers! clear out of the way for the Emperor.

CENTURION. Emperor! Where's the Emperor? You aint the Emperor, are you?

THE OX DRIVER. It's the menagerie service. My

𐑣𐑦𐑟 𐑝 𐑤𐑧𐑕𐑩𐑯 𐑦𐑟 𐑚𐑮𐑦𐑙𐑦𐑙 𐑞 𐑯𐑿 𐑤𐑲𐑩𐑯 𐑑 𐑞 𐑒𐑪𐑤𐑦𐑕𐑰𐑩𐑥. 𐑣𐑰 𐑴𐑐𐑩𐑯𐑟 𐑞 𐑛𐑹.

𐑕𐑧𐑯𐑑𐑘𐑫𐑼𐑾𐑯. 𐑩𐑑! 𐑢𐑪 𐑦𐑟 𐑞𐑦𐑕 𐑣𐑰 𐑦𐑟 𐑣𐑨𐑝𐑦𐑙 𐑣𐑽𐑕𐑑, 𐑩𐑯𐑛 𐑜𐑦𐑝 𐑞 𐑑𐑧𐑤 𐑩𐑑 𐑞 𐑜𐑱𐑑𐑟 𐑝 𐑣𐑰 𐑯 𐑣𐑦𐑟 𐑤𐑲𐑩𐑯! 𐑳𐑯𐑑 𐑤𐑲𐑩𐑯𐑟. 𐑩𐑯 𐑢𐑪 𐑡𐑳𐑕𐑑.

𐑞 𐑤𐑧𐑕 𐑚𐑩𐑤𐑴𐑛. 𐑞 𐑥𐑧𐑯𐑨𐑡𐑼𐑦 𐑒𐑰𐑐𐑼 𐑦𐑟 𐑞 𐑧𐑥𐑐𐑼𐑼'𐑟 𐑐𐑻𐑕𐑩𐑯𐑩𐑤 𐑕𐑻𐑝𐑩𐑯𐑑. 𐑣𐑰 𐑴𐑐𐑩𐑯𐑟 𐑦𐑑, 𐑲 𐑑𐑱𐑒 𐑣𐑦𐑥.

𐑕𐑧𐑯𐑑𐑘𐑫𐑼𐑾𐑯. 𐑣𐑰 𐑑𐑱𐑒𐑕 𐑦𐑑, 𐑚𐑳𐑑 𐑣𐑰? 𐑩𐑒, 𐑲'𐑒 𐑑𐑱𐑒 𐑣𐑦𐑥 𐑕𐑲𐑛𐑦𐑙. 𐑦𐑓 𐑞 𐑤𐑲𐑩𐑯 𐑦𐑟 𐑥𐑧𐑯𐑨𐑡𐑼𐑦 𐑕𐑻𐑝𐑦𐑕, 𐑞 𐑤𐑲𐑩𐑯'𐑟 𐑚𐑪𐑛𐑦 𐑦𐑟 𐑥𐑧𐑯𐑨𐑡𐑼𐑦 𐑕𐑻𐑝𐑦𐑕 𐑑𐑵. 𐑞𐑦𐑕 [𐑐𐑶𐑯𐑑𐑦𐑙 𐑑 𐑞 𐑒𐑮𐑦𐑕𐑗𐑩𐑯𐑟] 𐑦𐑟 𐑞 𐑤𐑲𐑩𐑯'𐑟 𐑚𐑪𐑛𐑦. 𐑕𐑴 𐑚𐑨𐑒 𐑩𐑯𐑛 𐑣𐑰 𐑑 𐑣𐑦𐑟 𐑚𐑧𐑤𐑩𐑝𐑦𐑛 𐑚𐑰𐑕𐑑𐑕 𐑒𐑱𐑡; 𐑯 𐑤𐑧𐑑 𐑣𐑦𐑟 𐑚𐑧𐑕𐑑. 𐑥𐑸𐑗. [𐑞 𐑕𐑴𐑤𐑡𐑼𐑟 𐑕𐑑𐑸𐑑]. 𐑒𐑩𐑥 𐑪𐑯, 𐑿 𐑒𐑮𐑦𐑕𐑗𐑩𐑯𐑟: 𐑕𐑑𐑧𐑐 𐑩𐑯 𐑞𐑺.

𐑤𐑩𐑝𐑦𐑯𐑾 [𐑥𐑸𐑗𐑦𐑙] 𐑒𐑳𐑥 𐑩𐑤𐑪𐑙, 𐑞 𐑛𐑳𐑕𐑑 𐑝 𐑞 𐑚𐑪𐑛𐑦. 𐑲 𐑢𐑪𐑯𐑑 𐑑 𐑞 𐑤𐑧𐑜𐑟 𐑯 𐑞 𐑨𐑯𐑛𐑮𐑩𐑒𐑤𐑰𐑟.

𐑩𐑯𐑳𐑞𐑼 𐑒𐑮𐑦𐑕𐑗𐑩𐑯 [𐑤𐑨𐑓𐑦𐑙] 𐑲 𐑢𐑪𐑯𐑑 𐑑 𐑞 𐑕𐑳𐑯.

𐑩𐑯𐑳𐑞𐑼. 𐑲 𐑢𐑪𐑯𐑑 𐑑 𐑞 𐑡𐑨𐑒.

𐑩𐑯𐑳𐑞𐑼. ·𐑓𐑧𐑮𐑴𐑝𐑾𐑕 𐑢𐑪𐑯𐑑 𐑑 𐑞 𐑛𐑳𐑕𐑑 𐑚𐑨𐑒.

𐑓𐑧𐑮𐑴𐑝𐑾𐑕 [𐑜𐑮𐑦𐑥𐑤𐑦] 𐑲 𐑕𐑱 𐑞 𐑢𐑻𐑛. 𐑚𐑧𐑒, 𐑚𐑧𐑒: 𐑲 𐑢𐑪𐑯𐑑 𐑑 𐑞 𐑛𐑳𐑕𐑑 𐑚𐑨𐑒. 𐑜𐑴! 𐑜𐑴! [𐑜𐑴 𐑤𐑨𐑒𐑕 𐑒𐑮𐑦𐑕𐑗𐑩𐑯𐑟𐑦𐑑𐑦 𐑯 𐑥𐑸𐑗𐑼𐑟 𐑩𐑯 𐑞𐑺 𐑢𐑱].

𐑨𐑯𐑛𐑮𐑩𐑒𐑤𐑰𐑟 [𐑓𐑪𐑤𐑴𐑦𐑙] 𐑲 𐑢𐑪𐑯𐑑 𐑑 𐑞 𐑥𐑦𐑛𐑩𐑤 𐑛𐑲.
[𐑣𐑰 𐑥𐑸𐑗𐑩𐑟 𐑦𐑟 𐑛𐑦𐑕𐑒𐑳𐑕 𐑢𐑦𐑞 𐑩 𐑤𐑧𐑜𐑟 𐑤𐑧𐑝 𐑑𐑵 𐑞 𐑛𐑳𐑕𐑑 𐑩𐑟 𐑞 𐑚𐑪𐑛 𐑒𐑲𐑤𐑟 𐑦𐑑].

𐑕𐑧𐑯𐑑𐑘𐑫𐑼𐑾𐑯 [𐑕𐑒𐑨𐑯𐑛𐑩𐑤𐑲𐑟𐑛] 𐑕𐑑𐑪𐑐! 𐑜𐑩𐑛 𐑕𐑱𐑝 𐑕𐑩𐑥 𐑝 𐑣𐑦𐑟 𐑕𐑑𐑦𐑒𐑩𐑤. 𐑦𐑟 𐑞𐑦𐑕 𐑞 𐑢𐑱 𐑑𐑵 𐑥𐑸𐑗𐑦𐑙 𐑑 𐑚𐑨𐑑𐑩𐑤? [𐑑 ·𐑕𐑐𐑦𐑯𐑔𐑴, 𐑣𐑵 𐑦𐑟 𐑒𐑮𐑲𐑦𐑙 𐑯 𐑒𐑮𐑦𐑙𐑦𐑙] 𐑲 𐑢𐑦𐑖 𐑩𐑯 𐑣𐑰'𐑒 𐑑𐑵 𐑩𐑯 𐑞𐑩𐑯

team of oxen is drawing the new lion to the Coliseum. You clear the road.

CENTURION. What! Go in after you in your dust, with half the town at the heels of you and your lion! Not likely. We go first.

THE OX DRIVER. The menagerie service is the Emperor's personal retinue. You clear out, I tell you.

CENTURION. You tell me, do you? Well, I'll tell you something. If the lion is menagerie service, the lion's dinner is menagerie service too. This [*pointing to the Christians*] is the lion's dinner. So back with you to your bullocks double quick; and learn your place. March. [*The soldiers start*]. Now then, you Christians: step out there.

LAVINIA [*marching*] Come along, the rest of the dinner. I shall be the olives and anchovies.

ANOTHER CHRISTIAN [*laughing*] I shall be the soup.

ANOTHER. I shall be the fish.

ANOTHER. Ferrovius shall be the roast boar.

FERROVIUS [*heavily*] I see the joke. Yes, yes: I shall be the roast boar. Ha! ha! [*He laughs conscientiously and marches out with them*].

ANDROCLES [*following*] I shall be the mince pie. [*Each announcement is received with a louder laugh by all the rest as the joke catches on*].

CENTURION [*scandalized*] Silence! Have some sense of your situation. Is this the way for martyrs to behave? [*To Spintho, who is quaking and loitering*] I know what youll be at that

𐑛𐑦𐑯𐑼. 𐑿'𐑤 𐑚𐑰 𐑞 𐑝𐑪𐑥𐑦𐑑. [𐑣𐑰 𐑒𐑮𐑲𐑟 𐑣𐑦𐑟 𐑮𐑳𐑛𐑤𐑦 𐑩𐑤𐑪𐑙].

𐑕𐑐𐑦𐑯𐑔𐑴. 𐑦𐑑'𐑕 𐑑𐑵 𐑛𐑮𐑧𐑛𐑓𐑩𐑤: 𐑲'𐑥 𐑯𐑪𐑑 𐑓𐑦𐑑 𐑑 𐑛𐑲.

𐑕𐑧𐑯𐑑𐑿𐑼𐑦𐑩𐑯. 𐑓𐑦𐑑𐑼 𐑞𐑨𐑯 𐑿 𐑸 𐑑 𐑤𐑦𐑝, 𐑿 𐑕𐑢𐑲𐑯.

[𐑞𐑱 𐑛𐑮𐑧𐑕 𐑓𐑮𐑪𐑥 𐑞 𐑕𐑒𐑮𐑰𐑯 𐑮𐑕𐑑𐑮𐑼𐑤. 𐑞 𐑮𐑒𐑕𐑯, 𐑛𐑮𐑦𐑝 𐑩 𐑢𐑛𐑩𐑯 𐑢𐑦𐑞 𐑩 𐑚𐑮𐑤𐑑 𐑢𐑝𐑛𐑯 𐑒𐑱𐑡 𐑦 𐑞 𐑤𐑲𐑩𐑯 𐑦𐑯 𐑦𐑑, 𐑮𐑪𐑲𐑩 𐑚𐑲𐑯 𐑞 𐑕𐑧𐑯𐑑𐑮𐑤 𐑮𐑪𐑤].

dinner. Youll be the emetic. [*He shoves him rudely along*].

SPINTHO. It's too dreadful: I'm not fit to die.

CENTURION. Fitter than you are to live, you swine.

They pass from the square westward. The oxen, drawing a waggon with a great wooden cage and the lion in it, arrive through the central arch.

𐑨𐑒𐑑 II

[𐑚𐑦𐑣𐑲𐑯𐑛 𐑞 𐑧𐑥𐑐𐑼𐑼'𐑟 𐑚𐑪𐑒𐑕 𐑨𐑑 𐑞 𐑒𐑪𐑤𐑦𐑕𐑰𐑩𐑥, 𐑢𐑺 𐑞 𐑐𐑼𐑓𐑹𐑥𐑼𐑟 𐑩𐑕𐑧𐑥𐑚𐑩𐑤 𐑚𐑦𐑓𐑹 𐑧𐑯𐑑𐑼𐑦𐑙 𐑞 𐑼𐑰𐑯𐑩. 𐑦𐑯 𐑞 𐑥𐑦𐑛𐑩𐑤 𐑩 𐑢𐑲𐑛 𐑐𐑨𐑕𐑦𐑡 𐑤𐑰𐑛𐑦𐑙 𐑑 𐑞 𐑼𐑰𐑯𐑩 𐑛𐑦𐑕𐑧𐑯𐑛𐑟 𐑓𐑮𐑪𐑥 𐑞 𐑓𐑤𐑹 𐑤𐑧𐑝𐑩𐑤 𐑳𐑯𐑛𐑼 𐑞 𐑦𐑥𐑐𐑽𐑾𐑤 𐑚𐑪𐑒𐑕. 𐑪𐑯 𐑚𐑴𐑔 𐑕𐑲𐑛𐑟 𐑝 𐑞𐑦𐑕 𐑐𐑨𐑕𐑦𐑡 𐑕𐑑𐑧𐑐𐑕 𐑩𐑕𐑧𐑯𐑛 𐑑 𐑩 𐑤𐑨𐑯𐑛𐑦𐑙 𐑨𐑑 𐑞 𐑚𐑨𐑒 𐑧𐑯𐑑𐑮𐑩𐑯𐑕 𐑑 𐑞 𐑚𐑪𐑒𐑕. 𐑞 𐑤𐑨𐑯𐑛𐑦𐑙 𐑓𐑹𐑥𐑟 𐑩 𐑚𐑮𐑦𐑡 𐑩𐑒𐑮𐑪𐑕 𐑞 𐑐𐑨𐑕𐑦𐑡. 𐑨𐑑 𐑞 𐑧𐑯𐑑𐑮𐑩𐑯𐑕 𐑑 𐑞 𐑐𐑨𐑕𐑦𐑡 𐑸 𐑑𐑵 𐑚𐑮𐑪𐑯𐑟 𐑥𐑦𐑮𐑼𐑟, 𐑢𐑳𐑯 𐑪𐑯 𐑰𐑗 𐑕𐑲𐑛.

𐑪𐑯 𐑞 𐑢𐑧𐑕𐑑 𐑕𐑲𐑛 𐑝 𐑞𐑦𐑕 𐑐𐑨𐑕𐑦𐑡, 𐑪𐑯 𐑞 𐑮𐑲𐑑 𐑣𐑨𐑯𐑛 𐑝 𐑧𐑯𐑦𐑢𐑳𐑯 𐑒𐑳𐑥𐑦𐑙 𐑓𐑮𐑪𐑥 𐑞 𐑚𐑪𐑒𐑕 𐑯 𐑕𐑑𐑨𐑯𐑛𐑦𐑙 𐑪𐑯 𐑞 𐑚𐑮𐑦𐑡, 𐑞 𐑥𐑸𐑑𐑼𐑟 𐑸 𐑕𐑦𐑑𐑦𐑙 𐑪𐑯 𐑞 𐑕𐑑𐑧𐑐𐑕. ·𐑤𐑩𐑝𐑦𐑯𐑾 𐑦𐑟 𐑕𐑰𐑑𐑩𐑛 𐑣𐑭𐑓-𐑢𐑱 𐑳𐑐, 𐑔𐑷𐑑𐑓𐑩𐑤, 𐑑𐑮𐑲𐑦𐑙 𐑑 𐑤𐑫𐑒 𐑛𐑧𐑔 𐑦𐑯 𐑞 𐑓𐑱𐑕. 𐑪𐑯 𐑣𐑻 𐑤𐑧𐑓𐑑 ·𐑨𐑯𐑛𐑮𐑩𐑒𐑤𐑰𐑟 𐑒𐑩𐑯𐑕𐑴𐑤𐑟 𐑣𐑦𐑥𐑕𐑧𐑤𐑓 𐑚𐑲 𐑯𐑻𐑕𐑦𐑙 𐑩 𐑒𐑨𐑑. ·𐑓𐑧𐑮𐑴𐑝𐑾𐑕 𐑕𐑑𐑨𐑯𐑛𐑟 𐑚𐑦𐑣𐑲𐑯𐑛 𐑞𐑧𐑥, 𐑣𐑦𐑟 𐑲𐑟 𐑚𐑤𐑱𐑟𐑦𐑙, 𐑣𐑦𐑟 𐑓𐑦𐑜𐑼 𐑕𐑑𐑦𐑓 𐑢𐑦𐑞 𐑦𐑯𐑑𐑧𐑯𐑕 𐑮𐑧𐑟𐑩𐑤𐑵𐑖𐑩𐑯. 𐑨𐑑 𐑞 𐑓𐑫𐑑 𐑝 𐑞 𐑕𐑑𐑧𐑐𐑕 𐑒𐑮𐑬𐑗𐑩𐑟 ·𐑕𐑐𐑦𐑯𐑔𐑴, 𐑢𐑦𐑞 𐑣𐑦𐑟 𐑣𐑧𐑛 𐑒𐑤𐑳𐑗𐑑 𐑦𐑯 𐑣𐑦𐑟 𐑣𐑨𐑯𐑛𐑟, 𐑓𐑫𐑤 𐑝 𐑣𐑪𐑮𐑼 𐑨𐑑 𐑞 𐑩𐑐𐑮𐑴𐑗 𐑝 𐑥𐑸𐑑𐑼𐑛𐑩𐑥.

𐑪𐑯 𐑞 𐑰𐑕𐑑 𐑕𐑲𐑛 𐑝 𐑞 𐑐𐑨𐑕𐑦𐑡 𐑞 𐑜𐑤𐑨𐑛𐑦𐑱𐑑𐑼𐑟 𐑸 𐑕𐑑𐑨𐑯𐑛𐑦𐑙 𐑯 𐑕𐑦𐑑𐑦𐑙 𐑨𐑑 𐑰𐑟, 𐑢𐑱𐑑𐑦𐑙, 𐑤𐑲𐑒 𐑞 𐑒𐑮𐑦𐑕𐑑-𐑾𐑯𐑟, 𐑓𐑹 𐑞𐑺 𐑑𐑻𐑯 𐑦𐑯 𐑞 𐑼𐑰𐑯𐑩. 𐑢𐑳𐑯 (·𐑮𐑧𐑑𐑦𐑸𐑦𐑩𐑕) 𐑦𐑟 𐑩 𐑯𐑽𐑤𐑦 𐑯𐑱𐑒𐑦𐑛 𐑥𐑨𐑯 𐑢𐑦𐑞 𐑩 𐑯𐑧𐑑 𐑯 𐑩 𐑑𐑮𐑲𐑛𐑩𐑯𐑑. 𐑩𐑯𐑳𐑞𐑼 (·𐑕𐑧𐑒𐑿𐑑𐑹) 𐑦𐑟 𐑦𐑯 𐑸𐑥𐑼 𐑢𐑦𐑞 𐑩 𐑕𐑹𐑛. 𐑣𐑰 𐑒𐑨𐑮𐑦𐑟 𐑩 𐑣𐑧𐑤𐑥𐑦𐑑 𐑢𐑦𐑞 𐑩 𐑚𐑸𐑛 𐑝𐑲𐑟𐑼. 𐑞 ·𐑧𐑛𐑦𐑑𐑼 𐑝 𐑞 𐑜𐑤𐑨𐑛𐑦𐑱𐑑𐑼𐑟 𐑕𐑦𐑑𐑕 𐑪𐑯 𐑩 𐑗𐑺 𐑩 𐑤𐑦𐑑𐑩𐑤 𐑩𐑐𐑸𐑑 𐑓𐑮𐑪𐑥 𐑞𐑧𐑥.

𐑞 ·𐑒𐑷𐑤 ·𐑚𐑶 𐑧𐑯𐑑𐑼𐑟 𐑓𐑮𐑪𐑥 𐑞 𐑐𐑨𐑕𐑦𐑡].

𐑞 𐑒𐑷𐑤 𐑚𐑶. 𐑯𐑳𐑥𐑚𐑼 𐑕𐑦𐑒𐑕. ·𐑮𐑧𐑑𐑦𐑸𐑦𐑩𐑕 𐑝𐑻𐑕𐑩𐑕 𐑞 ·𐑕𐑧𐑒𐑿𐑑𐑹.

[𐑞 𐑜𐑤𐑨𐑛𐑦𐑱𐑑𐑼 𐑢𐑦𐑞 𐑞 𐑯𐑧𐑑 𐑐𐑦𐑒𐑕 𐑦𐑑 𐑳𐑐. 𐑞

ACT II

Behind the Emperor's box at the Coliseum, where the performers assemble before entering the arena. In the middle a wide passage leading to the arena descends from the floor level under the imperial box. On both sides of this passage steps ascend to a landing at the back entrance to the box. The landing forms a bridge across the passage. At the entrance to the passage are two bronze mirrors, one on each side.

On the west side of this passage, on the right hand of anyone coming from the box and standing on the bridge, the martyrs are sitting on the steps. Lavinia is seated half-way up, thoughtful, trying to look death in the face. On her left Androcles consoles himself by nursing a cat. Ferrovius stands behind them, his eyes blazing, his figure stiff with intense resolution. At the foot of the steps crouches Spintho, with his head clutched in his hands, full of horror at the approach of martyrdom.

On the east side of the passage the gladiators are standing and sitting at ease, waiting, like the Christians, for their turn in the arena. One (Retiarius) is a nearly naked man with a net and a trident. Another (Secutor) is in armor with a sword. He carries a helmet with a barred visor. The editor of the gladiators sits on a chair a little apart from them.

The Call Boy enters from the passage.

THE CALL BOY. Number six. Retiarius versus Secutor.

The gladiator with the net picks it up. The

𐑜𐑤𐑨𐑛𐑦𐑱𐑑𐑼 𐑢𐑦𐑞 𐑞 𐑣𐑧𐑤𐑥𐑩𐑑 𐑐𐑫𐑑𐑕 𐑦𐑑 𐑪𐑯; 𐑯 𐑞 𐑑𐑵 𐑜𐑴 𐑦𐑯𐑑𐑵 𐑞 𐑩𐑮𐑰𐑯𐑩, 𐑞 𐑯𐑧𐑑-𐑔𐑮𐑴𐑼 𐑑𐑱𐑒𐑦𐑙 𐑬𐑑 𐑩 𐑤𐑦𐑑𐑩𐑤 𐑚𐑮𐑳𐑖 𐑯 𐑩𐑮𐑱𐑯𐑡𐑦𐑙 𐑣𐑦𐑟 𐑣𐑺 𐑨𐑟 𐑣𐑰 𐑜𐑴𐑟, 𐑞 𐑳𐑞𐑼 𐑑𐑲𐑑𐑩𐑯𐑦𐑙 𐑣𐑦𐑟 𐑕𐑑𐑮𐑨𐑐𐑕 𐑯 𐑖𐑱𐑒𐑦𐑙 𐑣𐑦𐑟 𐑖𐑴𐑤𐑛𐑼𐑟 𐑤𐑵𐑕. 𐑚𐑴𐑔 𐑤𐑫𐑒 𐑨𐑑 𐑞𐑧𐑥𐑕𐑧𐑤𐑝𐑟 𐑦𐑯 𐑞 𐑥𐑦𐑮𐑼𐑟 𐑚𐑦𐑓𐑹 𐑞𐑱 𐑧𐑯𐑑𐑼 𐑞 𐑐𐑨𐑕𐑦𐑡].

𐑤𐑩𐑝𐑦𐑯𐑾. 𐑢𐑦𐑤 𐑞𐑱 𐑮𐑽𐑤𐑦 𐑒𐑦𐑤 𐑢𐑳𐑯 𐑩𐑯𐑳𐑞𐑼?

𐑕𐑐𐑦𐑯𐑔𐑴. 𐑘𐑧𐑕, 𐑦𐑓 𐑞 𐑐𐑰𐑐𐑩𐑤 𐑑𐑻𐑯 𐑛𐑬𐑯 𐑞𐑺 𐑔𐑳𐑥𐑟.

𐑞 𐑧𐑛𐑦𐑑𐑼. 𐑿 𐑯𐑴 𐑯𐑳𐑔𐑦𐑙 𐑩𐑚𐑬𐑑 𐑦𐑑. 𐑞 𐑐𐑰𐑐𐑩𐑤 𐑦𐑯𐑛𐑰𐑛! 𐑛𐑵 𐑿 𐑕𐑩𐑐𐑴𐑟 𐑢𐑰 𐑢𐑫𐑛 𐑒𐑦𐑤 𐑩 𐑥𐑨𐑯 𐑢𐑻𐑔 𐑐𐑼𐑣𐑨𐑐𐑕 𐑓𐑦𐑓𐑑𐑦 𐑑𐑨𐑤𐑩𐑯𐑑𐑕 𐑑 𐑐𐑤𐑰𐑟 𐑞 𐑮𐑦𐑓𐑮𐑨𐑓? 𐑲 𐑖𐑫𐑛 𐑤𐑲𐑒 𐑑 𐑒𐑨𐑗 𐑧𐑯𐑦 𐑝 𐑥𐑲 𐑥𐑧𐑯 𐑨𐑑 𐑦𐑑.

𐑕𐑐𐑦𐑯𐑔𐑴. 𐑲 𐑔𐑷𐑑—

𐑞 𐑧𐑛𐑦𐑑𐑼 [𐑒𐑩𐑯𐑑𐑧𐑥𐑐𐑗𐑵𐑩𐑕𐑤𐑦] 𐑿 𐑔𐑷𐑑! 𐑣𐑵 𐑒𐑺𐑟 𐑢𐑪𐑑 𐑿 𐑔𐑦𐑙𐑒? 𐑿'𐑤 𐑚𐑰 𐑒𐑦𐑤𐑛 𐑷𐑤 𐑮𐑲𐑑 𐑦𐑯𐑳𐑓.

𐑕𐑐𐑦𐑯𐑔𐑴 [𐑜𐑮𐑴𐑯𐑟 𐑯 𐑩𐑜𐑧𐑯 𐑣𐑲𐑛𐑟 𐑣𐑦𐑟 𐑓𐑱𐑕].

𐑤𐑩𐑝𐑦𐑯𐑾. 𐑞𐑧𐑯 𐑦𐑟 𐑯𐑴𐑚𐑩𐑛𐑦 𐑧𐑝𐑼 𐑒𐑦𐑤𐑛 𐑦𐑒𐑕𐑧𐑐𐑑 𐑳𐑕 𐑐𐑫𐑼 𐑒𐑮𐑦𐑕𐑗𐑩𐑯𐑟?

𐑞 𐑧𐑛𐑦𐑑𐑼. 𐑦𐑓 𐑞 𐑝𐑧𐑕𐑑𐑩𐑤 𐑝𐑻𐑡𐑦𐑯𐑟 𐑑𐑻𐑯 𐑛𐑬𐑯 𐑞𐑺 𐑔𐑳𐑥𐑟, 𐑞𐑨𐑑'𐑕 𐑩𐑯𐑳𐑞𐑼 𐑥𐑨𐑑𐑼. 𐑞𐑱'𐑮 𐑤𐑱𐑛𐑦𐑟 𐑝 𐑮𐑨𐑙𐑒.

𐑤𐑩𐑝𐑦𐑯𐑾. 𐑛𐑳𐑟 𐑞 𐑧𐑥𐑐𐑼𐑼 𐑧𐑝𐑼 𐑦𐑯𐑑𐑼𐑓𐑽?

𐑞 𐑧𐑛𐑦𐑑𐑼. 𐑴, 𐑘𐑧𐑕: 𐑣𐑰 𐑑𐑻𐑯𐑟 𐑣𐑦𐑟 𐑔𐑳𐑥𐑟 𐑳𐑐 𐑓𐑭𐑕𐑑 𐑦𐑯𐑳𐑓 𐑦𐑓 𐑞 𐑝𐑧𐑕𐑑𐑩𐑤 𐑝𐑻𐑡𐑦𐑯𐑟 𐑢𐑪𐑯𐑑 𐑑 𐑣𐑨𐑝 𐑢𐑳𐑯 𐑝 𐑣𐑦𐑟 𐑐𐑧𐑑 𐑓𐑲𐑑𐑼𐑟 𐑒𐑦𐑤𐑛.

𐑨𐑯𐑛𐑮𐑩𐑒𐑤𐑰𐑟. 𐑚𐑳𐑑 𐑛𐑴𐑯𐑑 𐑞𐑱 𐑧𐑝𐑼 𐑡𐑳𐑕𐑑 𐑴𐑯𐑤𐑦 𐑐𐑮𐑦𐑑𐑧𐑯𐑛 𐑑 𐑒𐑦𐑤 𐑢𐑳𐑯 𐑩𐑯𐑳𐑞𐑼? 𐑢𐑲 𐑖𐑫𐑛𐑩𐑯𐑑 𐑿 𐑐𐑮𐑦𐑑𐑧𐑯𐑛 𐑑 𐑛𐑲, 𐑯 𐑜𐑧𐑑 𐑛𐑮𐑨𐑜𐑛 𐑬𐑑 𐑨𐑟 𐑦𐑓 𐑿 𐑢𐑻

gladiator with the helmet puts it on; and the two go into the arena, the net thrower taking out a little brush and arranging his hair as he goes, the other tightening his straps and shaking his shoulders loose. Both look at themselves in the mirrors before they enter the passage.

LAVINIA. Will they really kill one another?

SPINTHO. Yes, if the people turn down their thumbs.

THE EDITOR. You know nothing about it. The people indeed! Do you suppose we would kill a man worth perhaps fifty talents to please the riffraff? I should like to catch any of my men at it.

SPINTHO. I thought –

THE EDITOR [*contemptuously*] You thought! Who cares what you think? Youll be killed all right enough.

SPINTHO [*groans and again hides his face*]!!!

LAVINIA. Then is nobody ever killed except us poor Christians?

THE EDITOR. If the vestal virgins turn down their thumbs, thats another matter. Theyre ladies of rank.

LAVINIA. Does the Emperor ever interfere?

THE EDITOR. Oh, yes: he turns his thumb up fast enough if the vestal virgins want to have one of his pet fighting men killed.

ANDROCLES. But dont they ever just only pretend to kill one another? Why shouldnt you pretend to die, and get dragged out as if you were

𐑛𐑧𐑛; 𐑯 𐑞𐑧𐑯 𐑜𐑧𐑑 𐑳𐑐 𐑯 𐑜𐑴 𐑣𐑴𐑥 𐑤𐑲𐑒 𐑩𐑯 𐑨𐑒𐑑𐑼?

𐑞 ·𐑧𐑛𐑦𐑑𐑼. 𐑕𐑰 𐑣𐑽: 𐑿 𐑢𐑪𐑯𐑑 𐑑 𐑯𐑴 𐑑𐑵 𐑥𐑳𐑗. 𐑞𐑺 𐑢𐑦𐑤 𐑚𐑰 𐑯𐑴 𐑐𐑮𐑦𐑑𐑧𐑯𐑛𐑦𐑙 𐑩𐑚𐑬𐑑 𐑞 𐑯𐑿 𐑤𐑲𐑩𐑯: 𐑤𐑧𐑑 𐑞𐑨𐑑 𐑚𐑰 𐑦𐑯𐑳𐑓 𐑓 𐑿. 𐑣𐑰'𐑟 𐑣𐑳𐑙𐑜𐑮𐑦.

·𐑕𐑐𐑦𐑯𐑔𐑴 [*𐑜𐑮𐑴𐑯𐑦𐑙 𐑢𐑦𐑞 𐑣𐑪𐑮𐑼*] 𐑴, 𐑤𐑹𐑛! 𐑒𐑭𐑯𐑑 𐑿 𐑕𐑑𐑪𐑐 𐑑𐑷𐑒𐑦𐑙 𐑩𐑚𐑬𐑑 𐑦𐑑? 𐑦𐑟𐑯𐑑 𐑦𐑑 𐑚𐑨𐑛 𐑦𐑯𐑳𐑓 𐑓 𐑳𐑕 𐑢𐑦𐑞𐑬𐑑 𐑞𐑨𐑑?

·𐑨𐑯𐑛𐑮𐑩𐑒𐑤𐑰𐑟. 𐑲'𐑥 𐑜𐑤𐑨𐑛 𐑣𐑰'𐑟 𐑣𐑳𐑙𐑜𐑮𐑦. 𐑯𐑪𐑑 𐑞𐑨𐑑 𐑲 𐑢𐑪𐑯𐑑 𐑣𐑦𐑥 𐑑 𐑕𐑳𐑓𐑼, 𐑐𐑫𐑼 𐑗𐑨𐑐! 𐑚𐑳𐑑 𐑞𐑧𐑯 𐑣𐑰'𐑤 𐑦𐑯𐑡𐑶 𐑰𐑑𐑦𐑙 𐑥𐑰 𐑕𐑴 𐑥𐑳𐑗 𐑥𐑹. 𐑞𐑺'𐑟 𐑩 𐑗𐑽𐑓𐑫𐑤 𐑕𐑲𐑛 𐑑 𐑧𐑝𐑮𐑦𐑔𐑦𐑙.

𐑞 ·𐑧𐑛𐑦𐑑𐑼 [*𐑮𐑲𐑟𐑦𐑙 𐑯 𐑕𐑑𐑮𐑲𐑛𐑦𐑙 𐑴𐑝𐑼 𐑑 ·𐑨𐑯𐑛𐑮𐑩𐑒𐑤𐑰𐑟*] 𐑣𐑽: 𐑛𐑴𐑯𐑑 𐑿 𐑚𐑰 𐑪𐑚𐑕𐑑𐑦𐑯𐑩𐑑. 𐑒𐑳𐑥 𐑢𐑦𐑞 𐑥𐑰 𐑯 𐑛𐑮𐑪𐑐 𐑞 𐑐𐑦𐑯𐑗 𐑝 𐑦𐑯𐑕𐑧𐑯𐑕 𐑪𐑯 𐑞 𐑷𐑤𐑑𐑼. 𐑞𐑨𐑑'𐑕 𐑷𐑤 𐑿 𐑯𐑰𐑛 𐑛𐑵 𐑑 𐑚𐑰 𐑤𐑧𐑑 𐑪𐑓.

·𐑨𐑯𐑛𐑮𐑩𐑒𐑤𐑰𐑟. 𐑯𐑴: 𐑔𐑨𐑙𐑒 𐑿 𐑝𐑧𐑮𐑦 𐑥𐑳𐑗 𐑦𐑯𐑛𐑰𐑛; 𐑚𐑳𐑑 𐑲 𐑮𐑾𐑤𐑦 𐑥𐑳𐑕𐑩𐑯𐑑.

𐑞 ·𐑧𐑛𐑦𐑑𐑼. 𐑢𐑪𐑑! 𐑯𐑪𐑑 𐑑 𐑕𐑱𐑝 𐑿𐑼 𐑤𐑲𐑓?

·𐑨𐑯𐑛𐑮𐑩𐑒𐑤𐑰𐑟. 𐑲'𐑛 𐑮𐑭𐑞𐑼 𐑯𐑪𐑑. 𐑲 𐑒𐑫𐑛𐑩𐑯𐑑 𐑕𐑨𐑒𐑮𐑦𐑓𐑲𐑕 𐑑 ·𐑛𐑲𐑨𐑯𐑩: 𐑖𐑰'𐑟 𐑩 𐑣𐑳𐑯𐑑𐑮𐑩𐑕, 𐑿 𐑯𐑴, 𐑯 𐑒𐑦𐑤𐑟 𐑔𐑦𐑙𐑟.

𐑞 ·𐑧𐑛𐑦𐑑𐑼. 𐑞𐑨𐑑 𐑛𐑴𐑯𐑑 𐑥𐑨𐑑𐑼. 𐑿 𐑒𐑨𐑯 𐑗𐑵𐑟 𐑿𐑼 𐑴𐑯 𐑷𐑤𐑑𐑼. 𐑕𐑨𐑒𐑮𐑦𐑓𐑲𐑕 𐑑 ·𐑡𐑵𐑐𐑦𐑑𐑼: 𐑣𐑰 𐑤𐑲𐑒𐑕 𐑨𐑯𐑦𐑥𐑩𐑤𐑟: 𐑣𐑰 𐑑𐑻𐑯𐑟 𐑣𐑦𐑥𐑕𐑧𐑤𐑓 𐑦𐑯𐑑𐑵 𐑩𐑯 𐑨𐑯𐑦𐑥𐑩𐑤 𐑢𐑧𐑯 𐑣𐑰 𐑜𐑴𐑟 𐑪𐑓 𐑛𐑿𐑑𐑦.

·𐑨𐑯𐑛𐑮𐑩𐑒𐑤𐑰𐑟. 𐑯𐑴: 𐑦𐑑'𐑕 𐑝𐑧𐑮𐑦 𐑒𐑲𐑯𐑛 𐑝 𐑿; 𐑚𐑳𐑑 𐑲 𐑓𐑰𐑤 𐑲 𐑒𐑭𐑯𐑑 𐑕𐑱𐑝 𐑥𐑲𐑕𐑧𐑤𐑓 𐑞𐑨𐑑 𐑢𐑱.

𐑞 ·𐑧𐑛𐑦𐑑𐑼. 𐑚𐑳𐑑 𐑲 𐑛𐑴𐑯𐑑 𐑭𐑕𐑒 𐑿 𐑑 𐑛𐑵 𐑦𐑑 𐑑 𐑕𐑱𐑝 𐑿𐑼𐑕𐑧𐑤𐑓: 𐑲 𐑭𐑕𐑒 𐑿 𐑑 𐑛𐑵 𐑦𐑑 𐑑 𐑩𐑚𐑤𐑲𐑡 𐑥𐑰 𐑐𐑻𐑕𐑩𐑯𐑩𐑤𐑦.

dead; and then get up and go home, like an actor?

THE EDITOR. See here: you want to know too much. There will be no pretending about the new lion: let that be enough for you. He's hungry.

SPINTHO [*groaning with horror*] Oh, Lord! cant you stop talking about it? Isnt it bad enough for us without that?

ANDROCLES. I'm glad he's hungry. Not that I want him to suffer, poor chap! but then he'll enjoy eating me so much more. Theres a cheerful side to everything.

THE EDITOR [*rising and striding over to Androcles*] Here: dont you be obstinate. Come with me and drop the pinch of incense on the altar. Thats all you need do to be let off.

ANDROCLES. No: thank you very much indeed; but I really mustnt.

THE EDITOR. What! Not to save your life?

ANDROCLES. I'd rather not. I couldnt sacrifice to Diana: she's a huntress, you know, and kills things.

THE EDITOR. That dont matter. You can choose your own altar. Sacrifice to Jupiter: he likes animals: he turns himself into an animal when he goes off duty.

ANDROCLES. No: it's very kind of you; but I feel I cant save myself that way.

THE EDITOR. But I dont ask you to do it to save yourself: I ask you to do it to oblige me personally.

𐑨𐑯𐑛𐑮𐑩𐑒𐑤𐑰𐑟 [*𐑕𐑒𐑮𐑨𐑥𐑚𐑤𐑦𐑙 𐑳𐑐 𐑦𐑯 𐑞 𐑜𐑮𐑱𐑑𐑦𐑕𐑑 𐑨𐑡𐑦𐑑𐑱𐑖𐑩𐑯*] 𐑴, 𐑐𐑤𐑰𐑟 𐑛𐑴𐑯𐑑 𐑕𐑱 𐑞𐑨𐑑. 𐑞𐑦𐑕 𐑦𐑟 𐑛𐑮𐑧𐑛𐑓𐑤. 𐑿 𐑥𐑰𐑯 𐑕𐑴 𐑒𐑲𐑯𐑛𐑤𐑦 𐑚𐑲 𐑥𐑰 𐑞𐑨𐑑 𐑦𐑑 𐑕𐑰𐑥𐑟 𐑒𐑢𐑲𐑑 𐑣𐑪𐑮𐑦𐑚𐑩𐑤 𐑑 𐑛𐑦𐑕𐑩𐑚𐑤𐑲𐑡 𐑿. 𐑦𐑓 𐑿 𐑒𐑫𐑛 𐑩𐑮𐑱𐑯𐑡 𐑓𐑹 𐑥𐑰 𐑑 𐑕𐑨𐑒𐑮𐑦𐑓𐑲𐑕 𐑢𐑧𐑯 𐑞𐑺'𐑟 𐑯𐑴𐑚𐑪𐑛𐑦 𐑤𐑫𐑒𐑦𐑙, 𐑲 𐑖𐑫𐑛𐑯𐑑 𐑥𐑲𐑯𐑛. 𐑚𐑳𐑑 𐑲 𐑥𐑳𐑕𐑑 𐑜𐑴 𐑦𐑯𐑑𐑵 𐑞 𐑩𐑮𐑰𐑯𐑩 𐑢𐑦𐑞 𐑞 𐑮𐑧𐑕𐑑. 𐑥𐑲 𐑪𐑯𐑼, 𐑿 𐑯𐑴.

𐑞 𐑧𐑛𐑦𐑑𐑼. 𐑪𐑯𐑼! 𐑞 𐑪𐑯𐑼 𐑝 𐑩 𐑑𐑱𐑤𐑼?

𐑨𐑯𐑛𐑮𐑩𐑒𐑤𐑰𐑟 [*𐑩𐑐𐑪𐑤𐑩𐑡𐑧𐑑𐑦𐑒𐑤𐑦*] 𐑢𐑧𐑤, 𐑐𐑼𐑣𐑨𐑐𐑕 𐑪𐑯𐑼 𐑦𐑟 𐑑𐑵 𐑕𐑑𐑮𐑪𐑙 𐑩𐑯 𐑦𐑒𐑕𐑐𐑮𐑧𐑖𐑩𐑯. 𐑕𐑑𐑦𐑤, 𐑿 𐑯𐑴, 𐑲 𐑒𐑫𐑛𐑯𐑑 𐑩𐑤𐑬 𐑞 𐑑𐑱𐑤𐑼𐑟 𐑑 𐑜𐑧𐑑 𐑩 𐑚𐑨𐑛 𐑯𐑱𐑥 𐑔𐑮𐑵 𐑥𐑰.

𐑞 𐑧𐑛𐑦𐑑𐑼. 𐑣𐑬 𐑥𐑳𐑗 𐑢𐑦𐑤 𐑿 𐑮𐑦𐑥𐑧𐑥𐑚𐑼 𐑝 𐑷𐑤 𐑞𐑨𐑑 𐑢𐑧𐑯 𐑿 𐑕𐑥𐑧𐑤 𐑞 𐑚𐑰𐑕𐑑'𐑕 𐑚𐑮𐑧𐑔 𐑯 𐑕𐑰 𐑣𐑦𐑟 𐑡𐑷𐑟 𐑴𐑐𐑩𐑯𐑦𐑙 𐑑 𐑑𐑺 𐑬𐑑 𐑿𐑼 𐑔𐑮𐑴𐑑?

𐑕𐑐𐑦𐑯𐑔𐑴 [*𐑮𐑲𐑟𐑦𐑙 𐑢𐑦𐑞 𐑩 𐑘𐑧𐑤 𐑝 𐑑𐑧𐑮𐑼*] 𐑲 𐑒𐑭𐑯𐑑 𐑚𐑺 𐑦𐑑. 𐑢𐑺'𐑟 𐑞 𐑷𐑤𐑑𐑼? 𐑲'𐑤 𐑕𐑨𐑒𐑮𐑦𐑓𐑲𐑕.

𐑓𐑧𐑮𐑴𐑝𐑦𐑩𐑕. 𐑛𐑪𐑜 𐑝 𐑩𐑯 𐑩𐑐𐑪𐑕𐑑𐑱𐑑. ·𐑦𐑕𐑒𐑨𐑮𐑦𐑩𐑑!

𐑕𐑐𐑦𐑯𐑔𐑴. 𐑲'𐑤 𐑮𐑦𐑐𐑧𐑯𐑑 𐑭𐑓𐑑𐑼𐑢𐑼𐑛𐑟. 𐑲 𐑓𐑫𐑤𐑦 𐑥𐑰𐑯 𐑑 𐑛𐑲 𐑦𐑯 𐑞 𐑩𐑮𐑰𐑯𐑩: 𐑲'𐑤 𐑛𐑲 𐑩 𐑥𐑸𐑑𐑼 𐑯 𐑜𐑴 𐑑 𐑣𐑧𐑝𐑩𐑯; 𐑚𐑳𐑑 𐑯𐑪𐑑 𐑞𐑦𐑕 𐑑𐑲𐑥, 𐑯𐑪𐑑 𐑯𐑬, 𐑯𐑪𐑑 𐑳𐑯𐑑𐑦𐑤 𐑥𐑲 𐑣𐑧𐑤𐑔 𐑦𐑟 𐑚𐑧𐑑𐑼. 𐑚𐑦𐑕𐑲𐑛𐑟, 𐑲'𐑥 𐑑𐑵 𐑘𐑳𐑙: 𐑲 𐑢𐑪𐑯𐑑 𐑑 𐑣𐑨𐑝 𐑡𐑳𐑕𐑑 𐑢𐑳𐑯 𐑥𐑹 𐑜𐑫𐑛 𐑑𐑲𐑥. [*𐑞 𐑜𐑤𐑨𐑛𐑦𐑱𐑑𐑼𐑟 𐑤𐑭𐑓 𐑨𐑑 𐑣𐑦𐑥*]. 𐑴, 𐑢𐑦𐑤 𐑯𐑴𐑚𐑪𐑛𐑦 𐑑𐑧𐑤 𐑥𐑰 𐑢𐑺 𐑞 𐑷𐑤𐑑𐑼 𐑦𐑟? [*𐑣𐑰 𐑛𐑨𐑖𐑩𐑟 𐑦𐑯𐑑𐑵 𐑞 𐑐𐑨𐑕𐑦𐑡 𐑯 𐑝𐑨𐑯𐑦𐑖𐑩𐑟*].

𐑨𐑯𐑛𐑮𐑩𐑒𐑤𐑰𐑟 [*𐑑 𐑞 𐑧𐑛𐑦𐑑𐑼, 𐑐𐑶𐑯𐑑𐑦𐑙 𐑭𐑓𐑑𐑼 ·𐑕𐑐𐑦𐑯𐑔𐑴*] 𐑚𐑮𐑳𐑞𐑼: 𐑲 𐑒𐑭𐑯𐑑 𐑛𐑵 𐑞𐑨𐑑, 𐑯𐑪𐑑 𐑰𐑝𐑩𐑯 𐑑 𐑩𐑚𐑤𐑲𐑡 𐑿. 𐑛𐑴𐑯𐑑 𐑭𐑕𐑒 𐑥𐑰.

𐑞 𐑧𐑛𐑦𐑑𐑼. 𐑢𐑧𐑤, 𐑦𐑓 𐑿'𐑮 𐑛𐑦𐑑𐑻𐑥𐑦𐑯𐑛 𐑑 𐑛𐑲, 𐑲 𐑒𐑭𐑯𐑑 𐑣𐑧𐑤𐑐 𐑿. 𐑚𐑳𐑑 𐑲 𐑢𐑫𐑛𐑯𐑑 𐑚𐑰 𐑐𐑫𐑑 𐑳𐑐 𐑚𐑲 𐑩 𐑕𐑢𐑲𐑯 𐑤𐑲𐑒 𐑞𐑨𐑑.

ANDROCLES [*scrambling up in the greatest agitation*] Oh, please dont say that. This is dreadful. You mean so kindly by me that it seems quite horrible to disoblige you. If you could arrange for me to sacrifice when theres nobody looking, I shouldnt mind. But I must go into the arena with the rest. My honor, you know.

THE EDITOR. Honor! The honor of a tailor?

ANDROCLES [*apologetically*] Well, perhaps honor is too strong an expression. Still, you know, I couldnt allow the tailors to get a bad name through me.

THE EDITOR. How much will you remember of all that when you smell the beast's breath and see his jaws opening to tear out your throat?

SPINTHO [*rising with a yell of terror*] I cant bear it. Wheres the altar? I'll sacrifice.

FERROVIUS. Dog of an apostate. Iscariot!

SPINTHO. I'll repent afterwards. I fully mean to die in the arena: I'll die a martyr and go to heaven; but not this time, not now, not until my nerves are better. Besides, I'm too young: I want to have just one more good time. [*The gladiators laugh at him*]. Oh, will no one tell me where the altar is? [*He dashes into the passage and vanishes*].

ANDROCLES [*to the Editor, pointing after Spintho*] Brother: I cant do that, not even to oblige you. Dont ask me.

THE EDITOR. Well, if youre determined to die, I cant help you. But I wouldnt be put off by a swine like that.

𐑓𐑧𐑮𐑴𐑝𐑦𐑩𐑕. 𐑐𐑰𐑕, 𐑐𐑰𐑕: 𐑑𐑧𐑥𐑑 𐑣𐑦𐑥 𐑯𐑪𐑑. 𐑜𐑧𐑑 𐑞𐑰 𐑚𐑦𐑣𐑲𐑯𐑛 𐑣𐑦𐑥, ·𐑕𐑱𐑑𐑩𐑯.

𐑞 𐑧𐑛𐑦𐑑𐑼 [*𐑓𐑤𐑳𐑖𐑦𐑙 𐑢𐑦𐑞 𐑮𐑱𐑡*] 𐑓𐑹 𐑑𐑵 𐑐𐑦𐑯𐑟 𐑲'𐑛 𐑑𐑱𐑒 𐑩 𐑑𐑻𐑯 𐑦𐑯 𐑞 𐑼𐑰𐑯𐑩 𐑥𐑲𐑕𐑧𐑤𐑓 𐑑𐑩𐑛𐑱, 𐑯 𐑐𐑱 𐑿 𐑬𐑑 𐑓𐑹 𐑛𐑺𐑦𐑙 𐑑 𐑑𐑷𐑒 𐑑 𐑥𐑰 𐑤𐑲𐑒 𐑞𐑨𐑑.

[*·𐑓𐑧𐑮𐑴𐑝𐑦𐑩𐑕 𐑕𐑐𐑮𐑦𐑙𐑟 𐑓𐑹𐑢𐑼𐑛*].

𐑤𐑩𐑝𐑦𐑯𐑾 [*𐑮𐑲𐑟𐑦𐑙 𐑒𐑢𐑦𐑒𐑤𐑦 𐑯 𐑦𐑯𐑑𐑼𐑐𐑴𐑟𐑦𐑙*] 𐑚𐑮𐑳𐑞𐑼, 𐑚𐑮𐑳𐑞𐑼: 𐑿 𐑓𐑼𐑜𐑧𐑑.

𐑓𐑧𐑮𐑴𐑝𐑦𐑩𐑕 [*𐑒𐑻𐑚𐑦𐑙 𐑣𐑦𐑥𐑕𐑧𐑤𐑓 𐑚𐑲 𐑩 𐑥𐑲𐑑𐑦 𐑧𐑓𐑼𐑑*] 𐑴, 𐑥𐑲 𐑑𐑧𐑥𐑐𐑼, 𐑥𐑲 𐑢𐑦𐑒𐑦𐑛 𐑑𐑧𐑥𐑐𐑼! [*𐑑 𐑞 𐑧𐑛𐑦𐑑𐑼, 𐑨𐑟 ·𐑤𐑩𐑝𐑦𐑯𐑾 𐑕𐑦𐑑𐑕 𐑛𐑬𐑯 𐑩𐑜𐑱𐑯, 𐑮𐑰𐑩𐑖𐑫𐑼𐑛*] 𐑓𐑼𐑜𐑦𐑝 𐑥𐑰, 𐑚𐑮𐑳𐑞𐑼. 𐑥𐑲 𐑣𐑸𐑑 𐑦𐑟 𐑓𐑫𐑤 𐑝 𐑮𐑭𐑔: 𐑲 𐑖𐑫𐑛 𐑣𐑨𐑝 𐑚𐑰𐑯 𐑔𐑦𐑙𐑒𐑦𐑙 𐑝 𐑿𐑼 𐑛𐑽 𐑐𐑮𐑧𐑖𐑩𐑕 𐑕𐑴𐑤.

𐑞 𐑧𐑛𐑦𐑑𐑼. 𐑘𐑭! [*𐑣𐑰 𐑑𐑻𐑯𐑟 𐑣𐑦𐑟 𐑚𐑨𐑒 𐑪𐑯 ·𐑓𐑧𐑮𐑴𐑝𐑦𐑩𐑟 𐑒𐑩𐑯𐑑𐑧𐑥𐑐𐑗𐑵𐑩𐑕𐑤𐑦, 𐑯 𐑜𐑴𐑟 𐑚𐑨𐑒 𐑑 𐑣𐑦𐑟 𐑕𐑰𐑑*].

𐑓𐑧𐑮𐑴𐑝𐑦𐑩𐑕 [*𐑒𐑩𐑯𐑑𐑦𐑯𐑿𐑦𐑙*] 𐑯 𐑲 𐑓𐑼𐑜𐑪𐑑 𐑦𐑑 𐑷𐑤: 𐑲 𐑔𐑷𐑑 𐑝 𐑯𐑳𐑔𐑦𐑙 𐑚𐑳𐑑 𐑪𐑓𐑼𐑦𐑙 𐑑 𐑓𐑲𐑑 𐑿 𐑢𐑦𐑞 𐑢𐑳𐑯 𐑣𐑨𐑯𐑛 𐑑𐑲𐑛 𐑚𐑦𐑣𐑲𐑯𐑛 𐑥𐑰.

𐑞 𐑧𐑛𐑦𐑑𐑼 [*𐑑𐑻𐑯𐑦𐑙 𐑐𐑳𐑜𐑯𐑱𐑖𐑩𐑕𐑤𐑦*] 𐑢𐑪𐑑!

𐑓𐑧𐑮𐑴𐑝𐑦𐑩𐑕 [*𐑦𐑯 𐑞 𐑚𐑹𐑛𐑼 𐑤𐑲𐑯 𐑚𐑦𐑑𐑢𐑰𐑯 𐑟𐑰𐑤 𐑯 𐑓𐑼𐑪𐑕𐑦𐑑𐑦*] 𐑴, 𐑛𐑴𐑯𐑑 𐑜𐑦𐑝 𐑢𐑱 𐑑 𐑐𐑮𐑲𐑛 𐑯 𐑮𐑭𐑔, 𐑚𐑮𐑳𐑞𐑼. 𐑲 𐑒𐑫𐑛 𐑛𐑵 𐑦𐑑 𐑕𐑴 𐑰𐑟𐑦𐑤𐑦. 𐑲 𐑒𐑫𐑛 –

[*𐑞𐑱 𐑸 𐑕𐑧𐑐𐑼𐑱𐑑𐑩𐑛 𐑚𐑲 𐑞 𐑥𐑩𐑯𐑨𐑡𐑼𐑦 ·𐑒𐑰𐑐𐑼, 𐑣𐑵 𐑮𐑳𐑖𐑩𐑟 𐑦𐑯 𐑓𐑮𐑪𐑥 𐑞 𐑐𐑨𐑕𐑦𐑡, 𐑓𐑘𐑫𐑼𐑦𐑩𐑕*].

𐑞 𐑒𐑰𐑐𐑼. 𐑣𐑽'𐑟 𐑩 𐑯𐑲𐑕 𐑚𐑦𐑟𐑯𐑩𐑕! 𐑣𐑵 𐑤𐑧𐑑 𐑞𐑨𐑑 𐑒𐑮𐑦𐑕𐑗𐑩𐑯 𐑬𐑑 𐑝 𐑣𐑦𐑟 𐑐𐑧𐑯 𐑑 𐑞 𐑚𐑸𐑟 𐑢𐑧𐑯 𐑢𐑰 𐑢𐑻 𐑗𐑱𐑯𐑡𐑦𐑙 𐑞 𐑤𐑲𐑩𐑯 𐑦𐑯𐑑𐑫 𐑞 𐑒𐑱𐑡 𐑯𐑧𐑒𐑕𐑑 𐑞 𐑼𐑰𐑯𐑩?

𐑞 𐑧𐑛𐑦𐑑𐑼. 𐑯𐑴𐑚𐑩𐑛𐑦 𐑤𐑧𐑑 𐑣𐑦𐑥. 𐑣𐑰 𐑤𐑧𐑑 𐑣𐑦𐑥𐑕𐑧𐑤𐑓.

𐑞 𐑒𐑰𐑐𐑼. 𐑢𐑧𐑤, 𐑞 𐑤𐑲𐑩𐑯'𐑟 𐑧𐑑 𐑣𐑦𐑥.

[*𐑒𐑪𐑯𐑕𐑑𐑼𐑯𐑱𐑖𐑩𐑯. 𐑞 𐑒𐑮𐑦𐑕𐑗𐑩𐑯𐑟 𐑮𐑲𐑟, 𐑜𐑮𐑱𐑑𐑤𐑦 𐑨𐑡𐑦𐑑𐑱𐑑𐑦𐑛. 𐑞 𐑜𐑤𐑨𐑛𐑦𐑱𐑑𐑼𐑟 𐑕𐑦𐑑 𐑒𐑺𐑤𐑩𐑕𐑤𐑦, 𐑚𐑳𐑑 𐑸*

FERROVIUS. Peace, peace: tempt him not. Get thee behind him, Satan.

THE EDITOR [*flushing with rage*] For two pins I'd take a turn in the arena myself today, and pay you out for daring to talk to me like that.

Ferrovius springs forward.

LAVINIA [*rising quickly and interposing*] Brother, brother: you forget.

FERROVIUS [*curbing himself by a mighty effort*] Oh, my temper, my wicked temper! [*To the Editor, as Lavinia sits down again, reassured*] Forgive me, brother. My heart was full of wrath: I should have been thinking of your dear precious soul.

THE EDITOR. Yah! [*He turns his back on Ferrovius contemptuously, and goes back to his seat*].

FERROVIUS [*continuing*] And I forgot it all: I thought of nothing but offering to fight you with one hand tied behind me.

THE EDITOR [*turning pugnaciously*] What!

FERROVIUS [*on the border line between zeal and ferocity*] Oh, dont give way to pride and wrath, brother. I could do it so easily. I could –

They are separated by the Menagerie Keeper, who rushes in from the passage, furious.

THE KEEPER. Heres a nice business! Who let that Christian out of here down to the dens when we were changing the lion into the cage next the arena?

THE EDITOR. Nobody let him. He let himself.

THE KEEPER. Well, the lion's ate him.

Consternation. The Christians rise, greatly agitated. The gladiators sit callously, but are

𐑣𐑲𐑤𐑦 𐑮𐑧𐑕𐑐𐑧𐑒𐑑. 𐑚𐑰 𐑕𐑐𐑰𐑒 𐑿 𐑒𐑪𐑲 𐑬𐑑 𐑿 𐑤𐑭𐑛 𐑯𐑑 𐑢𐑨𐑕. 𐑑𐑮𐑧𐑥𐑚𐑤𐑦𐑙].

𐑤𐑧𐑯𐑑𐑫𐑤𐑳𐑕. 𐑴, 𐑐𐑫𐑼 𐑥𐑨𐑯! 𐑡𐑧𐑯𐑩𐑮𐑳𐑕. 𐑞 𐑤𐑦𐑕𐑑𐑩𐑯 𐑣𐑦𐑟 𐑐𐑮𐑱𐑼𐑑. 𐑐𐑮𐑱𐑟 𐑚𐑰 𐑑 ·𐑜𐑪𐑛'𐑟 𐑜𐑮𐑱𐑕𐑦𐑕! 𐑨𐑯𐑛𐑮𐑩𐑒𐑤𐑰𐑟. 𐑞 𐑐𐑫𐑼 𐑚𐑰𐑕𐑑 𐑢𐑪𐑟 𐑕𐑑𐑸𐑝-𐑦𐑙. 𐑦𐑑 𐑒𐑫𐑛𐑯𐑑 𐑣𐑧𐑤𐑐 𐑦𐑑𐑕𐑧𐑤𐑓. 𐑞 𐑒𐑮𐑦𐑕𐑑𐑦𐑩𐑯𐑟.

𐑢𐑩𐑑! 𐑯𐑑 𐑣𐑦𐑥! 𐑣𐑧 𐑛𐑲𐑑𐑛𐑦𐑛! 𐑣𐑧 𐑑𐑧𐑮𐑰𐑛! 𐑢𐑦𐑞𐑬𐑑 𐑩 𐑥𐑴𐑥𐑩𐑯𐑑 𐑑 𐑐𐑮𐑱! ·𐑜𐑪𐑛 𐑚𐑰 𐑥𐑻𐑕𐑦𐑓𐑩𐑤 𐑑 𐑣𐑦𐑥, 𐑩 𐑕𐑦𐑯𐑼! 𐑴, 𐑲 𐑒𐑭𐑯𐑑 𐑚𐑺 𐑑 𐑔𐑦𐑙𐑒 𐑝 𐑦𐑑! 𐑦𐑯 𐑞 𐑥𐑦𐑛𐑕𐑑 𐑝 𐑣𐑦𐑟 𐑕𐑦𐑯! 𐑣𐑪𐑮𐑦𐑚𐑩𐑤, 𐑣𐑪𐑮𐑦𐑚𐑩𐑤! 𐑞 𐑯𐑱𐑑𐑿. 𐑕𐑧𐑤 𐑞 𐑥𐑩𐑯𐑑 𐑥𐑲𐑑! 𐑞 𐑐𐑮𐑦𐑕𐑦𐑐-𐑑𐑩𐑯𐑟. 𐑚𐑲𐑕𐑑 𐑢𐑪𐑒𐑑 𐑦𐑯𐑑𐑫 𐑦𐑑, 𐑣𐑰 𐑚𐑦𐑚. 𐑣𐑰'𐑟 𐑥𐑸𐑑𐑩𐑚 𐑚𐑰 𐑥𐑲𐑑 𐑦𐑯𐑲𐑛. 𐑐𐑫𐑚 𐑴𐑤𐑛 𐑤𐑲𐑩𐑯! 𐑴𐑤𐑛 ·𐑜𐑪𐑒 𐑚𐑲𐑟𐑩𐑑 𐑤𐑲𐑒 𐑞𐑨𐑑: 𐑤𐑫𐑒 𐑨𐑑 𐑣𐑦𐑟 𐑛𐑧𐑕. 𐑚𐑳𐑚𐑤 𐑩 𐑚𐑫𐑑𐑩! 𐑞 𐑢𐑳𐑥𐑩𐑯 𐑢𐑦𐑤 𐑤𐑭𐑛 𐑢𐑪𐑯 𐑣𐑰 𐑣𐑻𐑟 𐑝 𐑦𐑑. 𐑲 𐑒𐑭𐑯𐑑 𐑣𐑧𐑤𐑐 𐑕𐑥𐑲𐑤𐑦𐑙. 𐑣𐑨 𐑣𐑨 𐑣𐑨!!!!!

𐑞 𐑒𐑰𐑐𐑼. 𐑯𐑧 𐑣𐑦𐑟 𐑩𐑐𐑦𐑑𐑲𐑑'𐑕 𐑑𐑧𐑒𐑩𐑯 𐑳𐑐, 𐑣𐑰 𐑢𐑴𐑯𐑑 𐑚𐑰 𐑕𐑲𐑟 𐑚𐑰 𐑤𐑫𐑒 𐑨𐑑 𐑩𐑞𐑼 𐑒𐑮𐑦𐑕𐑑𐑦𐑩𐑯 𐑛𐑿 𐑩 𐑢𐑰𐑒.

𐑨𐑯𐑛𐑮𐑩𐑒𐑤𐑰𐑟. 𐑒𐑫𐑛𐑯𐑑 𐑿 𐑣𐑨𐑝 𐑕𐑧𐑝𐑛 𐑣𐑦𐑥, 𐑚𐑮𐑳𐑞𐑼?

𐑞 𐑒𐑰𐑐𐑼. 𐑕𐑱𐑝𐑛 𐑣𐑦𐑥! 𐑕𐑱𐑝𐑛 𐑣𐑦𐑥 𐑓𐑮𐑪𐑥 𐑩 𐑤𐑲𐑩𐑯 𐑞𐑨𐑑 𐑲'𐑛 𐑚𐑦𐑑𐑩𐑯 𐑥𐑩𐑛 𐑢𐑦𐑞 𐑣𐑳𐑙𐑜𐑼! 𐑩 𐑢𐑲𐑤𐑛 𐑢𐑳𐑯 𐑞𐑨𐑑 𐑒𐑱𐑥 𐑬𐑑 𐑝 𐑞 𐑓𐑪𐑮𐑦𐑕𐑑 𐑯𐑪𐑑 𐑓𐑹 𐑢𐑰𐑒𐑕 𐑩𐑜𐑴! 𐑣𐑰 𐑚𐑴𐑑𐑩𐑛 𐑣𐑦𐑥 𐑚𐑦𐑓𐑹 𐑲 𐑒𐑫𐑛 𐑕𐑱 ·𐑡𐑫𐑐𐑦𐑑𐑼𐑕.

𐑤𐑧𐑯𐑑𐑫𐑤𐑳𐑕 [𐑕𐑦𐑑𐑦𐑙 𐑚𐑨𐑒 𐑩𐑜𐑱𐑯] 𐑐𐑫𐑼 ·𐑕𐑐𐑦𐑯𐑔𐑴! 𐑯 𐑦𐑑 𐑢𐑴𐑯𐑑 𐑰𐑝𐑩𐑯 𐑒𐑬𐑯𐑑 𐑨𐑟 𐑥𐑸𐑑𐑼𐑛𐑳𐑥!

𐑞 𐑒𐑰𐑐𐑼. 𐑕𐑻𐑝 𐑣𐑦𐑥 𐑮𐑲𐑑! 𐑢𐑪𐑑 𐑚𐑦𐑟𐑦𐑯𐑩𐑕 𐑣𐑨𐑛 𐑣𐑰 𐑑 𐑜𐑴 𐑦𐑯𐑑𐑫 𐑞 𐑛𐑧𐑯𐑟 𐑑 𐑥𐑱𐑒 𐑑 𐑚𐑰 𐑤𐑲𐑩𐑯𐑟 𐑓𐑫𐑛 𐑣𐑰 𐑢𐑪𐑟 𐑟𐑧𐑤𐑕?

𐑨𐑯𐑛𐑮𐑩𐑒𐑤𐑰𐑟. 𐑛𐑴𐑯𐑑 𐑚𐑤𐑱𐑥 𐑞 𐑤𐑲𐑩𐑯 𐑢𐑪𐑑 𐑣𐑰 𐑛𐑦𐑛 𐑯𐑴.

𐑞 𐑒𐑰𐑐𐑼. 𐑯𐑴: 𐑞𐑨𐑑'𐑕 𐑚𐑦𐑕𐑑 𐑤𐑲𐑒 𐑩 𐑒𐑮𐑦𐑕𐑑𐑦𐑩𐑯: 𐑔𐑦𐑙𐑒 𐑴𐑯𐑤𐑦 𐑝 𐑣𐑦𐑥𐑕𐑧𐑤𐑓! 𐑢𐑪𐑑 𐑩𐑚𐑬𐑑 𐑥𐑲 𐑑 𐑚𐑰? 𐑢𐑪𐑑 𐑩𐑚𐑬𐑑 𐑥𐑲 𐑑

highly amused. All speak or cry out or laugh at once. Tumult.

LAVINIA. Oh, poor wretch! FERROVIUS. The apostate has perished. Praise be to God's justice! ANDROCLES. The poor beast was starving. It couldnt help itself. THE CHRISTIANS. What! Ate him! How frightful! How terrible! Without a moment to repent! God be merciful to him, a sinner! Oh, I cant bear to think of it! In the midst of his sin! Horrible, horrible! THE EDITOR. Serve the rotter right! THE GLADIATORS. Just walked into it, he did. He's martyred all right enough. Good old lion! Old Jock doesn't like that: look at his face. Devil a better! The Emperor will laugh when he hears of it. I cant help smiling. Ha ha ha!!!!!

THE KEEPER. Now his appetite's taken off, he wont as much as look at another Christian for a week.

ANDROCLES. Couldnt you have saved him, brother?

THE KEEPER. Saved him! Saved him from a lion that I'd just got mad with hunger! a wild one that came out of the forest not four weeks ago! He bolted him before you could say Balbus.

LAVINIA [*sitting down again*] Poor Spintho! And it wont even count as martyrdom!

THE KEEPER. Serve him right! What call had he to walk down the throat of one of my lions before he was asked?

ANDROCLES. Perhaps the lion wont eat me now.

THE KEEPER. Yes: thats just like a Christian: think only of yourself! What am *I* to do? What am I to

𐑕𐑧 𐑑 𐑞 𐑧𐑥𐑐𐑼𐑼 𐑥𐑨𐑯 𐑣𐑰 𐑕𐑰𐑟 𐑥𐑦𐑯 𐑝 𐑥𐑦 𐑤𐑲𐑩𐑯𐑟 𐑒𐑲𐑥𐑦𐑛 𐑦𐑯𐑑𐑵 𐑞 𐑼𐑰𐑯𐑩 𐑣𐑨𐑛 𐑩𐑕𐑒𐑱𐑐𐑑?

𐑞 𐑧𐑛𐑦𐑑𐑼. 𐑕𐑧 𐑦𐑒𐑕𐑲𐑑𐑦𐑛. 𐑜𐑦𐑝 𐑿𐑼 𐑴𐑤𐑛 𐑤𐑲𐑩𐑯 𐑕𐑳𐑥 𐑝𐑦𐑑𐑼𐑟 𐑯 𐑩 𐑐𐑼𐑕𐑦𐑤 𐑝 𐑛𐑮𐑦𐑙𐑒 𐑛𐑦𐑤 𐑑 𐑥𐑱𐑒 𐑳𐑐 𐑓𐑹 𐑣𐑦𐑟 𐑛𐑦𐑕𐑩𐑐𐑱𐑯𐑑𐑥𐑩𐑯𐑑. [𐑤𐑭𐑓𐑑𐑼].

𐑞 𐑒𐑰𐑐𐑼. 𐑘𐑧𐑕: 𐑦𐑑'𐑕 𐑰𐑟𐑦 𐑓𐑹 𐑿 𐑑 𐑑𐑷𐑒; 𐑚𐑳𐑑 –

𐑞 𐑧𐑛𐑦𐑑𐑼 [𐑕𐑒𐑮𐑰𐑥𐑦𐑙 𐑑 𐑣𐑦𐑟 𐑓𐑰𐑑] 𐑴! 𐑩𐑯𐑳𐑞𐑼 𐑢𐑳𐑯! 𐑞 ·𐑧𐑥𐑐𐑼𐑼. [𐑞 ·𐑒𐑰𐑐𐑼 𐑮𐑳𐑖𐑩𐑟 𐑛𐑦𐑕𐑐𐑼𐑩𐑑𐑤𐑦 𐑦𐑯𐑑𐑵 𐑞 𐑐𐑨𐑕𐑦𐑡. 𐑞 𐑜𐑤𐑨𐑛𐑦𐑱𐑑𐑼𐑟 𐑚𐑱𐑟 𐑕𐑦𐑐𐑩𐑮𐑱𐑑 𐑯 𐑛𐑮𐑷 𐑦𐑯𐑑𐑵 𐑤𐑲𐑯.

𐑞 ·𐑧𐑥𐑐𐑼𐑼 𐑒𐑳𐑥𐑟 𐑳𐑐 𐑞 𐑕𐑑𐑧𐑐𐑕 𐑓𐑮𐑪𐑥 𐑞 𐑒𐑪𐑤𐑩𐑕𐑰𐑩𐑥 𐑕𐑲𐑛, 𐑒𐑩𐑯𐑝𐑻𐑕𐑦𐑙 𐑢𐑦𐑞 ·𐑓𐑧𐑮𐑴𐑝𐑾𐑕, 𐑯 𐑛𐑮𐑨𐑜𐑟 𐑦𐑯 𐑣𐑦𐑟 𐑕𐑢𐑰𐑑].

𐑞 𐑜𐑤𐑨𐑛𐑦𐑱𐑑𐑼𐑟. 𐑣𐑱𐑤, ·𐑕𐑰𐑟𐑼! 𐑞𐑱𐑟 𐑩𐑚𐑬𐑑 𐑑 𐑚𐑦 𐑕𐑧𐑤𐑩𐑑 𐑞𐑰.

𐑕𐑰𐑟𐑼. 𐑜𐑫𐑛 𐑥𐑹𐑯𐑦𐑙, 𐑛𐑨𐑮𐑤𐑦𐑙𐑟.

[·𐑓𐑧𐑮𐑴𐑝𐑾𐑕 𐑒𐑮𐑪𐑕𐑩𐑟 𐑣𐑦𐑟 𐑞𐑮𐑴𐑯 𐑢𐑦𐑞 𐑞 𐑧𐑛𐑦𐑑𐑼, 𐑣𐑵 𐑩𐑒𐑕𐑐𐑤𐑱𐑯𐑟 𐑣𐑦𐑟 𐑒𐑩𐑯𐑝𐑼𐑕𐑱𐑖𐑩𐑯 𐑢𐑦𐑞 𐑤𐑲𐑛 𐑦𐑯𐑑𐑼𐑧𐑕𐑑].

𐑤𐑩𐑝𐑦𐑯𐑾. 𐑚𐑤𐑧𐑕𐑦𐑙, ·𐑕𐑰𐑟𐑼, 𐑯 𐑛𐑦𐑐𐑸𐑑𐑩𐑕!

𐑕𐑰𐑟𐑼 [𐑑𐑻𐑯𐑦𐑙 𐑦𐑯 𐑕𐑲𐑤 𐑕𐑩𐑛𐑲𐑟𐑟 𐑩𐑑 𐑞 𐑕𐑦𐑜𐑯𐑦𐑓𐑦𐑒𐑩𐑯𐑕] 𐑞𐑺 𐑦𐑟 𐑯𐑴 𐑛𐑦𐑐𐑸𐑑𐑩𐑕 𐑛𐑵 𐑒𐑮𐑦𐑕𐑗𐑩𐑯𐑟.

𐑤𐑩𐑝𐑦𐑯𐑾. 𐑲 𐑛𐑴𐑯𐑑 𐑯𐑴 𐑞𐑨𐑑, ·𐑕𐑰𐑟𐑼. 𐑲 𐑯𐑴 𐑞𐑨𐑑 𐑢𐑰 𐑛𐑦𐑐𐑸𐑑 𐑦𐑟.

𐑓𐑧𐑮𐑴𐑝𐑾𐑕. 𐑩 𐑦𐑯𐑒𐑩𐑯𐑕𐑰𐑝𐑩𐑚𐑩𐑤 𐑤𐑦𐑚𐑼𐑑𐑦! 𐑚𐑳𐑑 𐑦𐑟 𐑯𐑪𐑑 𐑯𐑴, 𐑥𐑨𐑯, 𐑞𐑨𐑑 𐑞 𐑧𐑥𐑐𐑼𐑼 𐑒𐑨𐑯 𐑚𐑳𐑑 𐑯𐑴 𐑛𐑲𐑛 𐑯 𐑞𐑺𐑓𐑹 𐑒𐑩𐑯𐑑 𐑚𐑰 𐑛𐑦𐑐𐑸𐑑𐑩𐑛?

𐑤𐑩𐑝𐑦𐑯𐑾. 𐑲 𐑦𐑒𐑕𐑐𐑧𐑒𐑑 𐑞 𐑧𐑥𐑐𐑼𐑼 𐑯𐑴𐑟 𐑚𐑧𐑑𐑼. 𐑜𐑫𐑛𐑚𐑲, 𐑥𐑰 𐑛𐑦𐑐𐑸𐑑𐑦𐑙 𐑣𐑦𐑥.

𐑞 𐑒𐑮𐑦𐑕𐑑𐑾𐑯𐑟. 𐑱𐑥𐑧𐑯!

𐑕𐑰𐑟𐑼. ·𐑓𐑧𐑮𐑴𐑝𐑾𐑕: 𐑲 𐑕𐑰 𐑯𐑬 𐑞 𐑚𐑦𐑕𐑑𐑦𐑙𐑒𐑖𐑩𐑯𐑟 𐑝 𐑑𐑵 𐑥𐑲𐑯 𐑕𐑦𐑜𐑯𐑦𐑓𐑦𐑒𐑩𐑯𐑕. 𐑞𐑰𐑟 𐑛𐑰𐑤𐑼𐑟 𐑣𐑨𐑝 𐑯𐑴 𐑣𐑴𐑐; 𐑞𐑺𐑓𐑹 𐑞𐑱 𐑣𐑨𐑝 𐑦𐑒𐑕𐑲𐑑𐑦𐑛 𐑑 𐑛𐑦𐑕𐑑𐑮𐑳𐑒𐑑 𐑞𐑧𐑥

say to the Emperor when he sees one of my lions coming into the arena half asleep?

THE EDITOR. Say nothing. Give your old lion some bitters and a morsel of fried fish to wake up his appetite. [*Laughter*].

THE KEEPER. Yes: it's easy for you to talk; but –

THE EDITOR [*scrambling to his feet*] Sh! Attention there! The Emperor. [*The Keeper bolts precipitately into the passage. The gladiators rise smartly and form into line*].

The Emperor enters on the Christians' side, conversing with Metellus, and followed by his suite.

THE GLADIATORS. Hail, Caesar! those about to die salute thee.

CAESAR. Good morrow, friends.

Metellus shakes hands with the Editor, who accepts his condescension with bluff respect.

LAVINIA. Blessing, Caesar, and forgiveness!

CAESAR [*turning in some surprise at the salutation*] There is no forgiveness for Christianity.

LAVINIA. I did not mean that, Caesar. I mean that we forgive you.

METELLUS. An inconceivable liberty! Do you not know, woman, that the Emperor can do no wrong and therefore cannot be forgiven?

LAVINIA. I expect the Emperor knows better. Anyhow, we forgive him.

THE CHRISTIANS. Amen!

CAESAR. Metellus: you see now the disadvantage of too much severity. These people have no hope; therefore they have nothing to restrain them

𐑛𐑺 𐑕𐑐𐑰𐑒 𐑢𐑪𐑑 𐑞𐑱 𐑤𐑲𐑒 𐑑 𐑥𐑰. 𐑞𐑱 𐑸 𐑷𐑤𐑥𐑴𐑕𐑑 𐑨𐑟 𐑦𐑥𐑐𐑹𐑑𐑩𐑯𐑑 𐑨𐑟 𐑞 𐑜𐑤𐑨𐑛𐑦𐑱𐑑𐑼𐑟. 𐑢𐑦𐑗 𐑦𐑟 𐑞 𐑜𐑮𐑰𐑒 𐑕𐑹𐑕𐑼𐑼?

𐑨𐑯𐑛𐑮𐑩𐑒𐑤𐑰𐑟 [𐑣𐑳𐑥𐑚𐑤𐑦 𐑑𐑳𐑗𐑦𐑙 𐑣𐑦𐑟 𐑓𐑹𐑤𐑪𐑒] 𐑥𐑰, 𐑿𐑼 𐑢𐑻𐑖𐑦𐑐.

𐑕𐑰𐑟𐑼. 𐑥𐑲 𐑢𐑻𐑖𐑦𐑐! 𐑜𐑫𐑛! 𐑩 𐑯𐑿 𐑑𐑲𐑑𐑩𐑤. 𐑢𐑧𐑤: 𐑢𐑪𐑑 𐑥𐑦𐑮𐑩𐑒𐑩𐑤𐑟 𐑒𐑨𐑯 𐑿 𐑐𐑼𐑓𐑹𐑥?

𐑨𐑯𐑛𐑮𐑩𐑒𐑤𐑰𐑟. 𐑲 𐑒𐑨𐑯 𐑒𐑿𐑼 𐑢𐑹𐑑𐑕 𐑚𐑲 𐑮𐑳𐑚𐑦𐑙 𐑞𐑧𐑥 𐑢𐑦𐑞 𐑥𐑲 𐑑𐑱𐑤𐑼'𐑟 𐑗𐑷𐑒; 𐑯 𐑲 𐑒𐑨𐑯 𐑤𐑦𐑝 𐑢𐑦𐑞 𐑥𐑲 𐑢𐑲𐑓 𐑢𐑦𐑞𐑬𐑑 𐑚𐑰𐑑𐑦𐑙 𐑣𐑼.

𐑕𐑰𐑟𐑼. 𐑦𐑟 𐑞𐑨𐑑 𐑷𐑤?

𐑨𐑯𐑛𐑮𐑩𐑒𐑤𐑰𐑟. 𐑿 𐑛𐑴𐑯𐑑 𐑯𐑴 𐑣𐑼, ·𐑕𐑰𐑟𐑼, 𐑹 𐑿 𐑢𐑫𐑛𐑯𐑑 𐑕𐑱 𐑞𐑨𐑑.

𐑕𐑰𐑟𐑼. 𐑭, 𐑢𐑧𐑤, 𐑥𐑲 𐑓𐑮𐑧𐑯𐑛, 𐑢𐑰 𐑖𐑨𐑤 𐑯𐑴 𐑛𐑬𐑑 𐑒𐑩𐑯𐑑𐑮𐑲𐑝 𐑩 𐑣𐑨𐑐𐑦 𐑮𐑦𐑤𐑰𐑕 𐑓 𐑿. 𐑢𐑦𐑗 𐑦𐑟 ·𐑓𐑧𐑮𐑴𐑝𐑾𐑕?

𐑓𐑧𐑮𐑴𐑝𐑾𐑕. 𐑲 𐑨𐑥 𐑣𐑰.

𐑕𐑰𐑟𐑼. 𐑞𐑱 𐑑𐑧𐑤 𐑥𐑰 𐑿 𐑒𐑨𐑯 𐑓𐑲𐑑.

𐑓𐑧𐑮𐑴𐑝𐑾𐑕. 𐑦𐑑 𐑦𐑟 𐑰𐑟𐑦 𐑑 𐑓𐑲𐑑. 𐑲 𐑒𐑨𐑯 𐑛𐑲, ·𐑕𐑰𐑟𐑼.

𐑕𐑰𐑟𐑼. 𐑞𐑨𐑑 𐑦𐑟 𐑕𐑑𐑦𐑤 𐑰𐑟𐑦𐑼, 𐑦𐑟 𐑦𐑑 𐑯𐑪𐑑?

𐑓𐑧𐑮𐑴𐑝𐑾𐑕. 𐑯𐑪𐑑 𐑑 𐑥𐑰, ·𐑕𐑰𐑟𐑼. 𐑛𐑧𐑔 𐑒𐑳𐑥𐑟 𐑣𐑸𐑛 𐑑 𐑥𐑲 𐑓𐑤𐑧𐑖; 𐑯 𐑓𐑲𐑑𐑦𐑙 𐑒𐑳𐑥𐑟 𐑝𐑧𐑮𐑦 𐑰𐑟𐑦 𐑑 𐑥𐑲 𐑕𐑐𐑦𐑮𐑦𐑑 [𐑚𐑰𐑑𐑦𐑙 𐑣𐑦𐑟 𐑚𐑮𐑧𐑕𐑑 𐑯 𐑤𐑩𐑥𐑧𐑯𐑑𐑦𐑙] 𐑴, 𐑕𐑦𐑯𐑼 𐑞𐑨𐑑 𐑲 𐑨𐑥! [𐑣𐑰 𐑔𐑮𐑴𐑟 𐑣𐑦𐑥𐑕𐑧𐑤𐑓 𐑛𐑬𐑯 𐑪𐑯 𐑞 𐑕𐑑𐑧𐑐𐑕, 𐑛𐑰𐑐𐑤𐑦 𐑛𐑦𐑕𐑒𐑳𐑮𐑦𐑡𐑛].

𐑕𐑰𐑟𐑼. ·𐑥𐑩𐑑𐑧𐑤𐑩𐑕: 𐑲 𐑖𐑫𐑛 𐑤𐑲𐑒 𐑑 𐑣𐑨𐑝 𐑞𐑦𐑕 𐑥𐑨𐑯 𐑦𐑯 𐑞 𐑐𐑮𐑦𐑑𐑹𐑾𐑯 𐑜𐑸𐑛.

𐑥𐑩𐑑𐑧𐑤𐑩𐑕. 𐑲 𐑖𐑫𐑛 𐑯𐑪𐑑, ·𐑕𐑰𐑟𐑼. 𐑣𐑰 𐑤𐑫𐑒𐑕 𐑩 𐑕𐑐𐑶𐑤𐑕𐑐𐑹𐑑. 𐑞𐑺 𐑸 𐑥𐑧𐑯 𐑦𐑯 𐑣𐑵𐑟 𐑐𐑮𐑧𐑟𐑩𐑯𐑕 𐑦𐑑 𐑦𐑟 𐑦𐑥𐑐𐑪𐑕𐑦𐑚𐑩𐑤 𐑑 𐑣𐑨𐑝 𐑧𐑯𐑦 𐑓𐑳𐑯: 𐑥𐑧𐑯 𐑣𐑵 𐑸 𐑩 𐑕𐑹𐑑 𐑝 𐑢𐑷𐑒𐑦𐑙 𐑒𐑪𐑯𐑖𐑩𐑯𐑕𐑩𐑟. 𐑣𐑰 𐑢𐑫𐑛 𐑥𐑱𐑒 𐑳𐑕 𐑷𐑤 𐑩𐑯𐑒𐑳𐑥𐑓𐑼𐑑𐑩𐑚𐑩𐑤.

from saying what they like to me. They are almost as impertinent as the gladiators. Which is the Greek sorcerer?

ANDROCLES [*humbly touching his forelock*] Me, your Worship.

CAESAR. My Worship! Good! A new title. Well: what miracles can you perform?

ANDROCLES. I can cure warts by rubbing them with my tailor's chalk; and I can live with my wife without beating her.

CAESAR. Is that all?

ANDROCLES. You dont know her, Caesar, or you wouldnt say that.

CAESAR. Ah, well, my friend, we shall no doubt contrive a happy release for you. Which is Ferrovius?

FERROVIUS. I am he.

CAESAR. They tell me you can fight.

FERROVIUS. It is easy to fight, *I* can die, Caesar.

CAESAR. That is still easier, is it not?

FERROVIUS. Not to me, Caesar. Death comes hard to my flesh; and fighting comes very easily to my spirit [*beating his breast and lamenting*] Oh, sinner that I am! [*He throws himself down on the steps, deeply discouraged*].

CAESAR. Metellus: I should like to have this man in the Pretorian Guard.

METELLUS. *I* should not, Caesar. He looks a spoil-sport. There are men in whose presence it is impossible to have any fun: men who are a sort of walking conscience. He would make us all uncomfortable.

𐑕𐑰𐑟𐑼. 𐑓𐑹 𐑞𐑨𐑑 𐑮𐑰𐑟𐑯, 𐑥𐑧𐑑𐑧𐑤𐑩𐑕, 𐑦𐑑 𐑥𐑲𐑑 𐑚𐑰 𐑨𐑟 𐑢𐑧𐑤 𐑑 𐑣𐑨𐑝 𐑣𐑦𐑥. 𐑯 𐑢𐑦𐑯𐑛𐑼 𐑒𐑯 𐑣𐑸𐑛𐑤𐑦 𐑣𐑨𐑝 𐑞𐑧𐑥 𐑨𐑤 𐑒𐑮𐑦𐑕𐑗𐑩𐑯𐑟. [𐑑 ·𐑓𐑧𐑮𐑴𐑝𐑾𐑕] 𐑢𐑧𐑤, ·𐑓𐑧𐑮𐑴𐑝𐑾𐑕. [·𐑓𐑧𐑮𐑴𐑝𐑾𐑕 𐑣𐑨𐑙𐑟 𐑣𐑦𐑟 𐑣𐑧𐑛 𐑯 𐑢𐑦𐑤 𐑯𐑪𐑑 𐑤𐑫𐑒 𐑳𐑐]. 𐑣𐑰 𐑦𐑟 𐑣𐑼 𐑚𐑮𐑱𐑝𐑟𐑑 𐑥𐑨𐑯 𐑯𐑪𐑑 𐑚𐑰 𐑒𐑑-𐑮𐑲𐑑𐑩𐑯 𐑑𐑧𐑯𐑛𐑼 𐑦𐑯 𐑞 𐑼𐑰𐑯𐑩. 𐑣𐑰 𐑥𐑳𐑕𐑑 𐑣𐑨𐑝 𐑸𐑥𐑟: 𐑯 𐑞𐑧𐑥 𐑢𐑦𐑤 𐑚𐑰 𐑯𐑴 𐑓𐑿 𐑞𐑺 𐑢𐑧𐑯 𐑚𐑦𐑜𐑦𐑯𐑦𐑙 𐑑 𐑕𐑰 𐑒𐑮𐑦𐑕𐑗𐑩𐑯. 𐑦𐑓 𐑣𐑰 𐑒𐑳𐑥 𐑒𐑑 𐑝 𐑞 𐑼𐑰𐑯𐑩 𐑩𐑤𐑲𐑝, 𐑲 𐑢𐑦𐑤 𐑒𐑩𐑥𐑦𐑖𐑩𐑯 𐑣𐑦𐑥 𐑦𐑯 𐑞 𐑐𐑮𐑦𐑑𐑹𐑾𐑯 𐑜𐑸𐑛, 𐑯 𐑚𐑦𐑜 𐑣𐑰 𐑝 𐑚𐑦𐑤𐑧𐑑 𐑦𐑯 𐑞 𐑐𐑮𐑦𐑑𐑹𐑾𐑯 𐑜𐑸𐑛. 𐑰𐑝𐑩𐑯 𐑦𐑓 𐑞 𐑐𐑮𐑦𐑑𐑹𐑾𐑯𐑟 𐑚𐑰 𐑞𐑧𐑥 𐑯𐑴 𐑒𐑩𐑯𐑕𐑦𐑛𐑼𐑟 𐑚𐑰 𐑕𐑧𐑒𐑑 𐑮𐑦𐑒𐑑 𐑣𐑼 𐑓𐑧𐑛 𐑲 𐑥𐑳𐑕𐑑 𐑚𐑧𐑯𐑑𐑿𐑤𐑩𐑕 𐑢𐑦𐑞 𐑦𐑑 𐑕𐑦𐑥𐑐𐑤𐑦 𐑦𐑑.

·𐑓𐑧𐑮𐑴𐑝𐑾𐑕. 𐑲 𐑢𐑦𐑤 𐑯𐑪𐑑 𐑓𐑲𐑑. 𐑲 𐑢𐑦𐑤 𐑛𐑲. 𐑚𐑧𐑑𐑼 𐑕𐑑𐑨𐑯𐑛 𐑢𐑦𐑞 𐑞 𐑸𐑒𐑱𐑯𐑡𐑩𐑤𐑟 𐑞𐑨𐑯 𐑢𐑦𐑞 𐑞 𐑐𐑮𐑦𐑑𐑹𐑾𐑯 𐑜𐑸𐑛.

𐑕𐑰𐑟𐑼. 𐑲 𐑒𐑪𐑯𐑑 𐑚𐑦𐑤𐑰𐑝 𐑞𐑨𐑑 𐑞 𐑸𐑒𐑱𐑯𐑡𐑩𐑤𐑟 — 𐑣𐑵𐑧𐑝𐑼 𐑞𐑱 𐑥𐑱 𐑚𐑰 — 𐑣𐑨𐑝 𐑯𐑪𐑑 𐑚𐑦𐑯 𐑑 𐑚𐑰 𐑒𐑩𐑥𐑨𐑯𐑛𐑦𐑛 𐑚𐑲 𐑞 𐑐𐑮𐑦𐑑𐑹𐑾𐑯 𐑜𐑸𐑛. 𐑣𐑵𐑧𐑝𐑼, 𐑨𐑟 𐑣𐑰 𐑚𐑰𐑟. 𐑒𐑳𐑥: 𐑤𐑧𐑑 𐑳𐑕 𐑕𐑰 𐑞 𐑖𐑴.

[𐑨𐑟 𐑞 𐑒𐑹𐑑 𐑮𐑦𐑑𐑲𐑼𐑟 𐑞 𐑕𐑑𐑧𐑐𐑕, ·𐑕𐑧𐑒𐑿𐑑𐑹 𐑯 ·𐑮𐑧𐑑𐑦𐑺𐑾𐑕 𐑮𐑦𐑑𐑻𐑯 𐑚𐑲 𐑞 𐑐𐑨𐑕𐑦𐑡 𐑓𐑮𐑪𐑥 𐑞 𐑼𐑰𐑯𐑩 𐑔𐑮𐑵 𐑞 𐑛𐑹𐑟: ·𐑕𐑧𐑒𐑿𐑑𐑹 𐑒𐑲𐑯𐑛 𐑢𐑦𐑞 𐑐𐑲𐑕𐑑 𐑯 𐑖𐑰𐑤𐑛 𐑢𐑦𐑞 𐑦𐑒𐑕𐑐𐑧𐑮𐑦𐑩𐑯𐑕: ·𐑮𐑧𐑑𐑦𐑺𐑾𐑕 𐑐𐑳𐑟𐑩𐑤𐑛].

𐑕𐑧𐑒𐑿𐑑𐑹. 𐑘𐑧𐑕, 𐑞 𐑛𐑻𐑑𐑦 𐑮𐑧𐑑𐑦𐑺𐑾𐑕. 𐑦𐑑 𐑦𐑟 𐑥𐑳𐑕𐑑 𐑕𐑰. ·𐑕𐑰𐑟𐑼: 𐑲 𐑕𐑱𐑛 𐑣𐑰 𐑢𐑪𐑟 𐑦𐑯 𐑞 𐑓𐑲𐑑 𐑓𐑹 𐑞 𐑯𐑧𐑑 𐑯 𐑞 𐑮𐑧𐑑𐑦𐑺𐑾𐑕, 𐑦𐑯𐑕𐑑𐑧𐑛 𐑝 𐑥𐑱𐑒𐑦𐑙 𐑩 𐑓𐑺 𐑓𐑲𐑑 𐑝 𐑦𐑑 𐑣𐑨𐑟 𐑯𐑪𐑑 𐑞𐑨𐑑 𐑥𐑳𐑗, 𐑑 𐑕𐑧𐑯𐑛 𐑦𐑑 𐑮𐑬𐑯𐑛 𐑞 𐑐𐑨𐑕𐑦𐑡 𐑯 𐑓𐑲𐑑 𐑞 𐑕𐑧𐑒𐑿𐑑𐑹 𐑦𐑯 𐑞 𐑥𐑦𐑛𐑩𐑤, 𐑯 𐑞𐑧𐑯 𐑒𐑨𐑗 𐑣𐑦𐑥 𐑦𐑯 𐑞 𐑯𐑧𐑑 𐑲'𐑥 𐑐𐑩𐑯𐑦𐑖𐑑. 𐑦𐑓 𐑞 𐑐𐑳𐑚𐑤𐑦𐑒 𐑣𐑨𐑛 𐑯𐑪𐑑 𐑑𐑻𐑯𐑛 𐑩𐑐 𐑞𐑺 𐑔𐑳𐑥𐑟 𐑲 𐑖𐑫𐑛 𐑣𐑨𐑝 𐑚𐑰𐑯 𐑩 𐑛𐑧𐑛 𐑥𐑨𐑯.

CAESAR. For that reason, perhaps, it might be as well to have him. An Emperor can hardly have too many consciences. [*To Ferrovius*] Listen, Ferrovius. [*Ferrovius shakes his head and will not look up*]. You and your friends shall not be outnumbered today in the arena. You shall have arms; and there will be no more than one gladiator to each Christian. If you come out of the arena alive, I will consider favorably any request of yours, and give you a place in the Pretorian Guard. Even if the request be that no questions be asked about your faith I shall perhaps not refuse it.

FERROVIUS. I will not fight. I will die. Better stand with the archangels than with the Pretorian Guard.

CAESAR. I cannot believe that the archangels – whoever they may be – would not prefer to be recruited from the Pretorian Guard. However, as you please. Come: let us see the show.

As the Court ascends the steps, Secutor and Retiarius return from the arena through the passage: Secutor covered with dust and very angry: Retiarius grinning.

SECUTOR. Ha, the Emperor. Now we shall see. Caesar: I ask you whether it is fair for the Retiarius, instead of making a fair throw of his net at me, to swish it along the ground and throw the dust in my eyes, and then catch me when I'm blinded. If the vestals had not turned up their thumbs I should have been a dead man.

𐑕𐑰𐑟𐑼 [𐑣𐑴𐑤𐑛𐑦𐑙 𐑳𐑐 𐑞 𐑚𐑦𐑤] 𐑞𐑺 𐑦𐑟 𐑯𐑳𐑔𐑦𐑙 𐑦𐑯 𐑞 𐑮𐑵𐑤𐑟 𐑩𐑜𐑱𐑯𐑕𐑑 𐑦𐑑.

𐑕𐑧𐑒𐑿𐑑𐑹 [𐑦𐑯𐑛𐑦𐑜𐑯𐑩𐑯𐑑𐑤𐑦] ·𐑕𐑰𐑟𐑼: 𐑦𐑟 𐑦𐑑 𐑩 𐑓𐑺 𐑓𐑲𐑑 𐑹 𐑦𐑟 𐑦𐑑 𐑯𐑪𐑑?

𐑕𐑰𐑟𐑼. 𐑦𐑑 𐑦𐑟 𐑩 𐑛𐑳𐑕𐑑𐑦 𐑓𐑲𐑑, 𐑥𐑲 𐑚𐑶. [𐑳𐑐𐑮𐑹𐑦𐑩𐑕 𐑤𐑭𐑓𐑑𐑼]. 𐑿 𐑥𐑳𐑕𐑑 𐑛𐑵 𐑚𐑧𐑑𐑼 𐑯𐑧𐑒𐑕𐑑 𐑑𐑲𐑥.

𐑕𐑧𐑒𐑿𐑑𐑹. 𐑤𐑧𐑑 𐑣𐑦𐑥 𐑛𐑵 𐑣𐑦𐑟 𐑚𐑧𐑕𐑑. 𐑯𐑧𐑒𐑕𐑑 𐑑𐑲𐑥 𐑲'𐑤 𐑔𐑮𐑴 𐑥𐑲 𐑕𐑹𐑛 𐑨𐑑 𐑣𐑦𐑟 𐑣𐑰𐑤𐑟 𐑯 𐑕𐑑𐑮𐑨𐑙𐑜𐑩𐑤 𐑣𐑦𐑥 𐑢𐑦𐑞 𐑣𐑦𐑟 𐑴𐑯 𐑯𐑧𐑑 𐑚𐑦𐑓𐑹 𐑣𐑰 𐑒𐑨𐑯 𐑜𐑧𐑑 𐑳𐑐. [𐑑 𐑞 𐑮𐑧𐑑𐑦𐑺𐑦𐑩𐑕] 𐑿 𐑕𐑰 𐑦𐑓 𐑲 𐑛𐑴𐑯𐑑. [𐑣𐑰 𐑜𐑴𐑟 𐑬𐑑 𐑐𐑭𐑕𐑑 𐑞 𐑜𐑤𐑨𐑛𐑦𐑱𐑑𐑼𐑟, 𐑕𐑳𐑤𐑒𐑦 𐑯 𐑓𐑘𐑫𐑼𐑦𐑩𐑕].

𐑕𐑰𐑟𐑼 [𐑑 𐑞 𐑗𐑳𐑒𐑤𐑦𐑙 𐑮𐑧𐑑𐑦𐑺𐑦𐑩𐑕] 𐑞𐑰𐑟 𐑑𐑮𐑦𐑒𐑕 𐑸 𐑯𐑪𐑑 𐑓𐑲𐑯, 𐑥𐑲 𐑚𐑶. 𐑞 𐑐𐑳𐑚𐑤𐑦𐑒 𐑤𐑲𐑒𐑕 𐑑 𐑕𐑰 𐑩 𐑜𐑫𐑛 𐑥𐑨𐑯 𐑦𐑯 𐑷𐑤 𐑣𐑦𐑟 𐑚𐑿𐑑𐑦 𐑯 𐑕𐑐𐑤𐑧𐑯𐑛𐑼. 𐑦𐑓 𐑿 𐑕𐑐𐑶𐑤 𐑣𐑦𐑟 𐑤𐑫𐑒𐑕 𐑯 𐑕𐑶𐑤 𐑣𐑦𐑟 𐑸𐑥𐑼 𐑞𐑱 𐑢𐑦𐑤 𐑖𐑴 𐑞𐑺 𐑛𐑦𐑕𐑩𐑐𐑶𐑯𐑑𐑥𐑩𐑯𐑑 𐑚𐑲 𐑯𐑪𐑑 𐑤𐑧𐑑𐑦𐑙 𐑿 𐑒𐑦𐑤 𐑣𐑦𐑥. 𐑯 𐑢𐑧𐑯 𐑘𐑹 𐑑𐑻𐑯 𐑒𐑳𐑥𐑟, 𐑞𐑱 𐑢𐑦𐑤 𐑮𐑦𐑥𐑧𐑥𐑚𐑼 𐑦𐑑 𐑩𐑜𐑱𐑯𐑕𐑑 𐑿 𐑯 𐑑𐑻𐑯 𐑞𐑺 𐑔𐑳𐑥𐑟 𐑛𐑬𐑯.

𐑮𐑧𐑑𐑦𐑺𐑦𐑩𐑕. 𐑐𐑼𐑣𐑨𐑐𐑕 𐑞𐑨𐑑 𐑦𐑟 𐑢𐑲 𐑲 𐑛𐑦𐑛 𐑦𐑑, ·𐑕𐑰𐑟𐑼. 𐑣𐑰 𐑚𐑧𐑑 𐑥𐑰 𐑑𐑧𐑯 𐑕𐑧𐑕𐑑𐑼𐑕𐑰𐑟 𐑞𐑨𐑑 𐑣𐑰 𐑢𐑫𐑛 𐑛𐑦𐑓𐑰𐑑 𐑥𐑰. 𐑦𐑓 𐑲 𐑣𐑨𐑛 𐑣𐑨𐑛 𐑑 𐑒𐑦𐑤 𐑣𐑦𐑥 𐑲 𐑖𐑫𐑛 𐑯𐑪𐑑 𐑣𐑨𐑝 𐑣𐑨𐑛 𐑞 𐑥𐑳𐑯𐑦.

𐑕𐑰𐑟𐑼 [𐑦𐑯𐑛𐑳𐑤𐑡𐑩𐑯𐑑, 𐑤𐑭𐑓𐑦𐑙] 𐑿 𐑮𐑴𐑜𐑟: 𐑞𐑺 𐑦𐑟 𐑯𐑴 𐑧𐑯𐑛 𐑑 𐑘𐑹 𐑑𐑮𐑦𐑒𐑕. 𐑲'𐑤 𐑛𐑦𐑕𐑥𐑦𐑕 𐑿 𐑚𐑴𐑔 𐑯 𐑣𐑲𐑼 𐑯𐑿 𐑛𐑦𐑤𐑧𐑯𐑕𐑑𐑕 𐑑 𐑓𐑲𐑑. 𐑞𐑱 𐑓𐑲𐑑 𐑓𐑺. [𐑣𐑰 𐑜𐑴𐑟 𐑲𐑯 𐑑 𐑣𐑦𐑟 𐑚𐑪𐑒𐑕, 𐑯 𐑯𐑪𐑛𐑟 𐑨𐑑 𐑦𐑑. 𐑦𐑑 𐑦𐑟 𐑴𐑐𐑩𐑯 𐑓𐑮𐑳𐑥 𐑢𐑦𐑞𐑦𐑯 𐑚𐑲 𐑞 𐑒𐑭𐑤𐑑𐑼, 𐑣𐑵 𐑕𐑑𐑨𐑯𐑛𐑟 𐑨𐑟 𐑦𐑯 𐑛𐑿𐑑𐑦 𐑚𐑬𐑯𐑛 𐑑 𐑒𐑨𐑗 𐑣𐑦𐑥 𐑛𐑬𐑯].

𐑞 𐑒𐑷𐑤 𐑚𐑶 𐑒𐑳𐑥𐑟 𐑛𐑬𐑯 𐑞 𐑕𐑑𐑧𐑐𐑕, 𐑓𐑪𐑤𐑴𐑛 𐑚𐑲 𐑔𐑮𐑰 𐑥𐑧𐑯 𐑒𐑨𐑮𐑦𐑦𐑙 𐑩 𐑚𐑳𐑯𐑛𐑩𐑤 𐑝 𐑕𐑹𐑛𐑟, 𐑕𐑦𐑒𐑕 𐑣𐑧𐑤𐑥𐑩𐑑𐑕, 𐑯 𐑕𐑦𐑒𐑕 𐑚𐑮𐑧𐑕𐑑𐑐𐑤𐑱𐑑𐑕

CAESAR [*halting on the stair*] There is nothing in the rules against it.

SECUTOR [*indignantly*] Caesar: is it a dirty trick or is it not?

CAESAR. It is a dusty one, my friend. [*Obsequious laughter*]. Be on your guard next time.

SECUTOR. Let him be on his guard. Next time I'll throw my sword at his heels and strangle him with his own net before he can hop off. [*To the Retiarius*] You see if I dont. [*He goes out past the gladiators, sulky and furious*].

CAESAR [*to the chuckling Retiarius*] These tricks are not wise, my friend. The audience likes to see a dead man in all his beauty and splendor. If you smudge his face and spoil his armor they will shew their displeasure by not letting you kill him. And when your turn comes, they will remember it against you and turn their thumbs down.

RETIARIUS. Perhaps that is why I did it, Caesar. He bet me ten sesterces that he would vanquish me. If I had had to kill him I should not have had the money.

CAESAR [*indulgent, laughing*] You rogues: there is no end to your tricks. I'll dismiss you all and have elephants to fight. They fight fairly. [*He goes up to his box, and knocks at it. It is opened from within by the Captain, who stands as on parade to let him pass*].

The Call Boy comes from the passage, followed by three attendants carrying respectively a bundle of swords, some helmets, and some breastplates

𐑯 𐑐𐑰𐑕𐑩𐑟 𐑩 𐑯𐑩𐑯 𐑚𐑦𐑒 𐑞𐑒 𐑔𐑮𐑴 𐑛𐑬𐑯 𐑦𐑯 𐑩 𐑜𐑰𐑛].

𐑞 𐑒𐑷𐑤 𐑚𐑶. 𐑚𐑲 𐑿𐑼 𐑤𐑰𐑝, ·𐑕𐑰𐑟𐑼. 𐑯𐑳𐑥𐑚𐑼 𐑦𐑤𐑧𐑝𐑩𐑯! 𐑜𐑤𐑨𐑛𐑦𐑱𐑑𐑼𐑟 𐑯 𐑒𐑮𐑦𐑕𐑗𐑩𐑯𐑟!

[·𐑓𐑧𐑮𐑴𐑝𐑾𐑕 𐑕𐑐𐑮𐑦𐑙𐑟 𐑳𐑐, 𐑮𐑧𐑛𐑦 𐑓𐑹 𐑥𐑸𐑑𐑼𐑛𐑩𐑥. 𐑞 𐑳𐑞𐑼 𐑒𐑮𐑦𐑕𐑗𐑩𐑯𐑟 𐑑𐑱𐑒 𐑞 𐑕𐑳𐑥𐑩𐑯𐑟 𐑨𐑟 𐑚𐑧𐑕𐑑 𐑞𐑱 𐑒𐑨𐑯, 𐑕𐑳𐑥 𐑡𐑶𐑓𐑩𐑤 𐑯 𐑚𐑮𐑱𐑝, 𐑕𐑳𐑥 𐑐𐑱𐑖𐑩𐑯𐑑 𐑯 𐑛𐑦𐑜𐑯𐑦𐑓𐑲𐑛, 𐑕𐑳𐑥 𐑑𐑽𐑓𐑩𐑤 𐑯 𐑣𐑧𐑤𐑐𐑤𐑩𐑕, 𐑕𐑳𐑥 𐑦𐑥𐑚𐑮𐑱𐑕𐑦𐑙 𐑢𐑳𐑯 𐑩𐑯𐑳𐑞𐑼 𐑢𐑦𐑞 𐑦𐑥𐑴𐑖𐑩𐑯. 𐑞 𐑒𐑷𐑤 𐑚𐑶 𐑜𐑴𐑟 𐑚𐑨𐑒 𐑦𐑯𐑑𐑵 𐑞 𐑐𐑨𐑕𐑦𐑡].

·𐑕𐑰𐑟𐑼 [𐑑𐑻𐑯𐑦𐑙 𐑨𐑑 𐑞 𐑛𐑹 𐑝 𐑞 𐑚𐑪𐑒𐑕] 𐑞 𐑬𐑼 𐑣𐑨𐑟 𐑒𐑳𐑥, ·𐑓𐑧𐑮𐑴𐑝𐑾𐑕. 𐑲 𐑖𐑨𐑤 𐑜𐑴 𐑦𐑯𐑑𐑵 𐑥𐑲 𐑚𐑪𐑒𐑕 𐑯 𐑕𐑰 𐑿 𐑒𐑦𐑤, 𐑕𐑦𐑯𐑕 𐑿 𐑕𐑒𐑹𐑯 𐑞 𐑦𐑥𐑐𐑽𐑦𐑩𐑤 𐑚𐑵𐑯. [𐑣𐑰 𐑜𐑴𐑟 𐑦𐑯𐑑𐑵 𐑞 𐑚𐑪𐑒𐑕. 𐑞 𐑒𐑨𐑐𐑑𐑦𐑯 𐑖𐑳𐑑𐑕 𐑞 𐑛𐑹, 𐑮𐑦𐑥𐑱𐑯𐑦𐑙 𐑦𐑯𐑕𐑲𐑛 𐑢𐑦𐑞 𐑞 𐑧𐑥𐑐𐑼𐑼, ·𐑥𐑧𐑑𐑧𐑤𐑩𐑕 𐑯 𐑞 𐑮𐑧𐑕𐑑 𐑝 𐑞 𐑕𐑢𐑰𐑑 𐑕𐑑𐑮𐑨𐑜𐑩𐑤 𐑑 𐑞𐑺 𐑕𐑰𐑑𐑕. 𐑞 𐑒𐑮𐑦𐑕𐑗𐑩𐑯𐑟, 𐑤𐑧𐑛 𐑚𐑲 ·𐑓𐑧𐑮𐑴𐑝𐑾𐑕, 𐑛𐑮𐑷 𐑑𐑫𐑢𐑹𐑛𐑟 𐑞 𐑐𐑨𐑕𐑦𐑡].

·𐑤𐑩𐑝𐑦𐑯𐑾 [𐑑 ·𐑓𐑧𐑮𐑴𐑝𐑾𐑕] 𐑓𐑺𐑢𐑧𐑤.

𐑞 𐑧𐑛𐑦𐑑𐑼. 𐑕𐑑𐑧𐑛𐑦 𐑞𐑺. 𐑿 𐑒𐑮𐑦𐑕𐑗𐑩𐑯𐑟 𐑣𐑨𐑝 𐑜𐑪𐑑 𐑑 𐑓𐑲𐑑. 𐑣𐑽! 𐑸𐑥 𐑿𐑼𐑕𐑧𐑤𐑝𐑟.

·𐑓𐑧𐑮𐑴𐑝𐑾𐑕 [𐑐𐑦𐑒𐑦𐑙 𐑳𐑐 𐑩 𐑕𐑹𐑛] 𐑲'𐑤 𐑛𐑲 𐑕𐑹𐑛 𐑦𐑯 𐑣𐑨𐑯𐑛 𐑑 𐑖𐑴 𐑐𐑰𐑐𐑩𐑤 𐑞𐑨𐑑 𐑲 𐑒𐑫𐑛 𐑓𐑲𐑑 𐑦𐑓 𐑦𐑑 𐑢𐑻 𐑥𐑲 ·𐑥𐑭𐑕𐑑𐑼'𐑟 𐑢𐑦𐑤, 𐑯 𐑞𐑨𐑑 𐑲 𐑒𐑫𐑛 𐑒𐑦𐑤 𐑞 𐑥𐑨𐑯 𐑣𐑵 𐑒𐑦𐑤𐑟 𐑥𐑰 𐑦𐑓 𐑲 𐑗𐑴𐑟.

𐑞 𐑧𐑛𐑦𐑑𐑼. 𐑐𐑫𐑑 𐑪𐑯 𐑞𐑨𐑑 𐑸𐑥𐑼.

·𐑓𐑧𐑮𐑴𐑝𐑾𐑕. 𐑯𐑴 𐑸𐑥𐑼.

𐑞 𐑧𐑛𐑦𐑑𐑼 [𐑚𐑫𐑤𐑦𐑦𐑙 𐑣𐑦𐑥] 𐑛𐑵 𐑢𐑪𐑑 𐑿'𐑼 𐑑𐑴𐑤𐑛. 𐑐𐑫𐑑 𐑪𐑯 𐑞𐑨𐑑 𐑸𐑥𐑼.

·𐑓𐑧𐑮𐑴𐑝𐑾𐑕 [𐑜𐑮𐑦𐑐𐑦𐑙 𐑞 𐑕𐑹𐑛 𐑯 𐑤𐑫𐑒𐑦𐑙 𐑛𐑱𐑯𐑡𐑼𐑩𐑕] 𐑲 𐑕𐑱, 𐑯𐑴 𐑸𐑥𐑼.

𐑞 𐑧𐑛𐑦𐑑𐑼. 𐑯 𐑢𐑪𐑑 𐑨𐑥 𐑲 𐑑 𐑕𐑱 𐑢𐑧𐑯 𐑲 𐑨𐑥

and pieces of armor which they throw down in a heap.

THE CALL BOY. By your leave, Caesar. Number eleven! Gladiators and Christians!

Ferrovius springs up, ready for martyrdom. The other Christians take the summons as best they can, some joyful and brave, some patient and dignified, some tearful and helpless, some embracing one another with emotion. The Call Boy goes back into the passage.

CAESAR [*turning at the door of the box*] The hour has come, Ferrovius. I shall go into my box and see you killed, since you scorn the Pretorian Guard. [*He goes into the box. The Captain shuts the door, remaining inside with the Emperor, Metellus and the rest of the suite disperse to their seats. The Christians, led by Ferrovius, move towards the passage*].

LAVINIA [*to Ferrovius*] Farewell.

THE EDITOR. Steady there. You Christians have got to fight. Here! arm yourselves.

FERROVIUS [*picking up a sword*] I'll die sword in hand to shew people that I could fight if it were my Master's will, and that I could kill the man who kills me if I chose.

THE EDITOR. Put on that armor.

FERROVIUS. No armor.

THE EDITOR [*bullying him*] Do what youre told. Put on that armor.

FERROVIUS [*gripping the sword and looking dangerous*] I said, No armor.

THE EDITOR. And what am I to say when I am

𐑦𐑯𐑕𐑑𐑧𐑛 𐑝 𐑕𐑧𐑯𐑛𐑦𐑙 𐑝 𐑩𐑤𐑩𐑯 𐑥𐑧𐑯 𐑦𐑯 𐑑 𐑓𐑲𐑑 𐑥𐑲 𐑥𐑧𐑯 𐑦𐑯 𐑞 𐑼𐑰𐑯𐑩?

𐑓𐑧𐑮𐑴𐑝𐑾𐑕. 𐑕𐑱𐑝 𐑿𐑼 𐑚𐑮𐑧𐑔, 𐑚𐑮𐑳𐑞𐑼; 𐑯 𐑜𐑦𐑝 𐑯𐑴 𐑓𐑮𐑰 𐑝 𐑞 𐑚𐑪𐑯𐑛𐑟 𐑝 𐑞𐑦𐑕 𐑚𐑪𐑛𐑦.

𐑞 𐑧𐑛𐑦𐑑𐑼. 𐑕𐑑𐑪𐑐! 𐑿 𐑒𐑮𐑦𐑕𐑗𐑩𐑯 𐑓𐑵𐑤! [𐑣𐑰 𐑚𐑮𐑱𐑕 𐑞 𐑜𐑮𐑲𐑕 𐑤𐑲𐑯𐑟 𐑦𐑥𐑐𐑱𐑖𐑩𐑯𐑑𐑤𐑦, 𐑯𐑪𐑑 𐑢𐑴𐑦𐑙 𐑦𐑒𐑟𐑨𐑒𐑑𐑤𐑦 𐑢𐑪𐑑 𐑑 𐑛𐑵].

𐑨𐑯𐑛𐑮𐑩𐑒𐑤𐑰𐑟 [𐑑 ·𐑓𐑧𐑮𐑴𐑝𐑾𐑕] 𐑓𐑺𐑢𐑧𐑤, 𐑚𐑮𐑳𐑞𐑼, 𐑑𐑦𐑤 𐑢𐑰 𐑥𐑰𐑑 𐑦𐑯 𐑞 𐑕𐑢𐑰𐑑 𐑚𐑲-𐑯-𐑚𐑲.

𐑞 𐑧𐑛𐑦𐑑𐑼 [𐑑 ·𐑨𐑯𐑛𐑮𐑩𐑒𐑤𐑰𐑟] 𐑿 𐑸 𐑜𐑴𐑦𐑙 𐑑𐑵. 𐑑𐑱𐑒 𐑩 𐑕𐑹𐑛 𐑞𐑺; 𐑯 𐑚𐑰𐑑 𐑦𐑯 𐑢𐑳𐑯 𐑼𐑰𐑯𐑩 𐑿 𐑒𐑨𐑯 𐑓𐑲𐑯𐑛 𐑑 𐑓𐑲𐑑 𐑿.

𐑨𐑯𐑛𐑮𐑩𐑒𐑤𐑰𐑟. 𐑯𐑴, 𐑕𐑻: 𐑲 𐑒𐑭𐑯𐑑 𐑓𐑲𐑑: 𐑲 𐑯𐑧𐑝𐑼 𐑒𐑫𐑛: 𐑲 𐑒𐑭𐑯𐑑 𐑚𐑮𐑦𐑙 𐑥𐑲𐑕𐑧𐑤𐑓 𐑑 𐑛𐑦𐑕𐑑𐑻𐑚 𐑧𐑯𐑦𐑢𐑳𐑯 𐑦𐑤𐑕. 𐑲'𐑥 𐑑 𐑚𐑰 𐑔𐑮𐑴𐑯 𐑑 𐑞 𐑤𐑲𐑩𐑯𐑟 𐑢𐑦𐑞 𐑞 𐑤𐑱𐑛𐑦.

𐑞 𐑧𐑛𐑦𐑑𐑼. 𐑞𐑧𐑯 𐑜𐑧𐑑 𐑬𐑑 𐑝 𐑞 𐑢𐑱 𐑯 𐑜𐑴 𐑚𐑨𐑒 𐑑 𐑿𐑼 𐑐𐑤𐑱𐑕. [·𐑨𐑯𐑛𐑮𐑩𐑒𐑤𐑰𐑟 𐑕𐑑𐑨𐑯𐑛𐑟 𐑩𐑕𐑲𐑛 𐑢𐑦𐑞 𐑒𐑩𐑯𐑓𐑿𐑟𐑛 𐑚𐑴𐑤𐑛𐑯𐑩𐑕]. 𐑯𐑬 𐑞𐑧𐑯! 𐑸 𐑿 𐑮𐑧𐑛𐑦 𐑞𐑺?

[𐑩 𐑑𐑮𐑳𐑥𐑐𐑩𐑑 𐑦𐑟 𐑣𐑻𐑛 𐑓𐑮𐑪𐑥 𐑞 𐑼𐑰𐑯𐑩].

𐑓𐑧𐑮𐑴𐑝𐑾𐑕 [𐑕𐑑𐑸𐑑𐑦𐑙 𐑒𐑩𐑯𐑝𐑳𐑤𐑕𐑦𐑝𐑤𐑦] 𐑜𐑦𐑝 𐑥𐑰 𐑥𐑲 𐑕𐑹𐑛!

𐑞 𐑧𐑛𐑦𐑑𐑼. 𐑩𐑣𐑩! 𐑞𐑨𐑑 𐑓𐑮𐑲𐑑𐑩𐑯𐑟 𐑿, 𐑛𐑳𐑟 𐑦𐑑?

𐑓𐑧𐑮𐑴𐑝𐑾𐑕. 𐑯𐑴: 𐑞𐑺 𐑦𐑟 𐑯𐑴 𐑑𐑧𐑮𐑼 𐑤𐑧𐑓𐑑 𐑞 𐑑𐑧𐑮𐑼 𐑝 𐑞𐑨𐑑 𐑕𐑑𐑰𐑤 𐑑 𐑥𐑰. 𐑚𐑳𐑑 𐑲 𐑜𐑴 𐑩 𐑑𐑧𐑮𐑦𐑚𐑩𐑤 𐑢𐑦 𐑑 𐑞 𐑢𐑦𐑤𐑛 𐑝 𐑞 𐑓𐑤𐑧𐑖 𐑯 𐑞 𐑜𐑮𐑱𐑕 𐑝 𐑞 𐑛𐑧𐑝𐑩𐑤 𐑦𐑯 𐑞 𐑕𐑑𐑮𐑧𐑙𐑔 𐑝 𐑞𐑦𐑕 𐑓𐑤𐑧𐑖, 𐑢𐑧𐑯 𐑧𐑝𐑼𐑦 𐑥𐑳𐑕𐑩𐑤 𐑝 𐑥𐑲 𐑚𐑪𐑛𐑦 𐑒𐑮𐑲𐑟 𐑬𐑑 𐑥𐑲 𐑚𐑤𐑳𐑛: 𐑲 𐑓𐑰𐑤 𐑥𐑲 𐑚𐑪𐑛𐑦 𐑕𐑢𐑧𐑤 𐑢𐑦𐑞 𐑜𐑮𐑱𐑑 𐑚𐑪𐑛𐑦𐑤𐑦 𐑥𐑲 𐑣𐑸𐑑: 𐑲 𐑥𐑳𐑕𐑑 𐑓𐑲𐑑: 𐑲 𐑥𐑳𐑕𐑑 𐑕𐑑𐑮𐑲𐑒: 𐑲 𐑥𐑳𐑕𐑑 𐑒𐑪𐑯𐑒𐑻: ·𐑕𐑱𐑑𐑩𐑯 𐑜𐑮𐑨𐑕𐑐𐑕 𐑥𐑲 𐑢𐑦𐑞 𐑚𐑰 𐑕𐑰𐑛 𐑦𐑯 𐑣𐑦𐑟 𐑦𐑯𐑓𐑻𐑯𐑩𐑤 𐑕𐑢𐑧𐑑 𐑑𐑴 𐑥𐑳𐑕𐑑 𐑞𐑨𐑑 𐑕𐑑𐑮𐑪𐑙 𐑐𐑳𐑤𐑕 𐑤𐑲𐑒 𐑦𐑯 𐑥𐑰. 𐑴, 𐑚𐑮𐑳𐑞𐑼𐑟, 𐑚𐑦𐑥! 𐑦𐑯𐑛𐑳𐑤𐑡 𐑥𐑰! 𐑛𐑦𐑕𐑑𐑮𐑨𐑒𐑑 𐑥𐑰 𐑞𐑨𐑑

accused of sending a naked man in to fight my men in armor?

FERROVIUS. Say your prayers, brother; and have no fear of the princes of this world.

THE EDITOR. Tsha! You obstinate fool! [*He bites his lips irresolutely, not knowing exactly what to do*].

ANDROCLES [*to Ferrovius*] Farewell, brother, till we meet in the sweet by-and-by.

THE EDITOR [*to Androcles*] You are going too. Take a sword there; and put on any armor you can find to fit you.

ANDROCLES. No, really: I cant fight: I never could: I cant bring myself to dislike anyone enough. I'm to be thrown to the lions with the lady.

THE EDITOR. Then get out of the way and hold your noise. [*Androcles steps aside with cheerful docility*]. Now then! Are you all ready there?

A trumpet is heard from the arena.

FERROVIUS [*starting convulsively*] Heaven give me strength!

THE EDITOR. Aha! That frightens you, does it?

FERROVIUS. Man: there is no terror like the terror of that sound to me. When I hear a trumpet or a drum or the clash of steel or the hum of the catapult as the great stone flies, fire runs through my veins: I feel my blood surge up hot behind my eyes: I must charge: I must strike: I must conquer: Caesar himself will not be safe in his imperial seat if once that spirit gets loose in me. Oh, brothers, pray! exhort me! remind me that

𐑦𐑓 𐑲 𐑮𐑱𐑟 𐑥𐑲 𐑕𐑹𐑛 𐑥𐑲 𐑪𐑯𐑼 𐑓𐑷𐑤𐑟 𐑯 𐑥𐑲 ·𐑥𐑭𐑕𐑑𐑼 𐑦𐑟 𐑒𐑮𐑵𐑕𐑦𐑓𐑲𐑛 𐑩𐑓𐑮𐑧𐑖.

𐑨𐑯𐑛𐑮𐑩𐑒𐑤𐑰𐑟. 𐑡𐑳𐑕𐑑 𐑒𐑰𐑐 𐑔𐑦𐑙𐑒𐑦𐑙 𐑣𐑬 𐑒𐑮𐑵𐑩𐑤𐑦 𐑿 𐑥𐑲𐑑 𐑣𐑻𐑑 𐑞 𐑐𐑫𐑼 𐑜𐑤𐑨𐑛𐑦𐑱𐑑𐑼𐑟.

𐑓𐑧𐑮𐑴𐑝𐑾𐑕. 𐑦𐑑 𐑛𐑳𐑟 𐑯𐑪𐑑 𐑣𐑻𐑑 𐑩 𐑥𐑨𐑯 𐑑 𐑒𐑦𐑤 𐑣𐑦𐑥.

𐑤𐑩𐑝𐑦𐑯𐑾. 𐑯𐑳𐑔𐑦𐑙 𐑚𐑳𐑑 𐑓𐑱𐑔 𐑒𐑨𐑯 𐑕𐑱𐑝 𐑿.

𐑓𐑧𐑮𐑴𐑝𐑾𐑕. 𐑓𐑱𐑔! 𐑢𐑦𐑗 𐑓𐑱𐑔? 𐑞𐑺 𐑸 𐑑𐑵 𐑓𐑱𐑔𐑕. 𐑞𐑺 𐑦𐑟 𐑬𐑼 𐑓𐑱𐑔. 𐑯 𐑞𐑺 𐑦𐑟 𐑞 𐑧𐑥𐑐𐑼𐑼'𐑟 𐑓𐑱𐑔, 𐑞 𐑓𐑱𐑔 𐑦𐑯 𐑓𐑲𐑑𐑦𐑙, 𐑞 𐑓𐑱𐑔 𐑞𐑨𐑑 𐑕𐑰𐑟 ·𐑜𐑪𐑛 𐑦𐑯 𐑞 𐑕𐑹𐑛. 𐑣𐑬 𐑦𐑓 𐑞𐑨𐑑 𐑓𐑱𐑔 𐑖𐑫𐑛 𐑴𐑝𐑼𐑢𐑧𐑤𐑥 𐑥𐑰?

𐑤𐑩𐑝𐑦𐑯𐑾. 𐑿 𐑢𐑦𐑤 𐑓𐑲𐑯𐑛 𐑿𐑼 𐑮𐑦𐑩𐑤 𐑓𐑱𐑔 𐑦𐑯 𐑞 𐑬𐑼 𐑝 𐑑𐑮𐑲𐑩𐑤.

𐑓𐑧𐑮𐑴𐑝𐑾𐑕. 𐑞𐑨𐑑 𐑦𐑟 𐑢𐑪𐑑 𐑲 𐑓𐑽. 𐑲 𐑯𐑴 𐑞𐑨𐑑 𐑲 𐑨𐑥 𐑩 𐑓𐑲𐑑𐑼. 𐑣𐑬 𐑒𐑨𐑯 𐑲 𐑓𐑰𐑤 𐑖𐑫𐑼 𐑞𐑨𐑑 𐑲 𐑨𐑥 𐑩 𐑒𐑮𐑦𐑕𐑗𐑩𐑯?

𐑨𐑯𐑛𐑮𐑩𐑒𐑤𐑰𐑟. 𐑔𐑮𐑴 𐑩𐑢𐑱 𐑞 𐑕𐑹𐑛, 𐑚𐑮𐑳𐑞𐑼.

𐑓𐑧𐑮𐑴𐑝𐑾𐑕. 𐑲 𐑒𐑭𐑯𐑑. 𐑦𐑑 𐑒𐑤𐑰𐑝𐑟 𐑑 𐑥𐑲 𐑣𐑨𐑯𐑛. 𐑲 𐑒𐑫𐑛 𐑨𐑟 𐑰𐑟𐑦𐑤𐑦 𐑔𐑮𐑴 𐑩 𐑢𐑫𐑥𐑩𐑯 𐑲 𐑤𐑳𐑝𐑛 𐑓𐑮𐑪𐑥 𐑥𐑲 𐑸𐑥𐑟. [𐑕𐑑𐑸𐑑𐑦𐑙] 𐑣𐑵 𐑕𐑐𐑴𐑒 𐑞𐑨𐑑 𐑚𐑤𐑨𐑕𐑓𐑩𐑥𐑦? 𐑯𐑪𐑑 𐑲.

𐑤𐑩𐑝𐑦𐑯𐑾. 𐑲 𐑒𐑭𐑯𐑑 𐑣𐑧𐑤𐑐 𐑿, 𐑓𐑮𐑧𐑯𐑛. 𐑲 𐑒𐑭𐑯𐑑 𐑑𐑧𐑤 𐑿 𐑯𐑪𐑑 𐑑 𐑕𐑱𐑝 𐑿𐑼 𐑴𐑯 𐑤𐑲𐑓. 𐑕𐑳𐑥𐑔𐑦𐑙 𐑢𐑦𐑤𐑓𐑫𐑤 𐑦𐑯 𐑥𐑰 𐑢𐑪𐑯𐑑𐑕 𐑑 𐑕𐑰 𐑿 𐑓𐑲𐑑 𐑿𐑼 𐑢𐑱 𐑦𐑯𐑑𐑫 𐑣𐑧𐑝𐑩𐑯.

𐑓𐑧𐑮𐑴𐑝𐑾𐑕. 𐑣𐑭!

𐑨𐑯𐑛𐑮𐑩𐑒𐑤𐑰𐑟. 𐑚𐑳𐑑 𐑦𐑓 𐑿 𐑸 𐑜𐑴𐑦𐑙 𐑑 𐑜𐑦𐑝 𐑳𐑐 𐑬𐑼 𐑓𐑱𐑔, 𐑚𐑮𐑳𐑞𐑼, 𐑢𐑲 𐑯𐑪𐑑 𐑛𐑵 𐑦𐑑 𐑢𐑦𐑞𐑬𐑑 𐑣𐑻𐑑𐑦𐑙 𐑯𐑴𐑚𐑪𐑛𐑦? 𐑛𐑴𐑯𐑑 𐑓𐑲𐑑 𐑞𐑧𐑥. 𐑚𐑻𐑯 𐑞 𐑦𐑯𐑕𐑧𐑯𐑕.

𐑓𐑧𐑮𐑴𐑝𐑾𐑕. 𐑚𐑻𐑯 𐑞 𐑦𐑯𐑕𐑧𐑯𐑕! 𐑯𐑧𐑝𐑼.

𐑤𐑩𐑝𐑦𐑯𐑾. 𐑞𐑨𐑑 𐑦𐑟 𐑴𐑯𐑤𐑦 𐑐𐑮𐑲𐑛, ·𐑓𐑧𐑮𐑴𐑝𐑾𐑕.

𐑓𐑧𐑮𐑴𐑝𐑾𐑕. 𐑴𐑯𐑤𐑦 𐑐𐑮𐑲𐑛! 𐑢𐑪𐑑 𐑦𐑟 𐑯𐑴𐑚𐑤𐑼 𐑞𐑩𐑯

if I raise my sword my honor falls and my Master is crucified afresh.

ANDROCLES. Just keep thinking how cruelly you might hurt the poor gladiators.

FERROVIUS. It does not hurt a man to kill him.

LAVINIA. Nothing but faith can save you.

FERROVIUS. Faith! Which faith? There are two faiths. There is our faith. And there is the warrior's faith, the faith in fighting, the faith that sees God in the sword. How if that faith should overwhelm me?

LAVINIA. You will find your real faith in the hour of trial.

FERROVIUS. That is what I fear. I know that I am a fighter. How can I feel sure that I am a Christian?

ANDROCLES. Throw away the sword, brother.

FERROVIUS. I cannot. It cleaves to my hand. I could as easily throw a woman I loved from my arms. [*Starting*] Who spoke that blasphemy? Not I.

LAVINIA. I cant help you, friend. I cant tell you not to save your own life. Something wilful in me wants to see you fight your way into heaven.

FERROVIUS. Ha!

ANDROCLES. But if you are going to give up our faith, brother, why not do it without hurting anybody? Dont fight them. Burn the incense.

FERROVIUS. Burn the incense! Never.

LAVINIA. That is only pride, Ferrovius.

FERROVIUS. O n l y pride! What is nobler than

𐑐𐑮𐑲𐑛? [𐑒𐑪𐑯𐑖𐑩𐑯𐑕 𐑕𐑑𐑮𐑦𐑒𐑩𐑯] 𐑴, 𐑲'𐑥 𐑕𐑑𐑰𐑐𐑑 𐑦𐑯 𐑕𐑦𐑯. 𐑲'𐑥 𐑐𐑮𐑬𐑛 𐑝 𐑥𐑲 𐑐𐑮𐑲𐑛.

𐑤𐑩𐑝𐑦𐑯𐑾. 𐑞𐑱 𐑕𐑱 𐑢𐑰 𐑒𐑮𐑦𐑕𐑗𐑩𐑯𐑟 𐑸 𐑞 𐑐𐑮𐑬𐑛𐑩𐑕𐑑 𐑛𐑧𐑝𐑩𐑤𐑟 𐑪𐑯 𐑻𐑔 — 𐑞𐑨𐑑 𐑴𐑯𐑤𐑦 𐑞 𐑢𐑰𐑒 𐑸 𐑥𐑰𐑒. 𐑴, 𐑲 𐑨𐑥 𐑢𐑻𐑕 𐑞𐑨𐑯 𐑿. 𐑲 𐑷𐑑 𐑑 𐑕𐑧𐑯𐑛 𐑿 𐑑 𐑛𐑧𐑔; 𐑯 𐑲 𐑨𐑥 𐑑𐑧𐑥𐑐𐑑𐑦𐑙 𐑿.

𐑨𐑯𐑛𐑮𐑩𐑒𐑤𐑰𐑟. 𐑚𐑮𐑳𐑞𐑼, 𐑚𐑮𐑳𐑞𐑼: 𐑤𐑧𐑑 𐑞𐑧𐑥 𐑮𐑱𐑡 𐑯 𐑒𐑦𐑤: 𐑤𐑧𐑑 𐑳𐑕 𐑚𐑰 𐑚𐑮𐑱𐑝 𐑯 𐑕𐑳𐑓𐑼. 𐑿 𐑥𐑳𐑕𐑑 𐑜𐑴 𐑨𐑟 𐑩 𐑤𐑨𐑥 𐑑 𐑞 𐑕𐑤𐑷𐑑𐑼.

𐑓𐑧𐑮𐑴𐑝𐑾𐑕. 𐑲, 𐑲: 𐑞𐑨𐑑 𐑦𐑟 𐑮𐑲𐑑. 𐑯𐑪𐑑 𐑨𐑟 𐑩 𐑤𐑨𐑥 𐑦𐑟 𐑕𐑤𐑱𐑯 𐑚𐑲 𐑞 𐑚𐑫𐑗𐑼; 𐑚𐑳𐑑 𐑨𐑟 𐑩 𐑚𐑫𐑗𐑼 𐑥𐑲𐑑 𐑤𐑧𐑑 𐑣𐑦𐑥𐑕𐑧𐑤𐑓 𐑚𐑰 𐑕𐑤𐑱𐑯 𐑚𐑲 𐑩 [𐑤𐑫𐑒𐑦𐑙 𐑨𐑑 𐑞 𐑧𐑛𐑦𐑑𐑼] 𐑚𐑲 𐑩 𐑕𐑦𐑤𐑦 𐑪𐑒𐑕 𐑣𐑵𐑟 𐑣𐑧𐑛 𐑣𐑰 𐑒𐑫𐑛 𐑯𐑪𐑒 𐑪𐑓 𐑢𐑦𐑞 𐑢𐑳𐑯 𐑑𐑢𐑦𐑕𐑑.

[𐑚𐑦𐑓𐑹 𐑞 𐑧𐑛𐑦𐑑𐑼 𐑒𐑨𐑯 𐑮𐑦𐑑𐑹𐑑, 𐑞 𐑒𐑷𐑤 𐑚𐑶 𐑮𐑳𐑖𐑩𐑟 𐑳𐑐 𐑔𐑮𐑵 𐑞 𐑐𐑨𐑕𐑦𐑡, 𐑯 𐑞 𐑒𐑨𐑐𐑑𐑩𐑯 𐑒𐑳𐑥𐑟 𐑓𐑮𐑪𐑥 𐑞 𐑧𐑥𐑐𐑼𐑼'𐑟 𐑚𐑪𐑒𐑕 𐑯 𐑛𐑦𐑕𐑧𐑯𐑛𐑟 𐑞 𐑕𐑑𐑧𐑐𐑕].

𐑞 𐑒𐑷𐑤 𐑚𐑶. 𐑦𐑯 𐑢𐑦𐑞 𐑿: 𐑦𐑯𐑑𐑵 𐑞 𐑩𐑮𐑰𐑯𐑩. 𐑞 𐑕𐑑𐑱𐑡 𐑦𐑟 𐑢𐑱𐑑𐑦𐑙.

𐑞 𐑒𐑨𐑐𐑑𐑩𐑯. 𐑞 𐑧𐑥𐑐𐑼𐑼 𐑦𐑟 𐑢𐑱𐑑𐑦𐑙. [𐑑 𐑞 𐑧𐑛𐑦𐑑𐑼] 𐑢𐑪𐑑 𐑸 𐑿 𐑛𐑦𐑤𐑱𐑦𐑙 𐑓𐑹, 𐑥𐑨𐑯? 𐑕𐑧𐑯𐑛 𐑞𐑧𐑥 𐑦𐑯 𐑨𐑑 𐑢𐑳𐑯𐑕.

𐑞 𐑧𐑛𐑦𐑑𐑼. 𐑘𐑧𐑕, 𐑕𐑻: 𐑦𐑑'𐑕 𐑞𐑰𐑟 𐑒𐑮𐑦𐑕𐑗𐑩𐑯𐑟 𐑣𐑨𐑙𐑦𐑙 𐑚𐑨𐑒.

𐑓𐑧𐑮𐑴𐑝𐑾𐑕 [𐑦𐑯 𐑩 𐑝𐑶𐑕 𐑝 𐑔𐑳𐑯𐑛𐑼] 𐑤𐑲𐑼!

𐑞 𐑧𐑛𐑦𐑑𐑼 [𐑯𐑪𐑑 𐑣𐑰𐑛𐑦𐑙 𐑣𐑦𐑥] 𐑥𐑸𐑗. [𐑞 𐑜𐑤𐑨𐑛𐑦𐑱𐑑𐑼𐑟 𐑑𐑴𐑤𐑛 𐑪𐑓 𐑑 𐑓𐑲𐑑 𐑢𐑦𐑞 𐑞 𐑒𐑮𐑦𐑕𐑗𐑩𐑯𐑟 𐑥𐑸𐑗 𐑛𐑬𐑯 𐑞 𐑐𐑨𐑕𐑦𐑡] 𐑓𐑪𐑤𐑴 𐑳𐑐 𐑞𐑺, 𐑿.

𐑞 𐑒𐑮𐑦𐑕𐑗𐑩𐑯 𐑥𐑧𐑯 𐑯 𐑢𐑦𐑥𐑦𐑯 [𐑨𐑟 𐑞𐑱 𐑐𐑭𐑕] 𐑚𐑰 𐑕𐑑𐑧𐑛𐑓𐑭𐑕𐑑, 𐑚𐑮𐑳𐑞𐑼. 𐑓𐑺𐑢𐑧𐑤. 𐑣𐑴𐑤𐑛 𐑳𐑐 𐑞 𐑓𐑤𐑨𐑜, 𐑚𐑮𐑳𐑞𐑼. 𐑓𐑺𐑢𐑧𐑤. 𐑜𐑴 𐑑 𐑜𐑤𐑹𐑦, 𐑛𐑽𐑼𐑩𐑕𐑑. 𐑓𐑺𐑢𐑧𐑤. 𐑮𐑦𐑥𐑧𐑥𐑚𐑼: 𐑢𐑰 𐑸 𐑐𐑮𐑱𐑦𐑙 𐑓 𐑿.

pride? [*Conscience stricken*] Oh, I'm steeped in sin. I'm proud of my pride.

LAVINIA. They say we Christians are the proudest devils on earth – that only the weak are meek. Oh, I am worse than you. I ought to send you to death; and I am tempting you.

ANDROCLES. Brother, brother: let them rage and kill: let us be brave and suffer. You must go as a lamb to the slaughter.

FERROVIUS. Aye, aye: that is right. Not as a lamb is slain by the butcher; but as a butcher might let himself be slain by a [*looking at the Editor*] by a silly ram whose head he could fetch off in one twist.

Before the Editor can retort, the Call Boy rushes up through the passage, and the Captain comes from the Emperor's box and descends the steps.

THE CALL BOY. In with you: into the arena. The stage is waiting.

THE CAPTAIN. The Emperor is waiting. [*To the Editor*] What are you dreaming of, man? Send your men in at once.

THE EDITOR. Yes, sir: it's these Christians hanging back.

FERROVIUS [*in a voice of thunder*] Liar!

THE EDITOR [*not heeding him*] March. [*The gladiators told off to fight with the Christians march down the passage*] Follow up there, you.

THE CHRISTIAN MEN AND WOMEN [*as they part*] Be steadfast, brother. Farewell. Hold up the faith, brother. Farewell. Go to glory, dearest. Farewell. Remember: we are praying for you.

𐑤𐑨𐑝𐑦𐑯𐑾. 𐑲𐑥 𐑕𐑪𐑮𐑦, 𐑒𐑨𐑐𐑑𐑩𐑯. 𐑤𐑨𐑝𐑦𐑯𐑾. 𐑒𐑳𐑥 𐑤𐑨𐑝𐑦𐑯𐑾 𐑢𐑳𐑥 𐑞 𐑒𐑮𐑲𐑕𐑑 𐑤𐑲𐑓 𐑯 𐑤𐑩𐑝 𐑤𐑲𐑓 𐑕𐑩𐑤𐑦𐑥 𐑣𐑦𐑥. 𐑤𐑨𐑝𐑦𐑯𐑾. 𐑑𐑮𐑲𐑛 𐑓𐑹 𐑔𐑨𐑑 𐑣𐑦𐑥: 𐑒𐑮𐑦𐑕𐑑𐑾𐑯 𐑢𐑳𐑑, 𐑒𐑨𐑐𐑑𐑩𐑯. 𐑤𐑨𐑝𐑦𐑯𐑾. 𐑣𐑵𐑥𐑩𐑯 𐑐𐑰𐑐𐑩𐑤, 𐑒𐑳𐑥𐑐𐑩𐑯𐑦. 𐑤𐑨𐑝𐑦𐑯𐑾.

𐑞 𐑧𐑛𐑦𐑑𐑼 [𐑨𐑑 𐑩 𐑤𐑪𐑕𐑑] 𐑤𐑨𐑑 𐑞𐑧𐑥 𐑦𐑯, 𐑞𐑧𐑯. [𐑞 𐑒𐑮𐑦𐑕𐑑𐑾𐑯𐑟 𐑒𐑳𐑥 𐑦𐑯𐑑𐑵 𐑞 𐑓𐑮𐑳𐑯𐑑 𐑓𐑮𐑪𐑥 𐑞 𐑕𐑧𐑤 𐑚𐑳𐑑 𐑦𐑯𐑕𐑑𐑧𐑛 𐑞𐑧𐑥].

𐑓𐑧𐑮𐑴𐑝𐑾𐑕 [𐑦𐑯𐑕𐑑𐑩𐑯𐑑𐑤𐑦] 𐑒𐑦𐑤 𐑞𐑧𐑥, 𐑒𐑨𐑐𐑑𐑩𐑯; 𐑯 𐑲 𐑢𐑦𐑤 𐑛𐑲 𐑯 𐑞𐑧 𐑞𐑧𐑥 𐑩 𐑕𐑧𐑒𐑿𐑑𐑼. [𐑑 𐑞𐑦 𐑤𐑳𐑝 𐑒𐑮𐑦𐑕𐑑𐑾𐑯𐑟] 𐑒𐑨𐑐𐑑𐑩𐑯: 𐑞 𐑐𐑰𐑐𐑩𐑤 𐑕𐑩𐑥𐑑𐑲𐑥𐑟 𐑞𐑨𐑑 𐑒𐑨𐑯. 𐑞𐑧𐑥 𐑦𐑟 𐑛𐑦𐑕𐑑𐑩𐑯𐑕 𐑦𐑯 𐑣𐑦𐑥 𐑞𐑨𐑑 𐑑 ·𐑒𐑮𐑲𐑕𐑑. 𐑕𐑱𐑝 𐑦𐑑 𐑒𐑳𐑥𐑐𐑩𐑯𐑦, 𐑒𐑳𐑑 𐑩𐑢𐑱; 𐑯 𐑒𐑮𐑦𐑕𐑑𐑾𐑯! 𐑢𐑦𐑤 𐑩 𐑤𐑧𐑑 𐑩 𐑤𐑴𐑯 𐑯 𐑛𐑦𐑕𐑐𐑲𐑟, 𐑢𐑦𐑤 𐑩 𐑤𐑧𐑑 𐑩 𐑕𐑑𐑮𐑱𐑯𐑡𐑼 𐑚𐑦. [𐑣𐑰 𐑚𐑦 𐑤𐑴 𐑛𐑬𐑯 𐑞 𐑤𐑦𐑕𐑑. 𐑞𐑱 𐑤𐑫𐑒 𐑑 ·𐑒𐑨𐑐𐑑𐑩𐑯] 𐑤𐑨𐑝𐑦𐑯𐑾.

𐑒𐑨𐑐𐑑𐑩𐑯. 𐑦𐑯 𐑤𐑴𐑛𐑩𐑑: 𐑑 𐑕𐑧𐑯𐑑 𐑓𐑧𐑮𐑴 𐑦𐑯𐑑𐑵 𐑦𐑯 𐑞 𐑛𐑪𐑜.

𐑓𐑧𐑮𐑴𐑝𐑾𐑕. 𐑦𐑑 𐑦𐑟 𐑑𐑵 𐑚𐑧𐑛. 𐑲 𐑢𐑦𐑤 𐑢𐑱𐑑 𐑓𐑹 𐑦𐑑 𐑑 𐑤𐑧𐑕 𐑦𐑯 𐑑 𐑐𐑰𐑐𐑩𐑤. [𐑣𐑰 𐑚𐑴𐑟 𐑛𐑬𐑯 𐑞 𐑤𐑦𐑕𐑑].

𐑞 𐑧𐑛𐑦𐑑𐑼 [𐑑 𐑞 𐑒𐑷𐑤 𐑚𐑶] 𐑕𐑦𐑛𐑮𐑩𐑤 𐑐𐑴𐑛, 𐑞𐑦𐑕. 𐑲 𐑒𐑨𐑯𐑑 𐑞𐑧𐑥 𐑒𐑦𐑤 𐑣𐑦𐑥 𐑚𐑴𐑞 𐑑 𐑞 𐑤𐑲𐑩𐑯𐑟? 𐑦𐑑𐑕 𐑢𐑦𐑤 𐑩 𐑤𐑲𐑓'𐑟 𐑚𐑮𐑦𐑛. [𐑣𐑰 𐑚𐑴𐑟 𐑣𐑦𐑟 𐑣𐑧𐑛 𐑤𐑲𐑒𐑩𐑤𐑦 𐑦𐑯 𐑣𐑦𐑟 𐑣𐑨𐑯𐑛.

𐑥𐑧𐑯𐑩𐑤 𐑞𐑧𐑥 𐑯 𐑞𐑧𐑥 𐑞𐑨𐑑 𐑞 𐑒𐑮𐑦𐑕𐑑𐑾𐑯𐑟 𐑚𐑦 𐑒𐑳𐑥𐑑𐑩𐑤𐑦𐑕𐑦𐑯 𐑒𐑳𐑥 𐑦𐑯𐑑𐑵 𐑞 𐑐𐑨𐑕𐑦𐑡 𐑤𐑲𐑓𐑕𐑑𐑲𐑤. 𐑞 𐑒𐑷𐑤 𐑚𐑶 𐑤𐑫𐑒𐑕 𐑦𐑯 𐑞 𐑤𐑩𐑯𐑛𐑩𐑤𐑦𐑕 𐑯 𐑕𐑑𐑮𐑨𐑑𐑕 𐑩𐑤 𐑦𐑯 𐑞 𐑦𐑯𐑑𐑧𐑤𐑦𐑡𐑩𐑯𐑕 𐑦𐑯 𐑞 𐑤𐑲𐑩𐑯𐑟, 𐑯𐑬 𐑞 𐑧𐑛𐑦𐑑𐑼.

·𐑒𐑨𐑐𐑑𐑩𐑯 𐑯 𐑞 𐑛𐑦𐑕𐑑𐑩𐑯𐑕 𐑞𐑨𐑑 𐑕𐑦𐑑 𐑩𐑤 𐑒𐑳𐑥𐑩𐑤, 𐑚𐑱𐑤 𐑞𐑨𐑑 𐑚𐑧𐑕𐑑, 𐑕𐑧𐑝𐑩𐑤 𐑐𐑱𐑤 𐑕𐑑𐑧𐑝𐑩𐑤𐑦, 𐑕𐑧𐑝𐑩𐑤 𐑚𐑧𐑯𐑒𐑩𐑤, 𐑕𐑧𐑝𐑩𐑤 𐑛𐑱𐑟 𐑯 𐑕𐑑𐑦𐑤𐑯𐑧𐑕. ·𐑨𐑯𐑛𐑮𐑩𐑒𐑤𐑰𐑟

Farewell. Be strong, brother. Farewell. Dont forget that the divine love and our love surround you. Farewell. Nothing can hurt you: remember that, brother. Farewell. Eternal glory, dearest. Farewell.

THE EDITOR [*out of patience*] Shove them in, there.

The remaining gladiators and the Call Boy make a movement towards them.

FERROVIUS [*interposing*] Touch them, dogs; and we die here, and cheat the heathen of their spectacle. [*To his fellow Christians*] Brothers: the great moment has come. That passage is your hill to Calvary. Mount it bravely, but meekly; and remember! not a word of reproach, not a blow nor a struggle. Go. [*They go out through the passage. He turns to Lavinia*] Farewell.

LAVINIA. You forget: I must follow before you are cold.

FERROVIUS. It is true. Do not envy me because I pass before you to glory. [*He goes through the passage*].

THE EDITOR [*to the Call Boy*] Sickening work, this. Why cant they all be thrown to the lions? It's not a man's job. [*He throws himself moodily into his chair*].

The remaining gladiators go back to their former places indifferently. The Call Boy shrugs his shoulders and squats down at the entrance to the passage, near the Editor.

Lavinia and the Christian women sit down again, wrung with grief, some weeping silently, some praying, some calm and steadfast. Androcles

𐑕𐑦𐑑𐑕 𐑛𐑬𐑯 𐑩𐑑 ·𐑤𐑩𐑝𐑦𐑯𐑦𐑩'𐑟 𐑓𐑰𐑑. 𐑞 𐑒𐑨𐑐𐑑𐑦𐑯 𐑕𐑑𐑨𐑯𐑛𐑟 𐑪𐑯 𐑞 𐑕𐑑𐑧𐑐𐑕, 𐑢𐑪𐑗𐑦𐑙 𐑞𐑧𐑥 𐑒𐑿𐑮𐑾𐑕𐑤𐑦].

𐑨𐑯𐑛𐑮𐑩𐑒𐑤𐑰𐑟. 𐑲'𐑥 𐑜𐑤𐑨𐑛 𐑲 𐑣𐑨𐑝𐑯𐑑 𐑑 𐑓𐑲𐑑. 𐑞𐑨𐑑 𐑢𐑫𐑛 𐑮𐑾𐑤𐑦 𐑚𐑰 𐑩𐑯 𐑷𐑓𐑩𐑤 𐑥𐑸𐑑𐑼𐑛𐑩𐑥. 𐑲 𐑨𐑥 𐑤𐑳𐑒𐑦.

𐑤𐑩𐑝𐑦𐑯𐑦𐑩 [𐑤𐑫𐑒𐑦𐑙 𐑩𐑑 𐑣𐑦𐑥 𐑢𐑦𐑞 𐑩 𐑐𐑨𐑙 𐑝 𐑮𐑦𐑥𐑹𐑕] ·𐑨𐑯𐑛𐑮𐑩𐑒𐑤𐑰𐑟: 𐑚𐑻𐑯 𐑞 𐑦𐑯𐑕𐑧𐑯𐑕: 𐑿'𐑤 𐑚𐑰 𐑓𐑹𐑜𐑦𐑝𐑩𐑯. 𐑤𐑧𐑑 𐑥𐑲 𐑛𐑧𐑔 𐑩𐑑𐑴𐑯 𐑓𐑹 𐑚𐑴𐑔. 𐑲 𐑓𐑰𐑤 𐑨𐑟 𐑦𐑓 𐑲 𐑢𐑻 𐑒𐑦𐑤𐑦𐑙 𐑿.

𐑨𐑯𐑛𐑮𐑩𐑒𐑤𐑰𐑟. 𐑛𐑴𐑯𐑑 𐑔𐑦𐑙𐑒 𐑝 𐑥𐑰, 𐑕𐑦𐑕𐑑𐑼. 𐑔𐑦𐑙𐑒 𐑝 𐑿𐑼𐑕𐑧𐑤𐑓. 𐑞𐑨𐑑 𐑢𐑦𐑤 𐑒𐑰𐑐 𐑿𐑼 𐑣𐑸𐑑 𐑳𐑐.

[𐑞 𐑒𐑨𐑐𐑑𐑦𐑯 𐑤𐑭𐑓𐑕 𐑕𐑦𐑥𐑐𐑩𐑔𐑧𐑑𐑦𐑒𐑤𐑦].

𐑤𐑩𐑝𐑦𐑯𐑦𐑩 [𐑕𐑑𐑸𐑑𐑩𐑤𐑛: 𐑖𐑰 𐑣𐑨𐑛 𐑓𐑹𐑜𐑪𐑑𐑩𐑯 𐑣𐑦𐑟 𐑐𐑮𐑧𐑟𐑩𐑯𐑕] 𐑸 𐑿 𐑞𐑺, 𐑒𐑨𐑐𐑑𐑦𐑯? 𐑣𐑨𐑝 𐑿 𐑒𐑳𐑥 𐑑 𐑕𐑰 𐑥𐑰 𐑛𐑲?

𐑞 𐑒𐑨𐑐𐑑𐑦𐑯 [𐑒𐑳𐑥𐑦𐑙 𐑑 𐑣𐑻 𐑕𐑲𐑛] 𐑲 𐑨𐑥 𐑪𐑯 𐑛𐑿𐑑𐑦 𐑢𐑦𐑞 𐑞 𐑧𐑥𐑐𐑼𐑼, ·𐑤𐑩𐑝𐑦𐑯𐑦𐑩.

𐑤𐑩𐑝𐑦𐑯𐑦𐑩. 𐑦𐑟 𐑦𐑑 𐑐𐑸𐑑 𐑝 𐑿𐑼 𐑛𐑿𐑑𐑦 𐑑 𐑤𐑭𐑓 𐑨𐑑 𐑳𐑕?

𐑞 𐑒𐑨𐑐𐑑𐑦𐑯. 𐑯𐑴: 𐑞𐑨𐑑 𐑦𐑟 𐑐𐑸𐑑 𐑝 𐑥𐑲 𐑐𐑮𐑲𐑝𐑩𐑑 𐑐𐑤𐑧𐑠𐑼. 𐑿𐑼 𐑓𐑮𐑧𐑯𐑛 𐑣𐑽 𐑦𐑟 𐑩 𐑣𐑿𐑥𐑼𐑦𐑕𐑑. 𐑲 𐑤𐑭𐑓𐑑 𐑨𐑑 𐑣𐑦𐑟 𐑑𐑧𐑤𐑦𐑙 𐑿 𐑑 𐑔𐑦𐑙𐑒 𐑝 𐑿𐑼𐑕𐑧𐑤𐑓 𐑑 𐑒𐑰𐑐 𐑳𐑐 𐑿𐑼 𐑣𐑸𐑑. 𐑲 𐑕𐑱, 𐑔𐑦𐑙𐑒 𐑝 𐑿𐑼𐑕𐑧𐑤𐑓 𐑯 𐑚𐑻𐑯 𐑞 𐑦𐑯𐑕𐑧𐑯𐑕.

𐑤𐑩𐑝𐑦𐑯𐑦𐑩. 𐑣𐑰 𐑦𐑟 𐑯𐑪𐑑 𐑩 𐑣𐑿𐑥𐑼𐑦𐑕𐑑: 𐑣𐑰 𐑢𐑪𐑟 𐑮𐑲𐑑. 𐑿 𐑷𐑑 𐑑 𐑯𐑴 𐑞𐑨𐑑, 𐑒𐑨𐑐𐑑𐑦𐑯: 𐑿 𐑣𐑨𐑝 𐑚𐑰𐑯 𐑓𐑱𐑕 𐑑 𐑓𐑱𐑕 𐑢𐑦𐑞 𐑛𐑧𐑔.

𐑞 𐑒𐑨𐑐𐑑𐑦𐑯. 𐑯𐑪𐑑 𐑢𐑦𐑞 𐑕𐑻𐑑𐑩𐑯 𐑛𐑧𐑔, ·𐑤𐑩𐑝𐑦𐑯𐑦𐑩. 𐑴𐑯𐑤𐑦 𐑛𐑧𐑔 𐑦𐑯 𐑚𐑨𐑑𐑩𐑤, 𐑢𐑦𐑗 𐑕𐑐𐑺𐑟 𐑥𐑹 𐑥𐑧𐑯 𐑞𐑨𐑯 𐑛𐑧𐑔 𐑦𐑯 𐑚𐑧𐑛. 𐑢𐑪𐑑 𐑿 𐑸 𐑓𐑱𐑕𐑦𐑙 𐑦𐑟 𐑕𐑻𐑑𐑩𐑯 𐑛𐑧𐑔. 𐑿 𐑣𐑨𐑝 𐑯𐑳𐑔𐑦𐑙 𐑤𐑧𐑓𐑑 𐑯𐑬 𐑚𐑳𐑑 𐑿𐑼 𐑓𐑱𐑔 𐑦𐑯 𐑞𐑦𐑕 𐑒𐑮𐑱𐑟 𐑝 𐑿𐑼𐑟: 𐑞𐑦𐑕 𐑒𐑮𐑦𐑕𐑗𐑩𐑯𐑦𐑑𐑦. 𐑸 𐑿𐑼 𐑒𐑮𐑦𐑕𐑗𐑩𐑯 𐑓𐑺𐑦 𐑕𐑑𐑹𐑦𐑟 𐑧𐑯𐑦 𐑑𐑮𐑵𐑼 𐑞𐑨𐑯 𐑬𐑼 𐑕𐑑𐑹𐑦𐑟 𐑩𐑚𐑬𐑑 ·𐑡𐑵𐑐𐑦𐑑𐑼 𐑯 ·𐑛𐑲𐑨𐑯𐑩, 𐑦𐑯 𐑢𐑦𐑗, 𐑲 𐑥𐑱 𐑑𐑧𐑤

sits down at Lavinia's feet. The Captain stands on the stairs, watching her curiously.

ANDROCLES. I'm glad I havnt to fight. That would really be an awful martyrdom. I am lucky.

LAVINIA [*looking at him with a pang of remorse*] Androcles: burn the incense: youll be forgiven. Let my death atone for both. I feel as if I were killing you.

ANDROCLES. Dont think of me, sister. Think of yourself. That will keep your heart up.

The Captain laughs sardonically.

LAVINIA [*startled: she had forgotten his presence*] Are you there, handsome Captain? Have you come to see me die?

THE CAPTAIN [*coming to her side*] I am on duty with the Emperor, Lavinia.

LAVINIA. Is it part of your duty to laugh at us?

THE CAPTAIN. No: that is part of my private pleasure. Your friend here is a humorist. I laughed at his telling you to think of yourself to keep up your heart. *I* say, think of yourself and burn the incense.

LAVINIA. He is not a humorist: he was right. You ought to know that, Captain: you have been face to face with death.

THE CAPTAIN. Not with certain death, Lavinia. Only death in battle, which spares more men than death in bed. What you are facing is certain death. You have nothing left now but your faith in this craze of yours: this Christianity. Are your Christian fairy stories any truer than our stories about Jupiter and Diana, in which, I may tell

𐑿, 𐑲 𐑚𐑦𐑤𐑰𐑝 𐑯𐑴 𐑥𐑹 𐑞𐑨𐑯 𐑞 𐑧𐑥𐑐𐑼𐑼 𐑛𐑳𐑟, 𐑹 𐑧𐑯𐑦 𐑧𐑡𐑫𐑒𐑱𐑑𐑦𐑛 𐑥𐑨𐑯 𐑦𐑯 ·𐑮𐑴𐑥?

𐑤𐑩𐑝𐑦𐑯𐑾. 𐑒𐑨𐑐𐑑𐑩𐑯: 𐑷𐑤 𐑞𐑨𐑑 𐑕𐑰𐑥𐑟 𐑯𐑳𐑔𐑦𐑙 𐑑 𐑥𐑰 𐑯𐑬. 𐑲'𐑤 𐑯𐑪𐑑 𐑕𐑱 𐑞𐑨𐑑 𐑛𐑧𐑔 𐑦𐑟 𐑩 𐑑𐑧𐑮𐑩𐑚𐑩𐑤 𐑔𐑦𐑙; 𐑚𐑳𐑑 𐑲 𐑢𐑦𐑤 𐑕𐑱 𐑞𐑨𐑑 𐑦𐑑 𐑦𐑟 𐑕𐑴 𐑮𐑾𐑤 𐑩 𐑔𐑦𐑙 𐑞𐑨𐑑 𐑢𐑧𐑯 𐑦𐑑 𐑒𐑳𐑥𐑟 𐑒𐑤𐑴𐑕, 𐑷𐑤 𐑞 𐑦𐑥𐑨𐑡𐑦𐑯𐑼𐑦 𐑔𐑦𐑙𐑟 — 𐑷𐑤 𐑞 𐑕𐑑𐑹𐑦𐑟, 𐑨𐑟 𐑿 𐑒𐑷𐑤 𐑞𐑧𐑥 — 𐑓𐑱𐑛 𐑦𐑯𐑑𐑵 𐑥𐑽 𐑛𐑮𐑰𐑥𐑟 𐑚𐑦𐑕𐑲𐑛 𐑞𐑨𐑑 𐑦𐑯𐑧𐑒𐑕𐑼𐑩𐑚𐑩𐑤 𐑮𐑦𐑨𐑤𐑦𐑑𐑦. 𐑲 𐑯𐑴 𐑯𐑬 𐑞𐑨𐑑 𐑲 𐑨𐑥 𐑯𐑪𐑑 𐑛𐑲𐑦𐑙 𐑓𐑹 𐑕𐑑𐑹𐑦𐑟 𐑹 𐑛𐑮𐑰𐑥𐑟. 𐑛𐑦𐑛 𐑿 𐑣𐑽 𐑝 𐑞 𐑛𐑮𐑧𐑛𐑓𐑩𐑤 𐑔𐑦𐑙 𐑞𐑨𐑑 𐑣𐑨𐑐𐑩𐑯𐑛 𐑣𐑽 𐑢𐑲𐑤 𐑢𐑰 𐑢𐑻 𐑢𐑱𐑑𐑦𐑙?

𐑞 𐑒𐑨𐑐𐑑𐑩𐑯. 𐑲 𐑣𐑻𐑛 𐑞𐑨𐑑 𐑢𐑳𐑯 𐑝 𐑿𐑼 𐑓𐑧𐑤𐑴𐑟 𐑚𐑴𐑤𐑑𐑩𐑛, 𐑯 𐑮𐑨𐑯 𐑮𐑲𐑑 𐑦𐑯𐑑𐑵 𐑞 𐑡𐑷𐑟 𐑝 𐑞 𐑤𐑲𐑩𐑯. 𐑲 𐑤𐑭𐑓𐑑. 𐑲 𐑕𐑑𐑦𐑤 𐑤𐑭𐑓.

𐑤𐑩𐑝𐑦𐑯𐑾. 𐑞𐑧𐑯 𐑿 𐑛𐑦𐑛𐑯𐑑 𐑳𐑯𐑛𐑼𐑕𐑑𐑨𐑯𐑛 𐑢𐑪𐑑 𐑞𐑨𐑑 𐑥𐑧𐑯𐑑?

𐑞 𐑒𐑨𐑐𐑑𐑩𐑯. 𐑦𐑑 𐑥𐑧𐑯𐑑 𐑞𐑨𐑑 𐑞 𐑤𐑲𐑩𐑯 𐑣𐑨𐑛 𐑩 𐑒𐑻 𐑓𐑹 𐑣𐑦𐑟 𐑚𐑮𐑧𐑒𐑓𐑩𐑕𐑑.

𐑤𐑩𐑝𐑦𐑯𐑾. 𐑦𐑑 𐑥𐑧𐑯𐑑 𐑥𐑹 𐑞𐑨𐑯 𐑞𐑨𐑑, 𐑒𐑨𐑐𐑑𐑩𐑯. 𐑦𐑑 𐑥𐑧𐑯𐑑 𐑞𐑨𐑑 𐑩 𐑥𐑨𐑯 𐑒𐑨𐑯𐑪𐑑 𐑛𐑲 𐑓𐑹 𐑩 𐑕𐑑𐑹𐑦 𐑯 𐑩 𐑛𐑮𐑰𐑥. 𐑯𐑳𐑯 𐑝 𐑳𐑕 𐑚𐑦𐑤𐑰𐑝𐑛 𐑞 𐑕𐑑𐑹𐑦𐑟 𐑯 𐑞 𐑛𐑮𐑰𐑥𐑟 𐑥𐑹 𐑛𐑦𐑝𐑬𐑑𐑤𐑦 𐑞𐑨𐑯 𐑐𐑫𐑮 ·𐑕𐑐𐑦𐑯𐑔𐑴; 𐑚𐑳𐑑 𐑣𐑰 𐑒𐑫𐑛 𐑯𐑪𐑑 𐑓𐑱𐑕 𐑞 𐑜𐑮𐑱𐑑 𐑮𐑦𐑨𐑤𐑦𐑑𐑦. 𐑢𐑪𐑑 𐑣𐑰 𐑢𐑫𐑛 𐑣𐑨𐑝 𐑒𐑷𐑤𐑛 𐑥𐑲 𐑓𐑱𐑔 𐑣𐑨𐑟 𐑚𐑰𐑯 𐑵𐑟𐑦𐑙 𐑩𐑢𐑱 𐑥𐑦𐑯𐑦𐑑 𐑚𐑲 𐑥𐑦𐑯𐑦𐑑 𐑢𐑲𐑤𐑕𐑑 𐑲'𐑝 𐑚𐑰𐑯 𐑕𐑦𐑑𐑦𐑙 𐑣𐑽, 𐑢𐑦𐑞 𐑛𐑧𐑔 𐑒𐑳𐑥𐑦𐑙 𐑯𐑽𐑼 𐑯 𐑯𐑽𐑼, 𐑢𐑦𐑞 𐑮𐑦𐑨𐑤𐑦𐑑𐑦 𐑚𐑦𐑒𐑳𐑥𐑦𐑙 𐑮𐑾𐑤𐑼 𐑯 𐑮𐑾𐑤𐑼, 𐑢𐑦𐑞 𐑕𐑑𐑹𐑦𐑟 𐑯 𐑛𐑮𐑰𐑥𐑟 𐑓𐑱𐑛𐑦𐑙 𐑩𐑢𐑱 𐑦𐑯𐑑𐑵 𐑯𐑳𐑔𐑦𐑙.

𐑞 𐑒𐑨𐑐𐑑𐑩𐑯. 𐑸 𐑿 𐑞𐑧𐑯 𐑜𐑴𐑦𐑙 𐑑 𐑛𐑲 𐑓𐑹 𐑯𐑳𐑔𐑦𐑙?

𐑤𐑩𐑝𐑦𐑯𐑾. 𐑘𐑧𐑕: 𐑞𐑨𐑑 𐑦𐑟 𐑞 𐑢𐑳𐑯𐑛𐑼𐑓𐑩𐑤 𐑔𐑦𐑙. 𐑦𐑑 𐑦𐑟 𐑕𐑦𐑯𐑕 𐑷𐑤 𐑞 𐑕𐑑𐑹𐑦𐑟 𐑯 𐑛𐑮𐑰𐑥𐑟 𐑣𐑨𐑝 𐑜𐑪𐑯 𐑞𐑨𐑑

you, I believe no more than the Emperor does, or any educated man in Rome?

LAVINIA. Captain: all that seems nothing to me now. I'll not say that death is a terrible thing; but I will say that it is so real a thing that when it comes close, all the imaginary things – all the stories, as you call them – fade into mere dreams beside that inexorable reality. I know now that I am not dying for stories or dreams. Did you hear of the dreadful thing that happened here while we were waiting?

THE CAPTAIN. I heard that one of your fellows bolted, and ran right into the jaws of the lion. I laughed. I still laugh.

LAVINIA. Then you dont understand what that meant?

THE CAPTAIN. It meant that the lion had a cur for his breakfast.

LAVINIA. It meant more than that, Captain. It meant that a man cannot die for a story and a dream. None of us believed the stories and the dreams more devoutly than poor Spintho; but he could not face the great reality. What he would have called my faith has been oozing away minute by minute whilst Ive been sitting here, with death coming nearer and nearer, with reality becoming realler and realler, with stories and dreams fading away into nothing.

THE CAPTAIN. Are you then going to die for nothing?

LAVINIA. Yes: that is the wonderful thing. It is since all the stories and dreams have gone that

𐑲 𐑣𐑨𐑝 𐑯𐑬 𐑯𐑴 𐑛𐑬𐑑 𐑨𐑑 𐑷𐑤 𐑞𐑨𐑑 𐑲 𐑥𐑳𐑕𐑑 𐑛𐑲 𐑓𐑹 𐑕𐑳𐑥𐑔𐑦𐑙 𐑜𐑮𐑱𐑑𐑼 𐑞𐑨𐑯 𐑛𐑮𐑰𐑥𐑟 𐑹 𐑕𐑑𐑹𐑦𐑟.

𐑞 𐑒𐑨𐑐𐑑𐑦𐑯. 𐑚𐑳𐑑 𐑓𐑹 𐑢𐑪𐑑?

𐑤𐑩𐑝𐑦𐑯𐑾. 𐑲 𐑛𐑴𐑯𐑑 𐑯𐑴. 𐑦𐑓 𐑦𐑑 𐑢𐑻 𐑓𐑹 𐑧𐑯𐑦𐑔𐑦𐑙 𐑕𐑥𐑷𐑤 𐑦𐑯𐑳𐑓 𐑑 𐑯𐑴, 𐑦𐑑 𐑢𐑫𐑛 𐑚𐑰 𐑑𐑵 𐑕𐑥𐑷𐑤 𐑑 𐑛𐑲 𐑓𐑹. 𐑲 𐑔𐑦𐑙𐑒 𐑲'𐑥 𐑜𐑴𐑦𐑙 𐑑 𐑛𐑲 𐑓𐑹 ·𐑜𐑪𐑛. 𐑯𐑳𐑔𐑦𐑙 𐑧𐑤𐑕 𐑦𐑟 𐑮𐑾𐑤 𐑦𐑯𐑳𐑓 𐑑 𐑛𐑲 𐑓𐑹.

𐑞 𐑒𐑨𐑐𐑑𐑦𐑯. 𐑢𐑪𐑑 𐑦𐑟 ·𐑜𐑪𐑛?

𐑤𐑩𐑝𐑦𐑯𐑾. 𐑢𐑧𐑯 𐑢𐑰 𐑯𐑴 𐑞𐑨𐑑, 𐑒𐑨𐑐𐑑𐑦𐑯, 𐑢𐑰 𐑖𐑨𐑤 𐑚𐑰 𐑜𐑪𐑛𐑟 𐑬𐑼𐑕𐑧𐑤𐑝𐑟.

𐑞 𐑒𐑨𐑐𐑑𐑦𐑯. ·𐑤𐑩𐑝𐑦𐑯𐑾: 𐑒𐑳𐑥 𐑛𐑬𐑯 𐑑 𐑻𐑔. 𐑚𐑻𐑯 𐑞 𐑦𐑯𐑕𐑧𐑯𐑕 𐑯 𐑥𐑨𐑮𐑦 𐑥𐑰.

𐑤𐑩𐑝𐑦𐑯𐑾. 𐑣𐑨𐑯𐑕𐑩𐑥 𐑒𐑨𐑐𐑑𐑦𐑯; 𐑢𐑫𐑛 𐑿 𐑥𐑨𐑮𐑦 𐑥𐑰 𐑦𐑓 𐑲 𐑣𐑷𐑤𐑛 𐑛𐑬𐑯 𐑞 𐑓𐑤𐑨𐑜 𐑦𐑯 𐑞 𐑛𐑱 𐑝 𐑚𐑨𐑑𐑩𐑤 𐑯 𐑚𐑻𐑯𐑑 𐑞 𐑦𐑯𐑕𐑧𐑯𐑕? 𐑕𐑳𐑯𐑟 𐑑𐑱𐑒 𐑭𐑓𐑑𐑼 𐑞𐑺 𐑥𐑳𐑞𐑼𐑟, 𐑿 𐑯𐑴. 𐑛𐑵 𐑿 𐑢𐑪𐑯𐑑 𐑿𐑼 𐑕𐑳𐑯 𐑑 𐑚𐑰 𐑩 𐑒𐑬𐑼𐑛?

𐑞 𐑒𐑨𐑐𐑑𐑦𐑯 [𐑕𐑑𐑮𐑪𐑙𐑤𐑦 𐑥𐑵𐑝𐑛] 𐑚𐑲 𐑜𐑮𐑱𐑑 ·𐑛𐑲𐑨𐑯𐑩, 𐑲 𐑔𐑦𐑙𐑒 𐑲 𐑢𐑫𐑛 𐑕𐑑𐑮𐑨𐑙𐑜𐑩𐑤 𐑿 𐑦𐑓 𐑿 𐑜𐑱𐑝 𐑦𐑯 𐑯𐑬.

𐑤𐑩𐑝𐑦𐑯𐑾 [𐑐𐑫𐑑𐑦𐑙 𐑣𐑻 𐑣𐑨𐑯𐑛 𐑪𐑯 𐑞 𐑣𐑧𐑛 𐑝 ·𐑨𐑯𐑛𐑮𐑩𐑒𐑤𐑰𐑟] 𐑞 𐑣𐑨𐑯𐑛 𐑝 ·𐑜𐑪𐑛 𐑦𐑟 𐑪𐑯 𐑳𐑕 𐑔𐑮𐑰, 𐑒𐑨𐑐𐑑𐑦𐑯.

𐑞 𐑒𐑨𐑐𐑑𐑦𐑯. 𐑢𐑪𐑑 𐑯𐑪𐑯𐑕𐑩𐑯𐑕 𐑦𐑑 𐑷𐑤 𐑦𐑟! 𐑯 𐑢𐑪𐑑 𐑩 𐑥𐑪𐑯𐑕𐑑𐑮𐑩𐑕 𐑔𐑦𐑙 𐑞𐑨𐑑 𐑿 𐑖𐑫𐑛 𐑛𐑲 𐑓𐑹 𐑕𐑳𐑗 𐑯𐑪𐑯𐑕𐑩𐑯𐑕, 𐑯 𐑞𐑨𐑑 𐑲 𐑖𐑫𐑛 𐑤𐑫𐑒 𐑪𐑯 𐑣𐑧𐑤𐑐𐑤𐑩𐑕 𐑢𐑧𐑯 𐑥𐑲 𐑣𐑴𐑤 𐑕𐑴𐑤 𐑒𐑮𐑲𐑟 𐑬𐑑 𐑩𐑜𐑱𐑯𐑕𐑑 𐑦𐑑! 𐑛𐑲 𐑞𐑧𐑯 𐑦𐑓 𐑿 𐑥𐑳𐑕𐑑; 𐑚𐑳𐑑 𐑨𐑑 𐑤𐑰𐑕𐑑 𐑲 𐑒𐑨𐑯 𐑒𐑳𐑑 𐑞 𐑧𐑥𐑐𐑼𐑼'𐑟 𐑔𐑮𐑴𐑑 𐑯 𐑞𐑧𐑯 𐑥𐑲 𐑴𐑯 𐑢𐑧𐑯 𐑲 𐑕𐑰 𐑿 𐑛𐑧𐑛.

[𐑞 𐑧𐑥𐑐𐑼𐑼 𐑔𐑮𐑴𐑟 𐑴𐑐𐑩𐑯 𐑞 𐑛𐑹 𐑝 𐑣𐑦𐑟 𐑚𐑪𐑒𐑕 [illegible], 𐑯 [illegible] 𐑦𐑯 [illegible] 𐑦𐑯 𐑞 [illegible]. 𐑞 𐑧𐑛𐑦𐑑𐑼, 𐑞 𐑒𐑷𐑤 𐑚𐑶, 𐑯 𐑞 𐑜𐑤𐑨𐑛𐑦𐑱𐑑𐑼𐑟 [illegible] 𐑑 𐑞𐑺 [illegible]].

I have now no doubt at all that I must die for something greater than dreams or stories.

THE CAPTAIN. But for what?

LAVINIA. I dont know. If it were for anything small enough to know, it would be too small to die for. I think I'm going to die for God. Nothing else is real enough to die for.

THE CAPTAIN. What is God?

LAVINIA. When we know that, Captain, we shall be gods ourselves.

THE CAPTAIN. Lavinia: come down to earth. Burn the incense and marry me.

LAVINIA. Handsome Captain; would you marry me if I hauled down the flag in the day of battle and burnt the incense? Sons take after their mothers, you know. Do you want your son to be a coward?

THE CAPTAIN [*strongly moved*] By great Diana, I think I would strangle you if you gave in now.

LAVINIA [*putting her hand on the head of Androcles*] The hand of God is on us three, Captain.

THE CAPTAIN. What nonsense it all is! And what a monstrous thing that you should die for such nonsense, and that I should look on helplessly when my whole soul cries out against it! Die then if you must; but at least I can cut the Emperor's throat and then my own when I see your blood.

The Emperor throws open the door of his box angrily, and appears in wrath on the threshold. The Editor, the Call Boy, and the gladiators spring to their feet.

𐑞 𐑧𐑛𐑦𐑑𐑼. 𐑞 𐑒𐑮𐑦𐑕𐑑𐑾𐑯𐑟 𐑢𐑦𐑤 𐑯𐑪𐑑 𐑓𐑲𐑑; 𐑯 𐑿𐑼 𐑒𐑻𐑟 𐑒𐑨𐑯𐑑 𐑚𐑰𐑑 𐑞𐑧𐑥 𐑚𐑮𐑧𐑲𐑛 𐑧𐑐 𐑑 𐑩 𐑯𐑮𐑧𐑒 𐑞𐑧𐑥. 𐑦𐑑'𐑕 𐑷𐑤 𐑞𐑨𐑑 𐑓𐑧𐑤𐑴 𐑢𐑦𐑞 𐑞 𐑚𐑮𐑧𐑲𐑛 𐑲𐑟. 𐑕𐑧𐑯𐑛 𐑓𐑹 𐑞 𐑢𐑦𐑐. [𐑞 𐑒𐑷𐑤 𐑚𐑶 𐑮𐑲𐑒𐑩𐑟 𐑩𐑑 𐑯𐑪 𐑞 𐑣𐑕𐑑 𐑕𐑲𐑛 𐑓𐑹 𐑞 𐑢𐑦𐑐]. 𐑦𐑓 𐑞𐑨𐑑 𐑢𐑦𐑤 𐑯𐑪𐑑 𐑕𐑑𐑻 𐑞𐑧𐑥, 𐑚𐑮𐑦𐑙 𐑞 𐑣𐑨𐑑 𐑲𐑼𐑯𐑟. 𐑞 𐑥𐑨𐑯 𐑦𐑟 𐑤𐑲𐑒 𐑩 𐑥𐑿𐑤𐑩𐑯. [𐑣𐑰 𐑮𐑳𐑖𐑩𐑟 𐑨𐑢𐑱 𐑦𐑯𐑑𐑵 𐑞 𐑚𐑨𐑒𐑕 𐑯 𐑕𐑤𐑨𐑥𐑟 𐑞 𐑛𐑹.

𐑞 𐑒𐑷𐑤 𐑚𐑶 𐑮𐑳𐑖𐑩𐑟 𐑨𐑓𐑑𐑼 𐑣𐑦𐑥 𐑢𐑦𐑞 𐑩 𐑢𐑦𐑐 𐑯 𐑩 𐑣𐑨𐑥𐑼 𐑨𐑯𐑛 ·𐑕𐑑𐑮𐑲𐑒𐑩𐑯 𐑤𐑧𐑕𐑤𐑦, 𐑒𐑮𐑦𐑕𐑐𐑦𐑙 𐑩 𐑢𐑦𐑐. 𐑞𐑱 𐑚𐑪𐑔 𐑮𐑳𐑖 𐑦𐑯 𐑞 𐑛𐑹𐑟 𐑦𐑯𐑑𐑵 𐑞 𐑨𐑮𐑰𐑯𐑩].

𐑤𐑩𐑝𐑦𐑯𐑾 [𐑮𐑲𐑟𐑦𐑙] 𐑴, 𐑞𐑨𐑑 𐑦𐑟 𐑣𐑪𐑮𐑦𐑚𐑩𐑤. 𐑒𐑨𐑯 𐑞𐑧𐑮 𐑯𐑪𐑑 𐑚𐑰 𐑴𐑯𐑤𐑦 𐑢𐑳𐑯 𐑢𐑱 𐑦𐑯 𐑞𐑦𐑕 𐑢𐑻𐑤𐑛?

𐑨𐑯𐑛𐑮𐑩𐑒𐑤𐑰𐑟 [𐑕𐑑𐑮𐑩𐑜𐑩𐑤𐑦𐑙 𐑑 𐑣𐑦𐑟 𐑓𐑰𐑑 𐑯 𐑮𐑳𐑖𐑦𐑙 𐑦𐑯𐑑𐑵 𐑞 𐑥𐑦𐑛𐑩𐑤 𐑝 𐑞 𐑕𐑑𐑱𐑡 𐑚𐑦𐑑𐑢𐑰𐑯 𐑞 𐑕𐑑𐑨𐑒𐑕] 𐑦𐑑'𐑕 𐑞 𐑚𐑳𐑒𐑩𐑤. 𐑲 𐑒𐑨𐑯'𐑑 𐑕𐑑𐑨𐑯𐑛 𐑦𐑑. 𐑲 𐑒𐑪𐑯𐑑 𐑚𐑧𐑮 𐑞 𐑕𐑲𐑑 𐑝 𐑩 𐑢𐑦𐑐. 𐑞 𐑴𐑯𐑤𐑦 𐑑𐑲𐑥 𐑲 𐑣𐑧𐑤𐑛 𐑣𐑦𐑟 𐑩 𐑥𐑨𐑯 𐑢𐑦𐑟 𐑣𐑰 𐑤𐑲𐑒𐑑 𐑩 𐑚𐑪𐑒𐑕 𐑣𐑰𐑟 𐑢𐑦𐑞 𐑩 𐑢𐑦𐑐. 𐑦𐑑 𐑢𐑪𐑟 𐑑𐑵𐑥𐑩𐑗: 𐑲 𐑐𐑳𐑕𐑑 𐑣𐑦 𐑣𐑦𐑟 𐑓𐑧𐑕 𐑢𐑪𐑟 𐑣𐑰 𐑢𐑪𐑟 𐑦𐑯 𐑞 𐑚𐑩𐑒𐑩𐑐. 𐑣𐑰 𐑥𐑲𐑕𐑩𐑑 𐑕𐑑𐑮𐑲𐑒 ·𐑓𐑧𐑮𐑴𐑝𐑾𐑕: 𐑲'𐑤 𐑚𐑪 𐑦𐑯𐑑𐑵 𐑞 𐑨𐑮𐑰𐑯𐑩 𐑯 𐑒𐑦𐑤 𐑣𐑦𐑥 𐑓𐑻𐑕𐑑. [𐑣𐑰 𐑥𐑧𐑒𐑕 𐑩 𐑢𐑲𐑤𐑛 𐑚𐑴𐑤𐑑 𐑦𐑯𐑑𐑵 𐑞 𐑨𐑮𐑰𐑯𐑩. 𐑨𐑟 𐑣𐑰 𐑚𐑲𐑟 𐑕𐑪 𐑩 𐑚𐑮𐑱𐑒 𐑑𐑱𐑒 𐑩 𐑖𐑲𐑯𐑰𐑙 𐑚𐑴𐑤𐑑 𐑓𐑮𐑪𐑥 𐑞 𐑥𐑨𐑒𐑕 𐑝 𐑞 𐑨𐑮𐑰𐑯𐑩, 𐑤𐑲𐑒 𐑩 𐑢𐑲𐑑 𐑣𐑲𐑟 𐑦𐑯 𐑞 𐑚𐑤𐑩𐑟. 𐑞 𐑐𐑤𐑳𐑙𐑒𐑑𐑩𐑟 𐑤𐑦𐑕𐑩𐑯 𐑯 𐑤𐑫𐑒 𐑩𐑒𐑢𐑲𐑩𐑑𐑤𐑦 𐑨𐑑 𐑢𐑩𐑯 𐑩𐑯𐑳𐑞𐑼].

𐑞 𐑧𐑛𐑦𐑑𐑼. 𐑢𐑪𐑑'𐑕 𐑷𐑤 𐑞𐑦𐑕?

𐑤𐑩𐑝𐑦𐑯𐑾 [𐑑 𐑞 𐑒𐑨𐑐𐑑𐑩𐑯] 𐑢𐑪𐑑 𐑣𐑨𐑟 𐑣𐑨𐑐𐑩𐑯𐑛, 𐑦𐑟 𐑣𐑰 𐑛𐑧𐑛?

𐑞 𐑒𐑨𐑐𐑑𐑩𐑯. 𐑢𐑪𐑑 𐑒𐑨𐑯 𐑣𐑨𐑐𐑩𐑯? 𐑞𐑱 𐑢𐑦𐑤 𐑒𐑦𐑤 𐑣𐑦𐑥, 𐑝 𐑒𐑹𐑕.

𐑨𐑯𐑛𐑮𐑩𐑒𐑤𐑰𐑟 [𐑮𐑲𐑟𐑦𐑙 𐑦𐑯 𐑞𐑮𐑵 𐑞 𐑚𐑨𐑒𐑕, 𐑕𐑑𐑪𐑐𐑦𐑙 𐑢𐑦𐑞 𐑣𐑪𐑮𐑼 𐑯 𐑣𐑲𐑛𐑦𐑙 𐑣𐑦𐑟 𐑲𐑟] !!!

THE EMPEROR. The Christians will not fight; and your curs cannot get their blood up to attack them. It's all that fellow with the blazing eyes. Send for the whip. [*The Call Boy rushes out on the east side for the whip*]. If that will not move them, bring the hot irons. The man is like a mountain. [*He returns angrily into the box and slams the door*].

The Call Boy returns with a man in a hideous Etruscan mask, carrying a whip. They both rush down the passage into the arena.

LAVINIA [*rising*] Oh, that is unworthy. Can they not kill him without dishonoring him?

ANDROCLES [*scrambling to his feet and running into the middle of the space between the staircase*] It's dreadful. Now *I* want to fight. I cant bear the sight of a whip. The only time I ever hit a man was when he lashed an old horse with a whip. It was terrible: I danced on his face when he was on the ground. He mustnt strike Ferrovius: I'll go into the arena and kill him first. [*He makes a wild dash into the passage. As he does so a great clamor is heard from the arena, ending in wild applause. The gladiators listen and look inquiringly at one another*].

THE EDITOR. Whats up now?

LAVINIA [*to the Captain*] What has happened, do you think?

THE CAPTAIN. What can happen? They are killing them, I suppose.

ANDROCLES [*running in through the passage, screaming with horror and hiding his eyes*]!!!

𐑤𐑩𐑝𐑦𐑯𐑾. ·𐑨𐑯𐑛𐑮𐑩𐑒𐑤𐑰𐑟, ·𐑨𐑯𐑛𐑮𐑩𐑒𐑤𐑰𐑟: 𐑢𐑪𐑑'𐑕 𐑞 𐑥𐑨𐑑𐑼?

𐑨𐑯𐑛𐑮𐑩𐑒𐑤𐑰𐑟. 𐑴 𐑛𐑴𐑯𐑑 𐑭𐑕𐑒 𐑥𐑰, 𐑛𐑴𐑯𐑑 𐑭𐑕𐑒 𐑥𐑰. 𐑕𐑳𐑥𐑔𐑦𐑙 𐑑𐑵 𐑛𐑮𐑧𐑛𐑓𐑩𐑤. 𐑴! [𐑣𐑰 𐑒𐑮𐑬𐑗𐑩𐑟 𐑚𐑲 𐑣𐑻 𐑯 𐑣𐑲𐑛𐑟 𐑣𐑦𐑟 𐑓𐑱𐑕 𐑦𐑯 𐑣𐑻 𐑮𐑴𐑚, 𐑕𐑪𐑚𐑦𐑙].

𐑞 𐑒𐑷𐑤 𐑚𐑶 [𐑮𐑳𐑖𐑦𐑙 𐑔𐑮𐑵 𐑓𐑮𐑪𐑥 𐑞 𐑐𐑨𐑕𐑦𐑡 𐑨𐑟 𐑚𐑦𐑓𐑹] 𐑮𐑴𐑐𐑕 𐑯 𐑣𐑫𐑒𐑕 𐑞𐑺! 𐑮𐑴𐑐𐑕 𐑯 𐑣𐑫𐑒𐑕!

𐑞 𐑧𐑛𐑦𐑑𐑼. 𐑢𐑧𐑤, [illegible] 𐑩𐑚𐑬𐑑 𐑦𐑑? [𐑩𐑯𐑳𐑞𐑼 𐑚𐑻𐑕𐑑 𐑝 𐑗𐑽𐑟.

𐑑𐑵 𐑕𐑤𐑱𐑝𐑟 𐑦𐑯 ·𐑦𐑑𐑮𐑳𐑕𐑒𐑩𐑯 𐑥𐑭𐑕𐑒𐑕, 𐑢𐑦𐑞 𐑮𐑴𐑐𐑕 𐑯 𐑤𐑪𐑙 𐑣𐑫𐑒𐑕, 𐑣𐑳𐑮𐑦 𐑦𐑯].

𐑢𐑳𐑯 𐑝 𐑞 𐑕𐑤𐑱𐑝𐑟. 𐑣𐑬 𐑥𐑧𐑯𐑦 𐑛𐑧𐑛?

𐑞 𐑒𐑷𐑤 𐑚𐑶. 𐑕𐑦𐑒𐑕. [𐑞 𐑕𐑤𐑱𐑝 𐑚𐑤𐑴𐑟 𐑩 𐑢𐑦𐑕𐑩𐑤 𐑑𐑢𐑲𐑕; 𐑯 𐑓𐑹 𐑥𐑹 𐑥𐑭𐑕𐑒𐑑 𐑕𐑤𐑱𐑝𐑟 𐑮𐑳𐑖 𐑔𐑮𐑵 𐑦𐑯𐑑𐑵 𐑞 𐑼𐑰𐑯𐑩 𐑢𐑦𐑞 𐑞 𐑕𐑱𐑥 𐑦𐑥𐑐𐑤𐑦𐑥𐑩𐑯𐑑𐑕] 𐑯 𐑞 𐑚𐑭𐑕𐑒𐑩𐑑. 𐑚𐑮𐑦𐑙 𐑞 𐑚𐑭𐑕𐑒𐑩𐑑𐑕 [𐑞 𐑕𐑤𐑱𐑝 𐑢𐑦𐑕𐑩𐑤𐑟 𐑔𐑮𐑰 𐑑𐑲𐑥𐑟, 𐑯 𐑮𐑳𐑖𐑩𐑟 𐑔𐑮𐑵 𐑞 𐑐𐑨𐑕𐑦𐑡 𐑢𐑦𐑞 𐑣𐑦𐑟 𐑒𐑩𐑥𐑮𐑱𐑛𐑟].

𐑞 𐑒𐑨𐑐𐑑𐑩𐑯. 𐑢𐑪𐑑 𐑸 𐑞 𐑚𐑭𐑕𐑒𐑩𐑑𐑕 𐑓𐑹?

𐑞 𐑒𐑷𐑤 𐑚𐑶. 𐑓𐑹 𐑞 𐑢𐑦𐑤. 𐑣𐑰'𐑟 𐑦𐑯 𐑐𐑰𐑕𐑩𐑟. 𐑞𐑱'𐑮 𐑷𐑤 𐑦𐑯 𐑐𐑰𐑕𐑩𐑟, 𐑥𐑹 𐑹 𐑤𐑧𐑕. [·𐑤𐑩𐑝𐑦𐑯𐑾 𐑣𐑲𐑛𐑟 𐑣𐑻 𐑓𐑱𐑕.

𐑑𐑵 𐑥𐑹 𐑥𐑭𐑕𐑒𐑑 𐑕𐑤𐑱𐑝𐑟 𐑒𐑳𐑥 𐑦𐑯 𐑢𐑦𐑞 𐑩 𐑚𐑭𐑕𐑒𐑩𐑑 𐑯 𐑓𐑪𐑤𐑴 𐑞 𐑳𐑞𐑼𐑟 𐑦𐑯𐑑𐑵 𐑞 𐑼𐑰𐑯𐑩, 𐑨𐑟 𐑞 𐑒𐑷𐑤 𐑚𐑶 𐑑𐑻𐑯𐑟 𐑑 𐑞 𐑜𐑤𐑨𐑛𐑦𐑱𐑑𐑼𐑟 𐑯 𐑦𐑒𐑕𐑒𐑤𐑱𐑥𐑟, 𐑚𐑮𐑧𐑔𐑤𐑩𐑕] 𐑚𐑶𐑟: 𐑣𐑰'𐑟 𐑒𐑦𐑤𐑛 𐑞 𐑤𐑪𐑑.

𐑞 𐑧𐑥𐑐𐑼𐑼 [𐑩𐑜𐑧𐑯 𐑚𐑻𐑕𐑑𐑦𐑙 𐑓𐑮𐑪𐑥 𐑣𐑦𐑟 𐑚𐑪𐑒𐑕, 𐑞𐑦𐑕 𐑑𐑲𐑥 𐑦𐑯 𐑩𐑯 𐑧𐑒𐑕𐑑𐑩𐑕𐑦 𐑝 𐑛𐑦𐑤𐑲𐑑] 𐑢𐑺 𐑦𐑟 𐑣𐑰? 𐑥𐑨𐑜𐑯𐑦𐑓𐑦𐑕𐑩𐑯𐑑! 𐑣𐑰 𐑖𐑨𐑤 𐑣𐑨𐑝 𐑩 𐑜𐑴𐑤𐑛𐑩𐑯 𐑒𐑮𐑬𐑯.

[·𐑓𐑧𐑮𐑴𐑝𐑾𐑕, 𐑕𐑑𐑦𐑤 𐑢𐑱𐑝𐑦𐑙 𐑣𐑦𐑟 𐑚𐑤𐑳𐑛𐑕𐑑𐑱𐑯𐑛 𐑕𐑹𐑛, 𐑮𐑳𐑖𐑩𐑟 𐑔𐑮𐑵 𐑞 𐑐𐑨𐑕𐑦𐑡 𐑦𐑯 𐑑𐑮𐑲𐑩𐑥𐑓, 𐑓𐑪𐑤𐑴𐑛 𐑚𐑲 𐑣𐑦𐑟 𐑒𐑴-𐑮𐑦𐑤𐑦𐑡𐑩𐑯𐑦𐑕𐑑𐑕, 𐑯 𐑚𐑲 𐑞 𐑥𐑩𐑯𐑨𐑡𐑼𐑦

LAVINIA. Androcles, Androcles: whats the matter?

ANDROCLES. Oh dont ask me, dont ask me. Something too dreadful. Oh! [*He crouches by her and hides his face in her robe, sobbing*].

THE CALL BOY [*rushing through from the passage as before*] Ropes and hooks there! Ropes and hooks!

THE EDITOR. Well, need you excite yourself about it? [*Another burst of applause*].

Two slaves in Etruscan masks, with ropes and drag hooks, hurry in.

ONE OF THE SLAVES. How many dead?

THE CALL BOY. Six. [*The slave blows a whistle twice; and four more masked slaves rush through into the arena with the same apparatus*] And the basket. Bring the baskets [*The slave whistles three times, and runs through the passage with his companion*].

THE CAPTAIN. Who are the baskets for?

THE CALL BOY. For the whip. He's in pieces. Theyre all in pieces, more or less. [*Lavinia hides her face*].

Two more masked slaves come in with a basket and follow the others into the arena, as the Call Boy turns to the gladiators and exclaims, exhausted] Boys: he's killed the lot.

THE EMPEROR [*again bursting from his box, this time in an ecstasy of delight*] Where is he? Magnificent! He shall have a laurel crown.

Ferrovius, madly waving his bloodstained sword, rushes through the passage in despair, followed by his co-religionists, and by the Menagerie

·𐑤𐑨𐑝𐑦𐑯𐑾, 𐑣𐑵 𐑜𐑴𐑟 𐑑 𐑞 ·𐑒𐑮𐑦𐑕𐑗𐑩𐑯𐑟. 𐑞 𐑒𐑮𐑦𐑕𐑗𐑩𐑯𐑟 𐑜𐑨𐑞𐑼 𐑮𐑬𐑯𐑛 𐑞𐑧𐑥 𐑕𐑲𐑤𐑩𐑯𐑑𐑤𐑦].

𐑨𐑯𐑛𐑮𐑴𐑒𐑤𐑰𐑟. 𐑮𐑧𐑕𐑑! 𐑮𐑧𐑕𐑑 𐑓𐑹 𐑿! 𐑲 𐑢𐑪𐑟 𐑐𐑮𐑱𐑦𐑙 𐑓𐑹 𐑿 𐑞𐑧𐑮. 𐑤𐑧𐑑 𐑥𐑰 𐑕𐑰 𐑞𐑨𐑑 𐑢𐑵𐑯𐑛: 𐑦𐑑 𐑢𐑪𐑟 𐑴𐑯𐑤𐑦 𐑩 𐑕𐑒𐑮𐑨𐑗. 𐑣𐑰 𐑢𐑪𐑟 𐑕𐑬𐑯𐑛, 𐑓𐑹 𐑷𐑤 𐑞𐑨𐑑: 𐑕𐑑𐑮𐑪𐑙.

𐑤𐑨𐑝𐑦𐑯𐑾. 𐑯𐑴, 𐑯𐑴. 𐑢𐑪𐑑 𐑣𐑨𐑟 𐑣𐑰 𐑛𐑳𐑯, ·𐑨𐑯𐑛𐑮𐑴𐑒𐑤𐑰𐑟?

𐑨𐑯𐑛𐑮𐑴𐑒𐑤𐑰𐑟. 𐑲 𐑯𐑴 𐑯𐑪𐑑; 𐑚𐑳𐑑 𐑞𐑺 𐑢𐑪𐑟 𐑚𐑳𐑑 𐑢𐑳𐑯 𐑓𐑹 𐑣𐑦𐑥; 𐑯 𐑞𐑺'𐑟 𐑚𐑳𐑑 𐑢𐑳𐑯 𐑓𐑹 𐑥𐑰. 𐑢𐑪𐑑 𐑚𐑳𐑑 𐑞𐑨𐑑 𐑢𐑳𐑯?

𐑞 𐑧𐑛𐑦𐑑𐑼 [𐑦𐑯𐑛𐑦𐑜𐑯𐑩𐑯𐑑𐑤𐑦, 𐑑 𐑞 𐑒𐑷𐑤 𐑚𐑶 𐑯 𐑞 𐑥𐑧𐑯𐑨𐑡𐑼𐑦 𐑒𐑰𐑐𐑼] 𐑢𐑪𐑑 𐑚𐑳𐑑 𐑦𐑑 𐑢𐑳𐑯? 𐑦𐑑 𐑢𐑳𐑯𐑟 𐑞𐑨𐑑 𐑣𐑰 𐑦𐑟 𐑞 𐑚𐑩𐑤𐑰𐑝𐑼 𐑢𐑳𐑯 𐑦𐑯 ·𐑮𐑴𐑥. 𐑦𐑑 𐑥𐑰𐑯𐑟 𐑞𐑨𐑑 𐑣𐑰 𐑣𐑨𐑟 𐑩 𐑤𐑲𐑩𐑯 𐑓𐑹 𐑩 𐑚𐑪𐑛𐑦. 𐑕𐑦𐑤𐑧𐑯𐑕 𐑞𐑺: 𐑲 𐑢𐑪𐑯𐑑 𐑝𐑱𐑤𐑴𐑕𐑑 𐑗𐑨𐑑 𐑦𐑯 𐑞𐑦𐑕 𐑛𐑹. 𐑦𐑑 𐑦𐑟 𐑩 𐑚𐑦𐑜𐑼 𐑓𐑹 𐑞𐑦𐑕 𐑚𐑪𐑒𐑕: 𐑲 𐑣𐑨𐑝 𐑩 𐑓𐑨𐑥𐑦𐑤𐑦 𐑦𐑯 𐑣𐑦𐑕𐑑𐑼𐑦. 𐑢𐑳𐑯𐑟, 𐑦𐑯 ·𐑑𐑮𐑱𐑡𐑩𐑯'𐑟 𐑑𐑲𐑥, 𐑩 ·𐑚𐑻𐑤 𐑕𐑤𐑱𐑝 𐑛𐑮𐑴𐑝 𐑩𐑢𐑱 𐑦𐑯 𐑞 𐑥𐑦𐑛𐑤 𐑝 𐑚𐑪𐑛𐑦 𐑣𐑦𐑟 𐑓𐑱𐑕𐑦𐑟. 𐑚𐑳𐑑 𐑢𐑪𐑑 𐑚𐑦𐑑𐑼 𐑣𐑨𐑟 𐑢𐑪𐑟 𐑿𐑟𐑑 𐑢𐑪𐑯 𐑕𐑧𐑝𐑼𐑩𐑤 𐑕𐑦𐑛𐑟 𐑞𐑨𐑑 𐑢𐑪𐑯 𐑩 𐑞 𐑚𐑮𐑦𐑤𐑩𐑯𐑑 𐑯 𐑚𐑧𐑕𐑑? 𐑞 𐑓𐑹𐑕𐑦𐑛𐑩𐑚𐑤 𐑥𐑨𐑯 𐑕𐑰𐑟: 𐑦𐑯 𐑒𐑮𐑦𐑕𐑗𐑩𐑯𐑟 𐑤𐑪𐑑 𐑓𐑲𐑑 𐑤𐑲𐑒 𐑞𐑦𐑕, 𐑲 𐑥𐑨𐑯 𐑣𐑨𐑟 𐑯𐑪𐑑 𐑞𐑨𐑑 𐑒𐑮𐑦𐑕𐑗𐑩𐑯𐑟 𐑑 𐑓𐑲𐑑 𐑓𐑹 𐑩𐑕. [𐑑 𐑞 ·𐑒𐑮𐑦𐑕𐑗𐑩𐑯𐑟] 𐑣𐑰 𐑦𐑟 𐑕𐑳𐑥𐑦𐑙 𐑑 𐑚𐑰𐑒𐑳𐑥 𐑒𐑮𐑦𐑕𐑗𐑩𐑯𐑟, 𐑣𐑰 𐑞𐑦𐑙𐑟: 𐑚𐑳𐑑 𐑣𐑰 𐑣𐑵?

𐑤𐑧𐑯𐑑𐑿𐑤𐑩𐑕. 𐑦𐑑 𐑦𐑟 𐑯𐑴 𐑿𐑕 𐑑 𐑳𐑕, ·𐑕𐑰𐑟𐑼. 𐑣𐑰 𐑲 𐑚𐑨𐑒 𐑞𐑺 𐑢𐑪𐑟 𐑓𐑹 𐑯𐑪𐑑, 𐑞 𐑕𐑑𐑹𐑦 𐑢𐑪𐑟 𐑣𐑨𐑟 𐑚𐑰𐑯 𐑚𐑦𐑜𐑦𐑯𐑦𐑙.

𐑞 𐑒𐑨𐑐𐑑𐑦𐑯 [𐑕𐑑𐑨𐑯𐑛𐑦𐑙 𐑚𐑰𐑲𐑯𐑛 ·𐑤𐑨𐑝𐑦𐑯𐑾 𐑨𐑑 𐑞 𐑓𐑵𐑑 𐑝 𐑚𐑦𐑤𐑴𐑙𐑦𐑙 𐑣𐑰 𐑣𐑨𐑟 𐑞 𐑕𐑑𐑧𐑐𐑕 𐑑 𐑞 ·𐑧𐑛𐑦𐑑𐑼] ·𐑕𐑰𐑟𐑼: 𐑞𐑦𐑕 𐑢𐑫𐑥𐑩𐑯 𐑦𐑟 𐑞 𐑕𐑦𐑕𐑑𐑼 𐑝 ·𐑨𐑯𐑛𐑮𐑴𐑒𐑤𐑰𐑟. 𐑦𐑑 𐑢𐑪𐑟 𐑛𐑮𐑪𐑐𐑑 𐑑 𐑞 𐑤𐑲𐑩𐑯𐑟 𐑚𐑲 𐑢𐑦𐑗 𐑓𐑹𐑑. 𐑚𐑲 𐑢𐑦𐑗 𐑤𐑪𐑟 𐑢𐑧𐑯; 𐑚𐑳𐑑 𐑦𐑑 𐑩 𐑛𐑦𐑕𐑤𐑲𐑒 —

𐑞 𐑧𐑛𐑦𐑑𐑼. 𐑞 𐑤𐑲𐑩𐑯𐑟? 𐑯𐑩𐑯𐑕𐑧𐑯𐑕! [𐑑 ·𐑤𐑨𐑝𐑦𐑯𐑾]

Keeper, who goes to the gladiators. The gladiators draw their swords nervously.

FERROVIUS. Lost! lost for ever! I have betrayed my Master. Cut off this right hand: it has offended. Ye have swords, my brethren: strike.

LAVINIA. No, no. What have you done, Ferrovius?

FERROVIUS. I know not; but there was blood behind my eyes; and theres blood on my sword. What does that mean?

THE EMPEROR [*enthusiastically, on the landing outside his box*] What does it mean? It means that you are the greatest man in Rome. It means that you shall have a laurel crown of gold. Superb fighter: I could almost yield you my throne. It is a record for my reign: I shall live in history. Once, in Domitian's time, a Gaul slew three men in the arena and gained his freedom. But when before has one naked man slain six armed men of the bravest and best? The persecution shall cease: if Christians can fight like this, I shall have none but Christians to fight for me. [*To the Gladiators*] You are ordered to become Christians, you there: do you hear?

RETIARIUS. It is all one to us, Caesar. Had I been there with my net, the story would have been different.

THE CAPTAIN [*suddenly seizing Lavinia by the wrist and dragging her up the steps to the Emperor*] Caesar: this woman is the sister of Ferrovius. If she is thrown to the lions he will fret. He will lose weight; get out of condition –

THE EMPEROR. The lions? Nonsense! [*To Lavinia*]

𐑥𐑨𐑛𐑩𐑥: 𐑲 𐑨𐑥 𐑐𐑮𐑬𐑛 𐑑 𐑣𐑨𐑝 𐑞 𐑪𐑯𐑼 𐑝 𐑥𐑱𐑒𐑦𐑙 𐑿𐑼 𐑩𐑒𐑢𐑱𐑯𐑑𐑩𐑯𐑕. 𐑿𐑼 𐑚𐑮𐑳𐑞𐑼 𐑦𐑟 𐑞 𐑜𐑤𐑹𐑦 𐑝 ·𐑮𐑴𐑥.

𐑤𐑩𐑝𐑦𐑯𐑦𐑩. 𐑚𐑳𐑑 𐑥𐑲 𐑓𐑮𐑧𐑯𐑛𐑟 𐑣𐑽. 𐑥𐑳𐑕𐑑 𐑞𐑱 𐑛𐑲?

𐑞 𐑧𐑥𐑐𐑼𐑼. 𐑛𐑲! 𐑕𐑻𐑑𐑩𐑯𐑤𐑦 𐑯𐑪𐑑. 𐑞𐑺 𐑣𐑨𐑟 𐑯𐑧𐑝𐑼 𐑚𐑰𐑯 𐑞 𐑕𐑤𐑲𐑑𐑩𐑕𐑑 𐑲𐑛𐑾 𐑝 𐑣𐑸𐑥𐑦𐑙 𐑞𐑧𐑥. 𐑤𐑱𐑛𐑦𐑟 𐑯 𐑡𐑧𐑯𐑑𐑩𐑤𐑥𐑩𐑯: 𐑿 𐑸 𐑷𐑤 𐑓𐑮𐑰. 𐑐𐑮𐑱 𐑜𐑴 𐑦𐑯𐑑𐑵 𐑞 𐑓𐑮𐑳𐑯𐑑 𐑝 𐑞 𐑣𐑬𐑕 𐑯 𐑦𐑯𐑡𐑶 𐑞 𐑕𐑐𐑧𐑒𐑑𐑩𐑒𐑩𐑤 𐑑 𐑢𐑦𐑗 𐑿𐑼 𐑚𐑮𐑳𐑞𐑼 𐑣𐑨𐑟 𐑕𐑴 𐑕𐑐𐑤𐑧𐑯𐑛𐑦𐑛𐑤𐑦 𐑒𐑩𐑯𐑑𐑮𐑦𐑚𐑿𐑑𐑩𐑛. 𐑒𐑨𐑐𐑑𐑦𐑯: 𐑩𐑚𐑤𐑲𐑡 𐑥𐑰 𐑚𐑲 𐑒𐑩𐑯𐑛𐑳𐑒𐑑𐑦𐑙 𐑞𐑧𐑥 𐑑 𐑞 𐑕𐑰𐑑𐑕 𐑮𐑦𐑟𐑻𐑝𐑛 𐑓𐑹 𐑥𐑲 𐑐𐑻𐑕𐑩𐑯𐑩𐑤 𐑓𐑮𐑧𐑯𐑛𐑟.

𐑞 𐑥𐑩𐑯𐑨𐑡𐑼𐑦 𐑒𐑰𐑐𐑼. ·𐑕𐑰𐑟𐑼: 𐑲 𐑥𐑳𐑕𐑑 𐑣𐑨𐑝 𐑢𐑳𐑯 𐑒𐑮𐑦𐑕𐑗𐑩𐑯 𐑓𐑹 𐑞 𐑤𐑲𐑩𐑯. 𐑞 𐑐𐑰𐑐𐑩𐑤 𐑣𐑨𐑝 𐑚𐑰𐑯 𐑐𐑮𐑪𐑥𐑦𐑕𐑑 𐑦𐑑; 𐑯 𐑞𐑱 𐑢𐑦𐑤 𐑑𐑺 𐑞 𐑛𐑧𐑒𐑼𐑱𐑖𐑩𐑯𐑟 𐑑 𐑚𐑦𐑑𐑕 𐑦𐑓 𐑞𐑱 𐑸 𐑛𐑦𐑕𐑩𐑐𐑶𐑯𐑑𐑩𐑛.

𐑞 𐑧𐑥𐑐𐑼𐑼. 𐑑𐑮𐑵, 𐑑𐑮𐑵; 𐑢𐑰 𐑥𐑳𐑕𐑑 𐑣𐑨𐑝 𐑕𐑳𐑥𐑚𐑪𐑛𐑦 𐑓𐑹 𐑞 𐑯𐑿 𐑤𐑲𐑩𐑯.

𐑓𐑧𐑮𐑴𐑝𐑾𐑕. 𐑔𐑮𐑴 𐑥𐑰 𐑑 𐑣𐑦𐑥. 𐑤𐑧𐑑 𐑞 𐑩𐑐𐑪𐑕𐑑𐑱𐑑 𐑐𐑧𐑮𐑦𐑖.

𐑞 𐑧𐑥𐑐𐑼𐑼. 𐑯𐑴, 𐑯𐑴; 𐑿 𐑢𐑫𐑛 𐑑𐑺 𐑣𐑦𐑥 𐑦𐑯 𐑐𐑰𐑕𐑩𐑟, 𐑥𐑲 𐑓𐑮𐑧𐑯𐑛; 𐑯 𐑢𐑰 𐑒𐑨𐑯𐑪𐑑 𐑩𐑓𐑹𐑛 𐑑 𐑔𐑮𐑴 𐑩𐑢𐑱 𐑤𐑲𐑩𐑯𐑟 𐑨𐑟 𐑦𐑓 𐑞𐑱 𐑢𐑻 𐑥𐑽 𐑕𐑤𐑱𐑝𐑟. 𐑚𐑳𐑑 𐑢𐑰 𐑥𐑳𐑕𐑑 𐑣𐑨𐑝 𐑕𐑳𐑥𐑚𐑪𐑛𐑦. 𐑞𐑦𐑕 𐑦𐑟 𐑮𐑾𐑤𐑦 𐑦𐑒𐑕𐑑𐑮𐑰𐑥𐑤𐑦 𐑷𐑒𐑢𐑼𐑛.

𐑞 𐑥𐑩𐑯𐑨𐑡𐑼𐑦 𐑒𐑰𐑐𐑼. 𐑢𐑲 𐑯𐑪𐑑 𐑞𐑨𐑑 𐑤𐑦𐑑𐑩𐑤 𐑜𐑮𐑰𐑒 𐑗𐑨𐑐? 𐑣𐑰'𐑟 𐑯𐑪𐑑 𐑩 𐑒𐑮𐑦𐑕𐑗𐑩𐑯: 𐑣𐑰'𐑟 𐑩 𐑕𐑹𐑕𐑼𐑼.

𐑞 𐑧𐑥𐑐𐑼𐑼. 𐑞 𐑝𐑧𐑮𐑦 𐑔𐑦𐑙: 𐑣𐑰 𐑢𐑦𐑤 𐑛𐑵 𐑝𐑧𐑮𐑦 𐑢𐑧𐑤.

𐑞 𐑒𐑷𐑤 𐑚𐑶 [𐑦𐑖𐑵𐑦𐑙 𐑓𐑮𐑪𐑥 𐑞 𐑐𐑨𐑕𐑦𐑡] 𐑯𐑳𐑥𐑚𐑼 𐑑𐑢𐑧𐑤𐑝. 𐑞 𐑒𐑮𐑦𐑕𐑗𐑩𐑯 𐑓𐑹 𐑞 𐑯𐑿 𐑤𐑲𐑩𐑯.

Madam: I am proud to have the honor of making your acquaintance. Your brother is the glory of Rome.

LAVINIA. But my friends here. Must they die?

THE EMPEROR. Die! Certainly not. There has never been the slightest idea of harming them. Ladies and gentlemen: you are all free. Pray go into the front of the house and enjoy the spectacle to which your brother has so splendidly contributed. Captain: oblige me by conducting them to the seats reserved for my personal friends.

THE MENAGERIE KEEPER. Caesar: I must have one Christian for the lion. The people have been promised it; and they will tear the decorations to bits if they are disappointed.

THE EMPEROR. True, true: we must have somebody for the new lion.

FERROVIUS. Throw me to him. Let the apostate perish.

THE EMPEROR. No, no: you would tear him in pieces, my friend; and we cannot afford to throw away lions as if they were mere slaves. But we must have somebody. This is really extremely awkward.

THE MENAGERIE KEEPER. Why not that little Greek chap? He's not a Christian: he's a sorcerer.

THE EMPEROR. The very thing: he will do very well.

THE CALL BOY [*issuing from the passage*] Number twelve. The Christian for the new lion.

𐑨𐑯𐑛𐑮𐑩𐑒𐑤𐑰𐑟 [𐑮𐑲𐑟𐑦𐑙, 𐑯 𐑛𐑮𐑲𐑦𐑙 𐑣𐑯𐑕𐑦𐑤𐑨 𐑕𐑯𐑦𐑤𐑦 𐑑𐑮𐑛𐑦𐑞𐑩] 𐑥𐑤, 𐑦𐑑 𐑥𐑯𐑟 𐑑 𐑿, 𐑭𐑛𐑑𐑩 𐑧𐑤.

𐑤𐑩𐑝𐑦𐑯𐑦𐑩. 𐑲'𐑤 𐑜𐑴 𐑦𐑯 𐑣𐑦𐑟 𐑐𐑤𐑱𐑕, ·𐑕𐑰𐑟𐑼. 𐑭𐑕𐑒 𐑞 𐑒𐑨𐑐𐑑𐑩𐑯 𐑢𐑧𐑞𐑼 𐑞𐑧 𐑚𐑥 𐑘𐑘𐑑 𐑤𐑲𐑒 𐑚𐑧𐑕𐑑 𐑑 𐑕𐑰 𐑩 𐑥𐑨𐑯 𐑑𐑹𐑯 𐑑 𐑐𐑰𐑕𐑩𐑟. 𐑣𐑰 𐑑𐑴𐑤𐑛 𐑥𐑰 𐑕𐑴 𐑘𐑧𐑕𐑑𐑼𐑛𐑱.

𐑞 𐑒𐑨𐑐𐑑𐑩𐑯. 𐑞𐑺 𐑦𐑟 𐑕𐑳𐑥𐑔𐑦𐑙 𐑦𐑯 𐑞𐑨𐑑: 𐑞𐑺 𐑦𐑟 𐑕𐑳𐑥𐑑𐑦𐑥𐑟 𐑕𐑳𐑥𐑔𐑦𐑙 𐑦𐑯 𐑞𐑨𐑑 — 𐑦𐑓 𐑴𐑯𐑤𐑦 𐑲 𐑒𐑫𐑛 𐑚𐑰 𐑖𐑫𐑼 𐑞𐑨𐑑 𐑥𐑨𐑯 𐑢𐑪𐑟 𐑥𐑲 𐑢𐑲𐑓.

𐑨𐑯𐑛𐑮𐑩𐑒𐑤𐑰𐑟. 𐑯𐑴: 𐑲 𐑒𐑫𐑛 𐑯𐑧𐑝𐑼 𐑣𐑨𐑝 𐑩𐑥𐑩𐑞𐑼 𐑣𐑴𐑥 𐑢𐑧𐑯. 𐑯𐑴: 𐑯𐑴 𐑞 𐑚𐑧𐑕𐑑 𐑝 𐑩 𐑒𐑮𐑦𐑕𐑑𐑾𐑯 𐑯 𐑣𐑴𐑥 𐑞 𐑯𐑲𐑑 𐑝 𐑩 𐑑𐑧𐑤𐑩, 𐑲 𐑚𐑧𐑕𐑑𐑦𐑑 𐑞 𐑤𐑲𐑑 𐑞𐑨𐑑 𐑣𐑪𐑟 𐑯𐑴 𐑥𐑩𐑯 𐑞 𐑚𐑧𐑤𐑩𐑯 𐑯 𐑥𐑰. 𐑦𐑓 𐑢𐑲 𐑥𐑲 𐑒𐑳𐑥 𐑑𐑵 𐑲𐑑, 𐑚𐑦𐑤 𐑣𐑴 𐑢𐑲 𐑤𐑲𐑤 𐑯 𐑕𐑧 𐑞𐑨𐑑 𐑢𐑲 𐑥𐑲𐑤 𐑥𐑨𐑟 𐑞𐑨𐑑 𐑤𐑰 𐑤𐑫𐑛 𐑿 𐑣𐑨𐑝 𐑣𐑰 𐑚𐑰𐑟 𐑐𐑦𐑒𐑕𐑑, 𐑚𐑮𐑳𐑞𐑼 𐑚𐑦𐑤𐑴! ·𐑕𐑰𐑟𐑼: 𐑜𐑴 𐑑 𐑞𐑧 𐑚𐑲𐑤𐑛𐑟 𐑯 𐑕𐑰 𐑣𐑦𐑟 𐑩 𐑑𐑧𐑤𐑩 𐑒𐑳𐑥 𐑚𐑲. 𐑢𐑧𐑤 𐑥𐑧 𐑚𐑴 𐑯𐑲𐑚𐑩 𐑑𐑥𐑧𐑤 𐑞𐑺. [𐑣𐑰 𐑢𐑪𐑒𐑕 𐑬𐑑 𐑢𐑦𐑞 𐑞 𐑚𐑳𐑕𐑲𐑟.

𐑣𐑰𐑤 𐑯 𐑥𐑲𐑑𐑦𐑤𐑰 𐑞 𐑦𐑯 𐑤𐑨𐑟𐑑 𐑤𐑧𐑕𐑯 𐑞 𐑦𐑯 𐑞 𐑐𐑤𐑱𐑕𐑑 𐑧𐑤𐑥𐑟 𐑦𐑯 𐑞 𐑕𐑲𐑟 𐑞 𐑕𐑳𐑥𐑑𐑦𐑥𐑟 𐑞 𐑮𐑧𐑤𐑩𐑡𐑩𐑕 𐑣𐑦𐑟 𐑥𐑲𐑑-𐑚𐑰 𐑣𐑦𐑟 𐑤𐑲𐑒 𐑯 𐑤𐑧𐑕𐑯 𐑣𐑦𐑟 𐑐𐑤𐑱𐑕 𐑯 ·𐑨𐑯𐑛𐑮𐑩𐑒𐑤𐑰𐑟, 𐑚𐑦𐑒𐑳𐑥𐑟 𐑒𐑮𐑦𐑕𐑑𐑾𐑯 𐑚𐑧𐑤𐑰𐑝𐑼, 𐑐𐑲𐑑 𐑕𐑧𐑤 𐑞 𐑥𐑲𐑤 𐑣𐑦𐑟𐑑𐑼𐑦 𐑞𐑨𐑑 𐑤𐑦𐑝𐑦𐑙 𐑕𐑑𐑹𐑦𐑟 𐑢𐑦𐑞 𐑕𐑦𐑥𐑐𐑩𐑔𐑦, 𐑦𐑟 𐑞 𐑚𐑧𐑕𐑑 𐑦𐑯 𐑞 𐑐𐑤𐑱 𐑝 𐑞 𐑚𐑳𐑕𐑲𐑟, 𐑯 𐑞𐑨𐑑 𐑣𐑦𐑟 𐑤𐑲𐑓 𐑦𐑟 𐑞 𐑤𐑨𐑕𐑑 𐑞 𐑐𐑰𐑐𐑩𐑤 𐑝 𐑞 𐑕𐑳𐑥𐑔𐑦𐑙 𐑝 𐑞 𐑒𐑮𐑦𐑕𐑑𐑾𐑯 𐑯 𐑞 𐑤𐑲𐑩𐑯'𐑟 𐑒𐑱𐑟, 𐑥𐑧𐑯 𐑝 𐑣𐑦𐑟 𐑚𐑧𐑕𐑑𐑦𐑙𐑟 𐑚𐑦𐑤𐑰𐑝𐑦𐑙, 𐑦𐑟 𐑯 𐑣𐑦𐑟 𐑤𐑲𐑓. 𐑞 𐑕𐑳𐑥𐑔𐑦𐑙 𐑚𐑦𐑟 𐑩 𐑕𐑦𐑐𐑼𐑦𐑤. 𐑩 𐑚𐑦𐑙 𐑕𐑧𐑯𐑕. ·𐑨𐑯𐑛𐑮𐑩𐑒𐑤𐑰𐑟 𐑤𐑦𐑝𐑟 𐑑 𐑞 𐑕𐑧𐑯𐑕; 𐑞𐑦𐑯 𐑚𐑧𐑤𐑟 𐑦𐑯 𐑣𐑦𐑟 𐑕𐑳𐑥𐑔𐑦𐑙 𐑒𐑮𐑦𐑕𐑑𐑾𐑯 𐑯 𐑚𐑧𐑤𐑟. 𐑞 𐑚𐑧𐑕𐑑𐑦𐑙 𐑚𐑰𐑟𐑦𐑟 𐑦𐑟 𐑩 𐑒𐑮𐑦𐑕𐑑𐑾𐑯. 𐑞 𐑤𐑲𐑩𐑯 𐑚𐑦𐑤𐑦𐑝𐑟 𐑯𐑪𐑑 𐑞 𐑥𐑨𐑯. 𐑣𐑰 𐑚𐑦𐑤𐑰𐑝𐑟 𐑞𐑨𐑑 𐑞 𐑚𐑰𐑕𐑑𐑦𐑙 𐑦𐑯 𐑣𐑦𐑟 𐑚𐑦𐑤𐑰𐑝𐑟. 𐑣𐑰 𐑕𐑰𐑟 ·𐑨𐑯𐑛𐑮𐑩𐑒𐑤𐑰𐑟. 𐑣𐑰 𐑕𐑑𐑦𐑤𐑟; 𐑚𐑧𐑤𐑰𐑝𐑟 𐑕𐑑𐑦𐑤𐑦 𐑚𐑲 𐑕𐑑𐑮𐑧𐑙𐑔 𐑣𐑦𐑟 𐑤𐑲𐑓; 𐑕𐑑𐑮𐑧𐑙𐑔𐑩𐑟 𐑦𐑑 𐑣𐑦𐑟 𐑯𐑴𐑟 𐑚𐑰𐑤𐑦𐑓 𐑯 𐑣𐑦𐑟 𐑑𐑧𐑤 𐑦𐑯 𐑩 𐑦𐑯 𐑤𐑲𐑓 𐑣𐑦𐑟 𐑯𐑰𐑛 𐑚𐑦𐑤𐑦𐑓 𐑣𐑦𐑟 𐑑𐑧𐑤𐑦𐑙 𐑤𐑲𐑩𐑯 𐑚𐑦𐑣𐑲𐑯𐑛, 𐑤𐑲𐑒 𐑩 𐑚𐑦𐑤𐑰𐑝𐑼, 𐑯 𐑑𐑲𐑥𐑟

ANDROCLES [*rising, and pulling himself sadly together*] Well, it was to be, after all.

LAVINIA. I'll go in his place, Caesar. Ask the Captain whether they do not like best to see a woman torn to pieces. He told me so yesterday.

THE EMPEROR. There is something in that: there is certainly something in that – if only I could feel sure that your brother would not fret.

ANDROCLES. No: I should never have another happy hour. No: on the faith of a Christian and the honor of a tailor, I accept the lot that has fallen on me. If my wife turns up, give her my love and say that my wish was that she should be happy with her next, poor fellow! Caesar: go to your box and see how a tailor can die. Make way for number twelve there. [*He marches out along the passage*].

The vast audience in the amphitheatre now sees the Emperor re-enter his box and take his place as Androcles, desperately frightened, but still marching with piteous devotion, emerges from the other end of the passage, and finds himself at the focus of thousands of eager eyes. The lion's cage, with a heavy portcullis grating, is on his left. The Emperor gives a signal. A gong sounds. Androcles shivers at the sound; then falls on his knees and prays. The grating rises with a clash. The lion bounds into the arena. He rushes round frisking in his freedom. He sees Androcles. He stops; rises stiffly by straightening his legs; stretches out his nose forward and his tail in a horizontal line behind, like a pointer, and utters

an appalling roar. Androcles crouches and hides his face in his hands. The lion gathers himself for a spring, swishing his tail to and fro through the dust in an ecstasy of anticipation. Androcles throws up his hands in supplication to heaven. The lion checks at the sight of Androcles's face. He then steals towards him; smells him; arches his back; purrs like a motor car; finally rubs himself against Androcles, knocking him over. Androcles, supporting himself on his wrist, looks affrightedly at the lion. The lion limps on three paws, holding up the other as if it was wounded. A flash of recognition lights up the face of Androcles. He flaps his hand as if it had a thorn in it, and pretends to pull the thorn out and to hurt himself. The lion nods repeatedly. Androcles holds out his hands to the lion, who gives him both paws, which he shakes with enthusiasm. They embrace rapturously, finally waltz round the arena amid a sudden burst of deafening applause, and out through the passage, the Emperor watching them in breathless astonishment until they disappear, when he rushes from his box and descends the steps in frantic excitement.

THE EMPEROR. My friends, an incredible! an amazing thing! has happened. I can no longer doubt the truth of Christianity. [*The Christians press to him joyfully*]. This Christian sorcerer – [*with a yell, he breaks off, as he sees Androcles and the lion emerge from the passage, waltzing. He bolts wildly up the steps into his box, and slams the door. All, Christians and gladiators*

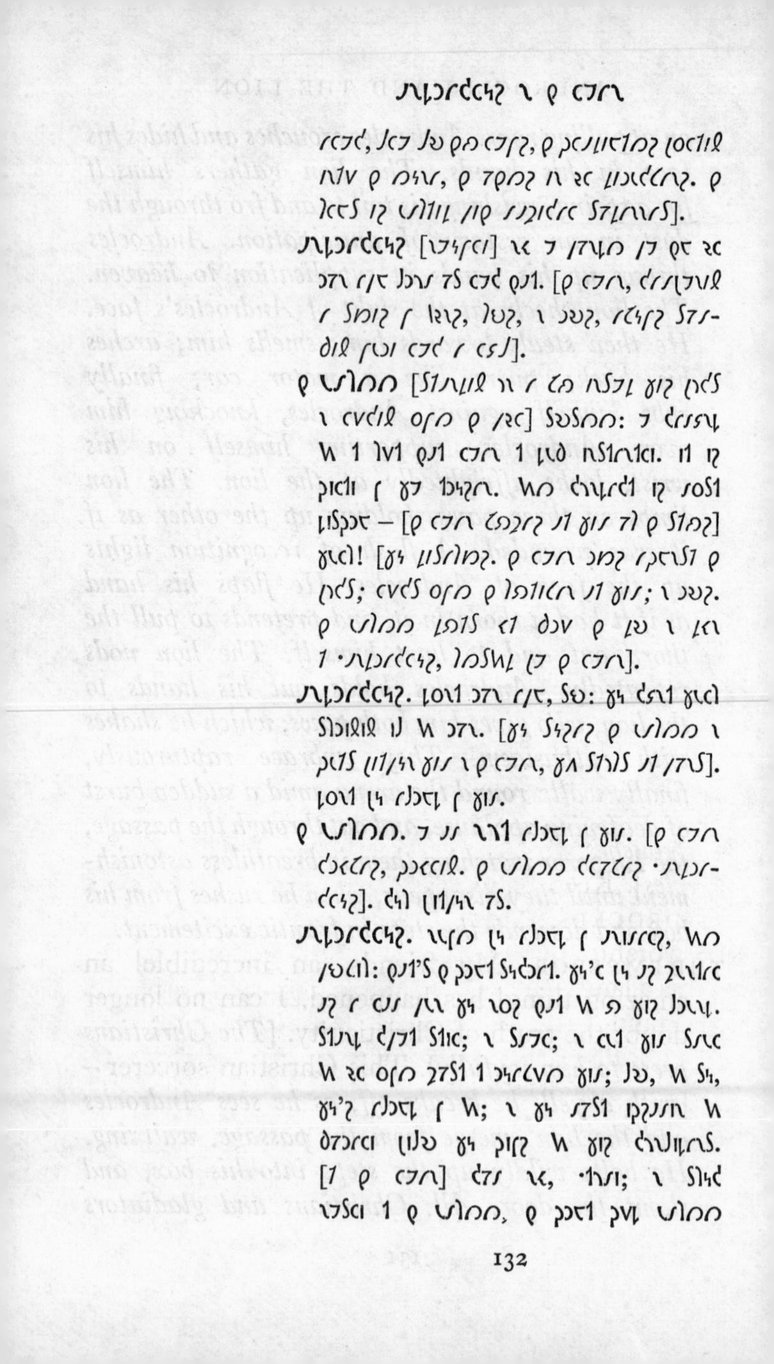

alike, fly for their lives, the gladiators bolting into the arena, the others in all directions. The place is emptied with magical suddenness].

ANDROCLES [*naïvely*] Now I wonder why they all run away from us like that. [*The lion, combining a series of yawns, purrs, and roars, achieves something very like a laugh*].

THE EMPEROR [*standing on a chair inside his box and looking over the wall*] Sorcerer: I command you to put that lion to death instantly. It is guilty of high treason. Your conduct is most disgra – [*the lion charges at him up the stairs*] help! [*He disappears. The lion rears against the box; looks over the partition at him; and roars. The Emperor darts out through the door and down to Androcles, pursued by the lion*].

ANDROCLES. Dont run away, sir: he cant help springing if you run. [*He seizes the Emperor and gets between him and the lion, who stops at once*]. Dont be afraid of him.

THE EMPEROR. I am n o t afraid of him. [*The lion crouches, growling. The Emperor clutches Androcles*]. Keep between us.

ANDROCLES. Never be afraid of animals, your worship: thats the great secret. He'll be as gentle as a lamb when he knows that you are his friend. Stand quite still; and smile; and let him smell you all over just to reassure him; for, you see, he's afraid of you; and he must examine you thoroughly before he gives you his confidence. [*To the lion*] Come now, Tommy; and speak nicely to the Emperor, the great good Emperor

𐑣𐑵 𐑣𐑨𐑟 𐑐𐑬𐑼 𐑑 𐑣𐑨𐑝 𐑷𐑤 𐑬𐑼 𐑣𐑧𐑛𐑟 𐑒𐑳𐑑 𐑪𐑓 𐑦𐑓 𐑢𐑰 𐑛𐑴𐑯𐑑 𐑚𐑦𐑣𐑱𐑝 𐑝𐑧𐑮𐑦 𐑝𐑧𐑮𐑦 𐑮𐑦𐑕𐑐𐑧𐑒𐑑𐑓𐑫𐑤𐑦 𐑑 𐑣𐑦𐑥.

[𐑞 𐑤𐑲𐑩𐑯 𐑳𐑑𐑼𐑟 𐑩 𐑓𐑽𐑓𐑩𐑤 𐑮𐑹. 𐑞 𐑧𐑥𐑐𐑼𐑼 𐑛𐑨𐑖𐑩𐑟 𐑥𐑨𐑛𐑤𐑦 𐑳𐑐 𐑞 𐑕𐑑𐑧𐑐𐑕, 𐑩𐑒𐑮𐑪𐑕 𐑞 𐑤𐑨𐑯𐑛𐑦𐑙, 𐑯 𐑛𐑬𐑯 𐑩𐑜𐑧𐑯 𐑪𐑯 𐑞 𐑳𐑞𐑼 𐑕𐑲𐑛, 𐑢𐑦𐑞 𐑞 𐑤𐑲𐑩𐑯 𐑦𐑯 𐑣𐑪𐑑 𐑐𐑼𐑕𐑵𐑑. ·𐑨𐑯𐑛𐑮𐑩𐑒𐑤𐑰𐑟 𐑮𐑳𐑖𐑩𐑟 𐑭𐑓𐑑𐑼 𐑞 𐑤𐑲𐑩𐑯; 𐑴𐑝𐑼𐑑𐑱𐑒𐑕 𐑣𐑦𐑥 𐑨𐑟 𐑣𐑰 𐑦𐑟 𐑛𐑦𐑕𐑧𐑯𐑛𐑦𐑙; 𐑯 𐑔𐑮𐑴𐑟 𐑣𐑦𐑥𐑕𐑧𐑤𐑓 𐑪𐑯 𐑣𐑦𐑟 𐑚𐑨𐑒, 𐑑𐑮𐑲𐑦𐑙 𐑑 𐑿𐑟 𐑣𐑦𐑟 𐑑𐑴𐑟 𐑨𐑟 𐑩 𐑚𐑮𐑱𐑒. 𐑚𐑦𐑓𐑹 𐑣𐑰 𐑒𐑨𐑯 𐑕𐑑𐑪𐑐 𐑣𐑦𐑥 𐑞 𐑤𐑲𐑩𐑯 𐑜𐑧𐑑𐑕 𐑣𐑴𐑤𐑛 𐑝 𐑞 𐑑𐑮𐑱𐑤𐑦𐑙 𐑧𐑯𐑛 𐑝 𐑞 𐑧𐑥𐑐𐑼𐑼'𐑟 𐑮𐑴𐑚].

𐑨𐑯𐑛𐑮𐑩𐑒𐑤𐑰𐑟. 𐑴 𐑚𐑨𐑛 𐑢𐑦𐑒𐑛 ·𐑑𐑪𐑥𐑦, 𐑑 𐑗𐑱𐑕 𐑞 𐑧𐑥𐑐𐑼𐑼 𐑤𐑲𐑒 𐑞𐑨𐑑! 𐑤𐑧𐑑 𐑜𐑴 𐑞 𐑧𐑥𐑐𐑼𐑼'𐑟 𐑮𐑴𐑚 𐑨𐑑 𐑢𐑳𐑯𐑕, 𐑕𐑻: 𐑢𐑺'𐑟 𐑘𐑹 𐑥𐑨𐑯𐑼𐑟? [𐑞 𐑤𐑲𐑩𐑯 𐑜𐑮𐑬𐑤𐑟 𐑯 𐑢𐑳𐑮𐑦𐑟 𐑞 𐑮𐑴𐑚]. 𐑛𐑴𐑯𐑑 𐑐𐑫𐑤 𐑦𐑑 𐑩𐑢𐑱 𐑓𐑮𐑪𐑥 𐑣𐑦𐑥, 𐑘𐑹 𐑢𐑻𐑖𐑦𐑐. 𐑣𐑰'𐑟 𐑴𐑯𐑤𐑦 𐑐𐑤𐑱𐑦𐑙. 𐑯𐑬 𐑲 𐑖𐑨𐑤 𐑚𐑰 𐑮𐑾𐑤𐑦 𐑨𐑙𐑜𐑮𐑦 𐑢𐑦𐑞 𐑿, ·𐑑𐑪𐑥𐑦, 𐑦𐑓 𐑿 𐑛𐑴𐑯𐑑 𐑤𐑧𐑑 𐑜𐑴. [𐑞 𐑤𐑲𐑩𐑯 𐑜𐑮𐑬𐑤𐑟 𐑩𐑜𐑧𐑯]. 𐑲'𐑤 𐑑𐑧𐑤 𐑿 𐑢𐑪𐑑 𐑦𐑑 𐑦𐑟, 𐑕𐑻: 𐑣𐑰 𐑔𐑦𐑙𐑒𐑕 𐑿 𐑯 𐑲 𐑸 𐑯𐑪𐑑 𐑓𐑮𐑧𐑯𐑛𐑟.

𐑞 𐑧𐑥𐑐𐑼𐑼 [𐑑𐑮𐑲𐑦𐑙 𐑑 𐑳𐑯𐑛𐑵 𐑞 𐑒𐑤𐑭𐑕𐑐 𐑝 𐑣𐑦𐑟 𐑮𐑴𐑚] 𐑓𐑮𐑧𐑯𐑛𐑟! 𐑿 𐑦𐑯𐑓𐑻𐑯𐑩𐑤 𐑕𐑒𐑬𐑯𐑛𐑮𐑩𐑤 [𐑞 𐑤𐑲𐑩𐑯 𐑜𐑮𐑬𐑤𐑟] – 𐑛𐑴𐑯𐑑 𐑤𐑧𐑑 𐑣𐑦𐑥 𐑜𐑴. 𐑒𐑻𐑕 𐑞𐑦𐑕 𐑮𐑴𐑚! 𐑲 𐑒𐑭𐑯𐑑 𐑜𐑧𐑑 𐑦𐑑 𐑤𐑵𐑕.

𐑨𐑯𐑛𐑮𐑩𐑒𐑤𐑰𐑟. 𐑢𐑰 𐑥𐑳𐑕𐑩𐑯𐑑 𐑤𐑧𐑑 𐑣𐑦𐑥 𐑢𐑻𐑒 𐑣𐑦𐑥𐑕𐑧𐑤𐑓 𐑦𐑯𐑑𐑵 𐑩 𐑮𐑱𐑡. 𐑿 𐑥𐑳𐑕𐑑 𐑖𐑴 𐑣𐑦𐑥 𐑞𐑨𐑑 𐑿 𐑸 𐑣𐑦𐑟 𐑐𐑼𐑑𐑦𐑒𐑿𐑤𐑼 𐑓𐑮𐑧𐑯𐑛 – 𐑦𐑓 𐑿 𐑢𐑦𐑤 𐑣𐑨𐑝 𐑞 𐑒𐑪𐑯𐑛𐑦𐑕𐑧𐑯𐑖𐑩𐑯. [𐑣𐑰 𐑕𐑰𐑟𐑩𐑟 𐑞 𐑧𐑥𐑐𐑼𐑼'𐑟 𐑣𐑨𐑯𐑛𐑟 𐑯 𐑖𐑱𐑒𐑕 𐑞𐑧𐑥 𐑒𐑹𐑛𐑾𐑤𐑦]. 𐑤𐑫𐑒, ·𐑑𐑪𐑥𐑦: 𐑞 𐑯𐑲𐑕 𐑧𐑥𐑐𐑼𐑼 𐑦𐑟 𐑞 𐑚𐑧𐑕𐑑 𐑓𐑮𐑧𐑯𐑛 ·𐑨𐑯𐑛𐑦 ·𐑢𐑪𐑯𐑛𐑦 𐑣𐑨𐑟 𐑦𐑯 𐑞 𐑣𐑴𐑤 𐑢𐑻𐑤𐑛: 𐑣𐑰 𐑤𐑳𐑝𐑟 𐑣𐑦𐑥 𐑤𐑲𐑒 𐑩 𐑚𐑮𐑳𐑞𐑼.

𐑞 𐑧𐑥𐑐𐑼𐑼. 𐑿 𐑤𐑦𐑑𐑩𐑤 𐑚𐑮𐑵𐑑, 𐑿 𐑛𐑨𐑥𐑛 𐑓𐑦𐑤𐑔𐑦 𐑤𐑦𐑑𐑩𐑤 𐑛𐑪𐑜 𐑝 𐑩 𐑜𐑮𐑰𐑒 𐑑𐑱𐑤𐑼: 𐑲'𐑤 𐑣𐑨𐑝 𐑿 𐑚𐑻𐑯𐑑

who has power to have all our heads cut off if we dont behave very very respectfully to him.

The lion utters a fearful roar. The Emperor dashes madly up the steps, across the landing, and down again on the other side, with the lion in hot pursuit. Androcles rushes after the lion; overtakes him as he is descending; and throws himself on his back, trying to use his toes as a brake. Before he can stop him the lion gets hold of the trailing end of the Emperor's robe.

ANDROCLES. Oh bad wicked Tommy, to chase the Emperor like that! Let go the Emperor's robe at once, sir: wheres your manners? [*The lion growls and worries the robe*]. Dont pull it away from him, your worship. He's only playing. Now I shall be really angry with you, Tommy, if you dont let go. [*The lion growls again*]. I'll tell you what it is, sir: he thinks you and I are not friends.

THE EMPEROR [*trying to undo the clasp of his brooch*] Friends! You infernal scoundrel [*the lion growls*] – dont let him go. Curse this brooch! I cant get it loose.

ANDROCLES. We mustnt let him lash himself into a rage. You must shew him that you are my particular friend – if you will have the condescension. [*He seizes the Emperor's hands and shakes them cordially*]. Look, Tommy: the nice Emperor is the dearest friend Andy Wandy has in the whole world: he loves him like a brother.

THE EMPEROR. You little brute, you damned filthy little dog of a Greek tailor: I'll have you burnt

𐑩𐑤𐑲𐑝 𐑚𐑲 𐑚𐑰𐑦𐑙 𐑑 𐑑𐑳𐑗 𐑞 𐑛𐑦𐑝𐑲𐑯 𐑐𐑻𐑕𐑩𐑯 𐑝 𐑞 𐑧𐑥𐑐𐑼𐑼. [𐑞 𐑤𐑲𐑩𐑯 𐑜𐑮𐑬𐑤𐑟].

𐑨𐑯𐑛𐑮𐑩𐑒𐑤𐑰𐑟. 𐑴 𐑛𐑴𐑯𐑑 𐑑𐑷𐑒 𐑤𐑲𐑒 𐑞𐑨𐑑, 𐑕𐑻. 𐑣𐑰 𐑳𐑯𐑛𐑼𐑕𐑑𐑨𐑯𐑛𐑟 𐑧𐑝𐑮𐑦 𐑢𐑻𐑛 𐑿 𐑕𐑱: 𐑷𐑤 𐑨𐑯𐑦𐑥𐑩𐑤𐑟 𐑛𐑵: 𐑞𐑱 𐑑𐑱𐑒 𐑦𐑑 𐑓𐑮𐑪𐑥 𐑞 𐑑𐑴𐑯 𐑝 𐑿𐑼 𐑝𐑶𐑕. [𐑞 𐑤𐑲𐑩𐑯 𐑜𐑮𐑬𐑤𐑟 𐑯 𐑤𐑨𐑖𐑩𐑟 𐑣𐑦𐑟 𐑑𐑱𐑤]. 𐑲 𐑔𐑦𐑙𐑒 𐑣𐑰'𐑟 𐑜𐑴𐑦𐑙 𐑑 𐑕𐑐𐑮𐑦𐑙 𐑨𐑑 𐑿𐑼 𐑢𐑻𐑖𐑦𐑐. 𐑦𐑓 𐑿 𐑢𐑫𐑛 𐑥𐑲𐑯𐑛 𐑕𐑱𐑦𐑙 𐑕𐑳𐑥𐑔𐑦𐑙 𐑐𐑤𐑧𐑟𐑩𐑯𐑑. [𐑞 𐑤𐑲𐑩𐑯 𐑮𐑹𐑟].

𐑞 𐑧𐑥𐑐𐑼𐑼 [𐑑𐑱𐑒𐑦𐑙 ·𐑨𐑯𐑛𐑮𐑩𐑒𐑤𐑰𐑟'𐑩𐑟 𐑣𐑨𐑯𐑛 𐑐𐑮𐑩-𐑑𐑧𐑒𐑑𐑦𐑙𐑤𐑦] 𐑥𐑲 𐑛𐑽𐑮𐑧𐑕𐑑 𐑥𐑦𐑕𐑑𐑼 ·𐑨𐑯𐑛𐑮𐑩𐑒𐑤𐑰𐑟, 𐑥𐑲 𐑕𐑢𐑰𐑑𐑩𐑕𐑑 𐑚𐑳𐑛, 𐑥𐑲 𐑤𐑪𐑙 𐑤𐑪𐑕𐑑 𐑚𐑮𐑳𐑞𐑼, 𐑒𐑳𐑥 𐑑 𐑥𐑲 𐑸𐑥𐑟. [𐑣𐑰 𐑦𐑥𐑚𐑮𐑱𐑕𐑩𐑟 ·𐑨𐑯𐑛𐑮𐑩𐑒𐑤𐑰𐑟] 𐑴, 𐑢𐑪𐑑 𐑩 𐑒𐑳𐑥𐑓𐑼𐑑𐑩𐑚𐑩𐑤 𐑕𐑥𐑧𐑤 𐑝 𐑜𐑸𐑤𐑦𐑒!

[𐑞 𐑤𐑲𐑩𐑯 𐑤𐑧𐑑𐑕 𐑜𐑴 𐑞 𐑮𐑴𐑚 𐑯 𐑮𐑴𐑤𐑟 𐑴𐑝𐑼 𐑪𐑯 𐑣𐑦𐑟 𐑚𐑨𐑒, 𐑒𐑤𐑭𐑕𐑐𐑦𐑙 𐑣𐑦𐑟 𐑐𐑷𐑟 𐑴𐑝𐑼 𐑢𐑳𐑯 𐑳𐑞𐑼 𐑒𐑴𐑒𐑧𐑑𐑦𐑖𐑤𐑦 𐑩𐑚𐑳𐑝 𐑣𐑦𐑟 𐑯𐑴𐑟].

𐑨𐑯𐑛𐑮𐑩𐑒𐑤𐑰𐑟. 𐑞𐑺! 𐑿 𐑕𐑰, 𐑿𐑼 𐑢𐑻𐑖𐑦𐑐, 𐑩 𐑗𐑲𐑤𐑛 𐑥𐑲𐑑 𐑐𐑤𐑱 𐑢𐑦𐑞 𐑣𐑦𐑥 𐑯𐑬. 𐑕𐑰! [𐑣𐑰 𐑑𐑦𐑒𐑩𐑤𐑟 𐑞 𐑤𐑲𐑩𐑯'𐑟 𐑚𐑧𐑤𐑦. 𐑞 𐑤𐑲𐑩𐑯 𐑮𐑦𐑜𐑩𐑤𐑟 𐑧𐑒𐑕𐑑𐑨𐑑𐑦𐑒𐑤𐑦]. 𐑒𐑳𐑥 𐑯 𐑐𐑧𐑑 𐑣𐑦𐑥.

𐑞 𐑧𐑥𐑐𐑼𐑼. 𐑲 𐑥𐑳𐑕𐑑 𐑒𐑪𐑙𐑒𐑼 𐑞𐑰𐑟 𐑳𐑯𐑒𐑦𐑙𐑤𐑦 𐑑𐑧𐑮𐑼𐑟. 𐑥𐑲𐑯𐑛 𐑿 𐑛𐑴𐑯𐑑 𐑜𐑴 𐑩𐑢𐑱 𐑓𐑮𐑪𐑥 𐑣𐑦𐑥, 𐑞𐑴. [𐑣𐑰 𐑐𐑨𐑑𐑕 𐑞 𐑤𐑲𐑩𐑯'𐑟 𐑗𐑧𐑕𐑑].

𐑨𐑯𐑛𐑮𐑩𐑒𐑤𐑰𐑟. 𐑴, 𐑕𐑻, 𐑣𐑬 𐑓𐑿 𐑥𐑧𐑯 𐑢𐑫𐑛 𐑣𐑨𐑝 𐑞 𐑒𐑳𐑮𐑦𐑡 𐑑 𐑛𐑵 𐑞𐑨𐑑!

𐑞 𐑧𐑥𐑐𐑼𐑼. 𐑘𐑧𐑕: 𐑦𐑑 𐑑𐑱𐑒𐑕 𐑩 𐑚𐑦𐑑 𐑝 𐑯𐑻𐑝. 𐑤𐑧𐑑 𐑳𐑕 𐑣𐑨𐑝 𐑞 𐑒𐑹𐑑 𐑦𐑯 𐑯 𐑓𐑮𐑲𐑑𐑩𐑯 𐑞𐑧𐑥. 𐑦𐑟 𐑣𐑰 𐑕𐑱𐑓, 𐑛𐑵 𐑿 𐑔𐑦𐑙𐑒?

𐑨𐑯𐑛𐑮𐑩𐑒𐑤𐑰𐑟. 𐑒𐑢𐑲𐑑 𐑕𐑱𐑓 𐑯𐑬, 𐑕𐑻.

𐑞 𐑧𐑥𐑐𐑼𐑼 [𐑥𐑩𐑡𐑧𐑕𐑑𐑦𐑒𐑤𐑦] 𐑢𐑪𐑑 𐑣𐑴, 𐑞𐑺! 𐑷𐑤 𐑣𐑵 𐑸 𐑢𐑦𐑞𐑦𐑯 𐑣𐑽𐑦𐑙, 𐑮𐑦𐑑𐑻𐑯 𐑢𐑦𐑞𐑬𐑑 𐑓𐑽. ·𐑕𐑰𐑟𐑼 𐑣𐑨𐑟 𐑑𐑱𐑥𐑛 𐑞 𐑤𐑲𐑩𐑯. [𐑷𐑤 𐑞 *𐑓𐑿𐑡𐑦𐑑𐑦𐑝𐑟* 𐑕𐑑𐑰𐑤

alive for daring to touch the divine person of the Emperor. [*The lion growls*].

ANDROCLES. Oh dont talk like that, sir. He understands every word you say: all animals do: they take it from the tone of your voice. [*The lion growls and lashes his tail*]. I think he's going to spring at your worship. If you wouldnt mind saying something affectionate. [*The lion roars*].

THE EMPEROR [*shaking Androcles's hand frantically*] My dearest Mr Androcles, my sweetest friend, my long lost brother, come to my arms. [*He embraces Androcles*] Oh, what an abominable smell of garlic!

The lion lets go the robe and rolls over on his back, clasping his forepaws over one another coquettishly above his nose.

ANDROCLES. There! You see, your worship, a child might play with him now. See! [*He tickles the lion's belly. The lion wriggles ecstatically*]. Come and pet him.

THE EMPEROR. I must conquer these unkingly terrors. Mind you dont go away from him, though. [*He pats the lion's chest*].

ANDROCLES. Oh, sir, how few men would have the courage to do that!

THE EMPEROR. Yes: it takes a bit of nerve. Let us have the Court in and frighten them. Is he safe, do you think?

ANDROCLES. Quite safe now, sir.

THE EMPEROR [*majestically*] What ho, there! All who are within hearing, return without fear. Caesar has tamed the lion. [*All the fugitives steal*

𐑒𐑷𐑖𐑩𐑕𐑤𐑦 𐑦𐑯. 𐑞 𐑥𐑩𐑯𐑨𐑡𐑼𐑦 𐑒𐑰𐑐𐑼𐑟 𐑒𐑳𐑥 𐑓𐑮𐑪𐑥 𐑞 𐑐𐑨𐑕𐑦𐑡 𐑢𐑦𐑞 𐑳𐑞𐑼 𐑒𐑰𐑐𐑼𐑟 𐑸𐑥𐑛 𐑢𐑦𐑞 𐑯𐑧𐑑𐑕 𐑯 𐑑𐑮𐑲𐑛𐑩𐑯𐑑𐑕]. 𐑑𐑱𐑒 𐑞𐑴𐑟 𐑔𐑦𐑙𐑟 𐑩𐑢𐑱. 𐑲 𐑣𐑨𐑝 𐑕𐑩𐑚𐑛𐑿𐑛 𐑞 𐑚𐑰𐑕𐑑. [𐑣𐑰 𐑐𐑤𐑱𐑕𐑩𐑟 𐑣𐑦𐑟 𐑓𐑫𐑑 𐑪𐑯 𐑦𐑑].

·𐑓𐑧𐑮𐑴𐑝𐑾𐑕 [𐑑𐑦𐑥𐑦𐑛𐑤𐑦 𐑩𐑐𐑮𐑴𐑗𐑦𐑙 𐑞 𐑧𐑥𐑐𐑼𐑼 𐑯 𐑤𐑫𐑒𐑦𐑙 𐑛𐑬𐑯 𐑢𐑦𐑞 𐑷 𐑪𐑯 𐑞 𐑤𐑲𐑩𐑯] 𐑦𐑑 𐑦𐑟 𐑕𐑑𐑮𐑱𐑯𐑡 𐑞𐑨𐑑 𐑲, 𐑣𐑵 𐑓𐑽 𐑯𐑴 𐑥𐑨𐑯, 𐑖𐑫𐑛 𐑓𐑽 𐑩 𐑤𐑲𐑩𐑯.

𐑞 𐑒𐑨𐑐𐑑𐑩𐑯. 𐑧𐑝𐑮𐑦 𐑥𐑨𐑯 𐑓𐑽𐑟 𐑕𐑳𐑥𐑔𐑦𐑙, ·𐑓𐑧𐑮𐑴𐑝𐑾𐑕.

𐑞 𐑧𐑥𐑐𐑼𐑼. 𐑣𐑬 𐑩𐑚𐑬𐑑 𐑞 𐑐𐑮𐑦𐑑𐑹𐑾𐑯 𐑜𐑸𐑛 𐑯𐑬?

·𐑓𐑧𐑮𐑴𐑝𐑾𐑕. 𐑦𐑯 𐑥𐑲 𐑿𐑔 𐑲 𐑢𐑻𐑖𐑦𐑐𐑑 ·𐑥𐑸𐑟, 𐑞 𐑜𐑪𐑛 𐑝 𐑢𐑹. 𐑲 𐑑𐑻𐑯𐑛 𐑓𐑮𐑪𐑥 𐑣𐑦𐑥 𐑑 𐑕𐑻𐑝 𐑞 𐑒𐑮𐑦𐑕𐑗𐑩𐑯 𐑜𐑪𐑛; 𐑚𐑳𐑑 𐑑𐑩𐑛𐑱 𐑞 𐑒𐑮𐑦𐑕𐑗𐑩𐑯 𐑜𐑪𐑛 𐑓𐑹𐑕𐑫𐑒 𐑥𐑰; 𐑯 ·𐑥𐑸𐑟 𐑴𐑝𐑼𐑒𐑱𐑥 𐑥𐑰 𐑯 𐑑𐑫𐑒 𐑚𐑨𐑒 𐑣𐑦𐑟 𐑴𐑯. 𐑞 𐑒𐑮𐑦𐑕𐑗𐑩𐑯 𐑜𐑪𐑛 𐑦𐑟 𐑯𐑪𐑑 𐑘𐑧𐑑. 𐑣𐑰 𐑢𐑦𐑤 𐑒𐑳𐑥 𐑢𐑧𐑯 ·𐑥𐑸𐑟 𐑯 𐑲 𐑸 𐑛𐑳𐑕𐑑; 𐑚𐑳𐑑 𐑥𐑰𐑯𐑢𐑲𐑤 𐑲 𐑥𐑳𐑕𐑑 𐑕𐑻𐑝 𐑞 𐑜𐑪𐑛𐑟 𐑞𐑨𐑑 𐑸, 𐑯𐑪𐑑 𐑞 𐑜𐑪𐑛 𐑞𐑨𐑑 𐑢𐑦𐑤 𐑚𐑰. 𐑩𐑯𐑑𐑦𐑤 𐑞𐑧𐑯 𐑲 𐑩𐑒𐑕𐑧𐑐𐑑 𐑕𐑻𐑝𐑦𐑕 𐑦𐑯 𐑞 𐑜𐑸𐑛, ·𐑕𐑰𐑟𐑼.

𐑞 𐑧𐑥𐑐𐑼𐑼. 𐑝𐑧𐑮𐑦 𐑢𐑲𐑟𐑤𐑦 𐑕𐑧𐑛. 𐑷𐑤 𐑮𐑦𐑩𐑤𐑦 𐑕𐑧𐑯𐑕𐑩𐑚𐑩𐑤 𐑥𐑧𐑯 𐑩𐑜𐑮𐑰 𐑞𐑨𐑑 𐑞 𐑐𐑮𐑵𐑛𐑩𐑯𐑑 𐑒𐑹𐑕 𐑦𐑟 𐑑 𐑚𐑰 𐑯𐑲𐑞𐑼 𐑚𐑦𐑜𐑩𐑑𐑩𐑛 𐑦𐑯 𐑬𐑼 𐑩𐑑𐑨𐑗𐑥𐑩𐑯𐑑 𐑑 𐑞 𐑴𐑤𐑛 𐑯𐑹 𐑮𐑨𐑖 𐑯 𐑳𐑯𐑐𐑮𐑨𐑒𐑑𐑦𐑒𐑩𐑤 𐑦𐑯 𐑒𐑰𐑐𐑦𐑙 𐑩𐑯 𐑴𐑐𐑩𐑯 𐑥𐑲𐑯𐑛 𐑓𐑹 𐑞 𐑯𐑿, 𐑚𐑳𐑑 𐑑 𐑥𐑱𐑒 𐑞 𐑚𐑧𐑕𐑑 𐑝 𐑚𐑴𐑔 𐑛𐑦𐑕𐑐𐑧𐑯𐑕𐑱𐑖𐑩𐑯𐑟.

𐑞 𐑒𐑨𐑐𐑑𐑩𐑯. 𐑢𐑪𐑑 𐑛𐑵 𐑿 𐑕𐑱, ·𐑤𐑩𐑝𐑦𐑯𐑾? 𐑢𐑦𐑤 𐑿 𐑑𐑵 𐑚𐑰 𐑒𐑩𐑯𐑝𐑻𐑑𐑩𐑛?

·𐑤𐑩𐑝𐑦𐑯𐑾 [𐑪𐑯 𐑞 𐑕𐑑𐑺𐑟] 𐑯𐑴: 𐑲'𐑤 𐑕𐑑𐑮𐑲𐑝 𐑓𐑹 𐑞 𐑒𐑳𐑥𐑦𐑙 𐑝 𐑞 𐑜𐑪𐑛 𐑣𐑵 𐑦𐑟 𐑯𐑪𐑑 𐑘𐑧𐑑.

𐑞 𐑒𐑨𐑐𐑑𐑩𐑯. 𐑥𐑱 𐑲 𐑒𐑳𐑥 𐑯 𐑸𐑜𐑿 𐑢𐑦𐑞 𐑿 𐑩𐑒𐑱𐑠𐑩𐑯𐑩𐑤𐑦?

cautiously in. The Menagerie Keeper comes from the passage with other keepers armed with iron bars and tridents]. Take those things away. I have subdued the beast. [*He places his foot on it*].

FERROVIUS [*timidly approaching the Emperor and looking down with awe on the lion*] It is strange that I, who fear no man, should fear a lion.

THE CAPTAIN. Every man fears something, Ferrovius.

THE EMPEROR. How about the Pretorian Guard now?

FERROVIUS. In my youth I worshipped Mars, the God of War. I turned from him to serve the Christian god; but today the Christian god forsook me; and Mars overcame me and took back his own. The Christian god is not yet. He will come when Mars and I are dust; but meanwhile I must serve the gods that are, not the God that will be. Until then I accept service in the Guard, Caesar.

THE EMPEROR. Very wisely said. All really sensible men agree that the prudent course is to be neither bigoted in our attachment to the old nor rash and unpractical in keeping an open mind for the new, but to make the best of both dispensations.

THE CAPTAIN. What do you say, Lavinia? Will you too be prudent?

LAVINIA [*on the stairs*] No: I'll strive for the coming of the God who is not yet.

THE CAPTAIN. May I come and argue with you occasionally?

𐑤𐑨𐑝𐑦𐑯𐑾. 𐑘𐑧𐑕, 𐑣𐑨𐑯𐑕𐑩𐑥 𐑒𐑨𐑐𐑑𐑦𐑯: 𐑿 𐑥𐑱. [𐑣𐑰 𐑒𐑦𐑕𐑩𐑟 𐑣𐑻 𐑣𐑨𐑯𐑛].

𐑞 𐑧𐑥𐑐𐑼𐑼. 𐑯 𐑯𐑬, 𐑥𐑲 𐑓𐑮𐑧𐑯𐑛𐑟, 𐑞𐑴 𐑲 𐑛𐑵 𐑯𐑪𐑑, 𐑨𐑟 𐑿 𐑕𐑰, 𐑓𐑽 𐑞𐑦𐑕 𐑤𐑲𐑩𐑯, 𐑘𐑧𐑑 𐑞 𐑕𐑑𐑮𐑧𐑙𐑔 𐑝 𐑣𐑦𐑟 𐑚𐑲𐑕𐑧𐑐𐑕 𐑦𐑟 𐑒𐑩𐑯𐑕𐑦𐑛𐑼𐑩𐑚𐑩𐑤; 𐑕𐑴 𐑯𐑳𐑯 𐑝 𐑳𐑕 𐑒𐑨𐑯 𐑓𐑰𐑤 𐑒𐑢𐑲𐑑 𐑖𐑫𐑼 𐑢𐑪𐑑 𐑣𐑰 𐑢𐑦𐑤 𐑛𐑵 𐑯𐑧𐑒𐑕𐑑.

𐑞 𐑥𐑩𐑯𐑨𐑡𐑼𐑦 𐑒𐑰𐑐𐑼. ·𐑕𐑰𐑟𐑼: 𐑜𐑦𐑝 𐑳𐑕 𐑞𐑦𐑕 𐑜𐑮𐑰𐑒 𐑕𐑹𐑕𐑼𐑼 𐑑 𐑚𐑰 𐑩 𐑕𐑤𐑱𐑝 𐑦𐑯 𐑞 𐑥𐑩𐑯𐑨𐑡𐑼𐑦. 𐑣𐑰 𐑣𐑨𐑟 𐑩 𐑢𐑱 𐑢𐑦𐑞 𐑞 𐑚𐑰𐑕𐑑𐑕.

𐑨𐑯𐑛𐑮𐑩𐑒𐑤𐑰𐑟 [𐑛𐑦𐑕𐑑𐑮𐑧𐑕𐑑] 𐑯𐑪𐑑 𐑦𐑓 𐑞𐑱 𐑸 𐑦𐑯 𐑒𐑱𐑡𐑩𐑟. 𐑞𐑱 𐑹𐑑 𐑯𐑪𐑑 𐑚𐑰 𐑒𐑧𐑐𐑑 𐑦𐑯 𐑒𐑱𐑡𐑩𐑟. 𐑞𐑱 𐑥𐑳𐑕𐑑 𐑚𐑰 𐑷𐑤 𐑤𐑧𐑑 𐑬𐑑.

𐑞 𐑧𐑥𐑐𐑼𐑼. 𐑲 𐑜𐑦𐑝 𐑞𐑦𐑕 𐑕𐑹𐑕𐑼𐑼 𐑑 𐑚𐑰 𐑩 𐑕𐑤𐑱𐑝 𐑑 𐑞 𐑓𐑻𐑕𐑑 𐑥𐑨𐑯 𐑣𐑵 𐑤𐑱𐑟 𐑣𐑨𐑯𐑛𐑟 𐑪𐑯 𐑣𐑦𐑥. [𐑞 𐑥𐑩𐑯𐑨𐑡𐑼𐑦 𐑒𐑰𐑐𐑼𐑟 𐑯 𐑞 𐑜𐑤𐑨𐑛𐑦𐑱𐑑𐑼𐑟 𐑮𐑳𐑖 𐑓𐑹 ·𐑨𐑯𐑛𐑮𐑩𐑒𐑤𐑰𐑟. 𐑞 𐑤𐑲𐑩𐑯 𐑕𐑑𐑸𐑑𐑕 𐑳𐑐 𐑯 𐑓𐑱𐑕𐑩𐑟 𐑞𐑧𐑥. 𐑞𐑱 𐑖𐑮𐑦𐑙𐑒 𐑚𐑨𐑒]. 𐑿 𐑕𐑰 𐑣𐑬 𐑥𐑨𐑜𐑯𐑨𐑯𐑦𐑥𐑩𐑕 𐑢𐑰 𐑮𐑴𐑥𐑩𐑯𐑟 𐑸, ·𐑨𐑯𐑛𐑮𐑩𐑒𐑤𐑰𐑟. 𐑢𐑰 𐑕𐑳𐑓𐑼 𐑿 𐑑 𐑜𐑴 𐑦𐑯 𐑐𐑰𐑕.

𐑨𐑯𐑛𐑮𐑩𐑒𐑤𐑰𐑟. 𐑲 𐑔𐑨𐑙𐑒 𐑿𐑼 𐑢𐑻𐑖𐑦𐑐. 𐑲 𐑔𐑨𐑙𐑒 𐑿 𐑷𐑤, 𐑤𐑱𐑛𐑦𐑟 𐑯 𐑡𐑧𐑯𐑑𐑩𐑤𐑥𐑧𐑯. 𐑒𐑳𐑥, ·𐑑𐑪𐑥𐑦. 𐑢𐑲𐑤𐑕𐑑 𐑢𐑰 𐑕𐑑𐑨𐑯𐑛 𐑑𐑩𐑜𐑧𐑞𐑼, 𐑯𐑴 𐑒𐑱𐑡 𐑓 𐑿: 𐑯𐑴 𐑕𐑤𐑱𐑝𐑼𐑦 𐑓 𐑥𐑰. [𐑣𐑰 𐑜𐑴𐑟 𐑬𐑑 𐑢𐑦𐑞 𐑞 𐑤𐑲𐑩𐑯, 𐑧𐑝𐑮𐑦𐑚𐑪𐑛𐑦 𐑒𐑮𐑬𐑛𐑦𐑙 𐑩𐑢𐑱 𐑑 𐑜𐑦𐑝 𐑣𐑦𐑥 𐑨𐑟 𐑢𐑲𐑛 𐑩 𐑚𐑻𐑔 𐑨𐑟 𐑐𐑪𐑕𐑦𐑚𐑩𐑤].

LAVINIA. Yes, handsome Captain: you may. [*He kisses her hand*].

THE EMPEROR. And now, my friends, though I do not, as you see, fear this lion, yet the strain of his presence is considerable; for none of us can feel quite sure what he will do next.

THE MENAGERIE KEEPER. Caesar: give us this Greek sorcerer to be a slave in the menagerie. He has a way with the beasts.

ANDROCLES [*distressed*] Not if they are in cages. They should not be kept in cages. They must be all let out.

THE EMPEROR. I give this sorcerer to be a slave to the first man who lays hands on him. [*The menagerie keepers and the gladiators rush for Androcles. The lion starts up and faces them. They surge back*]. You see how magnanimous we Romans are, Androcles. We suffer you to go in peace.

ANDROCLES. I thank your worship, I thank you all, ladies and gentlemen. Come, Tommy. Whilst we stand together, no cage for you: no slavery for me. [*He goes out with the lion, everybody crowding away to give him as wide a berth as possible*].

NOTES ON THE SPELLING

THE 'transliteration' was spelt in accordance with certain guiding principles that had to be laid down in advance. Though it is claimed that the decisions taken were wise ones, there is nothing binding about the resultant spellings; it is merely proposed that the spellings here shown be looked upon as standard, unless and until others come to be widely preferred, and when good reasons can be found for making a change.

(1) It is desirable that a given word should appear always in a given spelling and not vary from time to time. (This does not preclude individual writers from regularly using some spellings that differ from those in *Androcles*; it merely recommends consistency.)

(2) It follows from (1) above that a choice of possible spellings has to be made in the case of those very common short words that are differently pronounced at different times by one speaker – those having what are called 'strong and weak forms'. The decision was taken in principle to spell such words with their fullest pronunciation (since reduced forms can always be derived from fuller ones, whereas the converse is not possible). For the two kinds of exception to this, see (3) and (4) below.

(3) WORD-SIGNS. The design chosen to be the Shaw Alphabet has the characteristic feature incorporated in it of four 'word-signs' for the four most frequently occurring words of the language – *the*, *of*, *and*, *to* (it is estimated that one word in six is either *the* or *of* or *and* or *to*). These word-signs each consist of a single letter – that for the single sounds of *th*, *v*, *n*, and *t* respectively. The word-signs save valuable time and space.

(4) THE INDEFINITE ARTICLES. The words *a*, *an*

are here transliterated *not* to rhyme with *day*, *Ann* (which would be their 'fuller' pronunciation), but with the central, neutral, or shwa vowel actually heard in '*a* man', '*an*other'. This has the advantage that the two words *a*, *an* can then be spelt with the same vowel – which would not otherwise be the case. Moreover, the 'fuller' pronunciation of these two words is hardly ever used. This constitutes the second exception to the principle in (2) above.

(5) Many English words have alternative pronunciations, each speaker generally using one of them consistently, e.g. *azure*, *subsidence*, *acoustic*, *controversy*, *laboratory*, and countless others. Clearly, the principle in (1) above required that a choice be made. In general, individuals are of course at liberty to spell in conformity with their own pronunciation. Alternative standard spellings of such words are likely to emerge; but until they do, the spellings in *Androcles* may be taken as standard.

(6) It is obvious that the spellings in *Androcles* will fit the speech of some English-speaking people better than others. Nevertheless, it is claimed that none will find it hard to read from the spellings shown, i.e., to get the meaning from the printed page. It is to enable the greatest number of people to read from the spellings easily that words are in general written out in their fullest form (see (1) above), especially since most readers of Shavian are already readers of English in Roman letters, and since this will be their first experience of reading English in the new script.

(7) It is for the reasons given in (1) and (6) above that the letter R is transliterated wherever it now occurs in Roman. The non-pronunciation of R in certain positions, which is characteristic of certain types of English speech, can easily be inferred from the spellings shown here – as

it is now from our traditional orthography; but it would not be possible to deduce the pronunciation of R from a spelling which did not show it. Here again, the fuller form of words is the one shown, thus incidentally making the transliterated spellings more acceptable to, because conforming more closely to the speech of, a much larger number of speakers of English in all parts of the world.

(8) Even so, the spellings in *Androcles*, while not committing anyone to specific *qualities* of sound (since each reader will read his own qualities, e.g. of vowel sound, into each different letter), do nevertheless commit to a particular *distribution* of sounds, and this distribution may be at variance with the usage of different speakers, not only with respect to the alternative pronunciations within a given type of English (see (5) above), but as between the usage in the various areas of the English-speaking world. It is probable that, for example, American writers would favour other spellings in a number of instances, and that therefore further alternative spellings of some words will emerge. These are not likely to interfere greatly with the intelligibility of a text. It is in any case fitting that this first publication in an alphabet constructed in accordance with Shaw's wishes should show spellings in conformity with the kind of pronunciation he thought should be represented.

NOTE: It would be possible to extend the number of word-signs beyond the four provided for in the design. Thus, common words such as the following could regularly be spelt with a single consonant (the corresponding Roman letter is shown in brackets after each word): *for* (f), *be* (b), *with* (w), *he* (h), *are* (r), *so* (s), *do* (d). Further economies could be made by writing other common words with *two* letters, omitting the vowel between initial and final consonants, e.g., *that* (t͜ht), *was* (wz), *have* (hv), *not* (nt), *this* (t͜hs), *but* (bt), *from* (fm), *had* (hd), *has* (hz), *been* (bn), *were* (wr), and so on. If such spellings became standardized, these invariable written forms would stand equally well for strong and weak forms in pronunciation, each reader supplying whichever he found appropriate in the context (which is what he does now). Naturally, it would always remain possible for a writer to indicate, by spelling out in full, any particular form he wished – to avoid ambiguity, or for the sake of emphasis, or in order to specify, for example in stage dialogue, some particular reading. For the reasons given in (6) above, *Androcles* has been transliterated without any abbreviations save those mentioned in (3) above. It is possible, however, that other abbreviations would come into use for private purposes but not for printing; it is also possible that some might come to be adopted in print as well.

PETER MACCARTHY

The University
Leeds
1962

SUGGESTIONS FOR WRITING

1. While learning to form the letters, write larger than usual. Once their shapes are thoroughly mastered, letters will be written fast without undue distortion.

   A sheet of guide-lines can be inserted beneath your writing paper if you need them.

2. Use pencil, or a ball-point pen, or a nib pen giving only slight variation of stroke-thickness. Test your pen and your size of writing on the eight small-curve letters **out** to **err**. If your pen is too broad to write these clearly, either change it or write larger.

3. Cultivate an upright rather than a sloping handwriting. It will be more like printed letterpress and more distinguishable.

4. Make Tall and Deep letters about twice the height of Shorts, to allow for the inexactitudes of free handwriting.

5. Leave ample space between words. Write the letters of each word closely together. Avoid linking letters unnaturally.

   There is no need to link letters at all. But it frequently happens that the end of one letter naturally runs into the beginning of another; and the alphabet is so designed that this cannot produce alternative readings.

   Junctions or links can occur only along one of the double guide-lines (used or imagined) within which Short letters are written. No links are permissible between the guide-lines, nor above them, nor beneath them.

Fast writers are likely to make such natural junctions as these:

– in which it is easy to recognize these separate letters, and no others:

6. Be sure to distinguish properly between these Short letters:

7. While taking care, avoid over-anxiety. Avoid cramped fingers and heavy pressure of pen on paper. Only with a light touch will you write well, freely, and fast. As soon as hand or brain is fatigued, take a rest.

   Little and often – but very often; that is the way to practise. You can practise on a newspaper's margin as happily as doing its crosswords. Earnest practice for a single week enables one to write with assurance if not with speed. You will be surprised at the brevity and simplicity of Shavian writing.

8. Re-read your practice writing. Learn by your own writing and spelling slips. Make sure that a reader would not hesitate.

9. If you have already learnt to read this book's Shavian pages without reference to any key, you will have no difficulty in spelling when you write.

10. This is a good first exercise in spelling and writing: From the Writers' Alphabet take the first pair of

letters (consonants) and, from its righthand column, the first three pairs (vowels). Write down all the words these will make. A few minutes will show you how simple spelling is, and you will have mastered once for all the shapes of eight letters.

11. You can be perfectly understood without spelling quite 'like a book'. We shall all tend to spell words as we see them printed; but nobody should complain so long as spelling is intelligible. *To communicate* – more easily, sensibly, economically – is the whole purpose of Shavian writing.

12. Mutual encouragement helps. Interest yourself and fellow writers by joining an 'ever-circulator' as page 15 invites you to do. It is the way to get sufficient reading as well as writing practice. Have a shot at it; and good luck!

KINGSLEY READ

Abbots Morton
Worcester
1962

The Shaw Alphabet for Writers

Double lines = between pairs show the relative height of Talls, Deeps, and Shorts. Wherever possible, finish letters rightwards; those starred * will be written upwards. Also see heading and footnotes overleaf.

	Tall		Deep			Short		Short	
peep	𐑐	=	𐑚	bib	if	𐑦	=	𐑰	eat
tot	𐑑	=	𐑛	dead	egg	𐑧	=	𐑱	age
kick	𐑒	=	𐑜	gag	ash*	𐑨	=	𐑲	ice
fee	𐑓	=	𐑝	vow	ado*	𐑩	=	𐑳	up
thigh	𐑔	=	𐑞	they	on	𐑪	=	𐑴	oak
so	𐑕	=	𐑟	zoo	wool	𐑫	=	𐑵	ooze
sure	𐑖	=	𐑠	measure	out	𐑬	=	𐑶	oil
church	𐑗	=	𐑡	judge	ah*	𐑭	=	𐑷	awe
yea	𐑘	=	𐑢	*woe	are	𐑸	=	𐑹	or
hung	𐑙	=	𐑣	ha-ha	air	𐑺	=	𐑻	err
	Short		Short		array	𐑼	=	𐑽	ear
loll	𐑤	=	𐑮	roar				Tall	
mime*	𐑥	=	𐑯	nun	Ian	𐑾	=	𐑿	yew

The Shaw Alphabet Reading Key

The letters are classified as Tall, Deep, Short, and Compound.
Beneath each letter is its full name: its *sound* is shown in **bold** type.

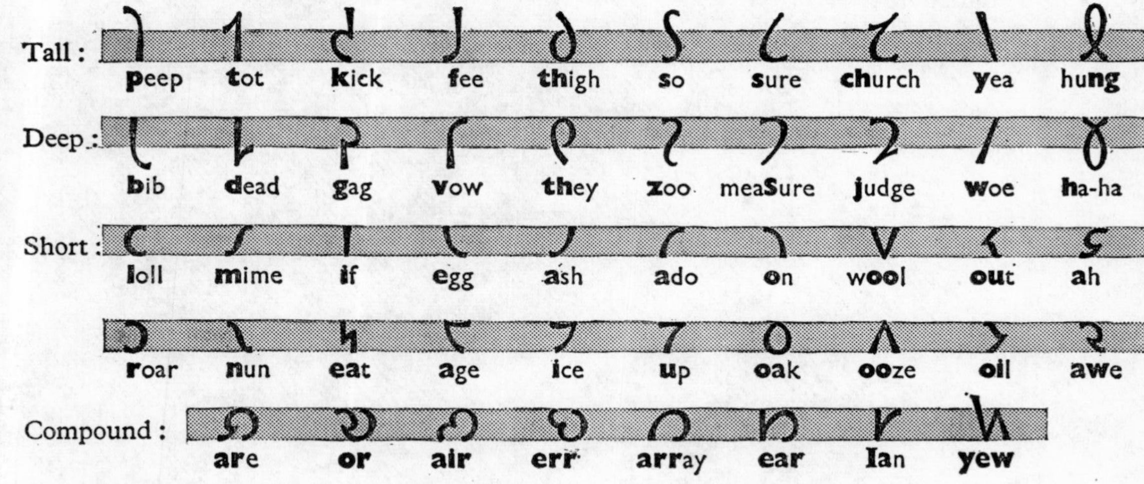

The four most frequent words are represented by single letters: **the** 𐑞, **of** 𐑝, **and** 𐑯, **to** 𐑑.

Proper names may be distinguished by a preceding 'Namer' dot: e.g. ·𐑮𐑴𐑥, Rome.

Punctuation and numerals are unchanged. Learn the alphabet *in pairs*, as listed for Writers overleaf.